# Progress Chart

This chart lists the topics in the book. Once you have completed each page, stick a star in the correct box below.

| Page | Topic | Star | Page | Topic | Star | Page | Topic | Star |
|------|-------|------|------|-------|------|------|-------|------|
| 2 | Counting by 1s, 10s, and 100s | ☆ | 13 | Subtracting | ☆ | 24 | Naming 2-dimensional shapes | ☆ |
| 3 | Counting by 2s | ☆ | 14 | Subtracting | ☆ | 25 | Sorting 2-dimensional shapes | ☆ |
| 4 | Odd and even | ☆ | 15 | Estimating length | ☆ | 26 | Picture graphs | ☆ |
| 5 | Reading and writing numbers | ☆ | 16 | Addition properties | ☆ | 27 | Equations | ☆ |
| 6 | Place value | ☆ | 17 | Add or subtract? | ☆ | 28 | 3-dimensional shapes | ☆ |
| 7 | More and less | ☆ | 18 | Subtracting | ☆ | 29 | Sorting 3-dimensional shapes | ☆ |
| 8 | Fact families | ☆ | 19 | Working with coins | ☆ | 30 | Location on a grid | ☆ |
| 9 | Fractions | ☆ | 20 | Money problems | ☆ | 31 | Placing on a grid | ☆ |
| 10 | Money | ☆ | 21 | Measurement problems | ☆ | 32 | Counting by 3s, 4s, and 5s | ☆ |
| 11 | Adding | ☆ | 22 | Telling time | ☆ | 33 | Adding | ☆ |
| 12 | Adding | ☆ | 23 | Simple tally charts and bar graphs | ☆ | 34 | Comparing and ordering | ☆ |

| 0 | 1 | 2 | 3 | 4 | 5 | 6 | 7 | 8 | 9 | 10 |
|---|---|---|---|---|---|---|---|---|---|----|
| zero | one | two | three | four | five | six | seven | eight | nine | ten |

| Page | Topic | Star | Page | Topic | Star | Page | Topic | Star |
|------|-------|------|------|-------|------|------|-------|------|
| 119 | Tables and graphs | ☆ | 133 | Multiplying by 5 | ☆ | 145 | Multiplying by 3 | ☆ |
| 120 | Identifying patterns | ☆ | 134 | Dividing by 5 | ☆ | 146 | Dividing by 3 | ☆ |
| 121 | Odds and evens | ☆ | 135 | Using the 5 times table | ☆ | 147 | 4 times table | ☆ |
| 122 | Real-life problems | ☆ | 136 | Using the 5 times table | ☆ | 148 | Multiplying by 4 | ☆ |
| 123 | Symmetry | ☆ | 137 | Using the 5 times table | ☆ | 149 | Dividing by 4 | ☆ |
| 124 | Adding | ☆ | 138 | 10 times table | ☆ | 150 | Mixed tables | ☆ |
| 125 | Subtracting | ☆ | 139 | Multiplying and dividing | ☆ | 151 | Mixed tables | ☆ |
| 126 | 2 times table | ☆ | 140 | Dividing by 10 | ☆ | 152 | Mixed tables | ☆ |
| 127 | Multiplying by 2 | ☆ | 141 | Using the 10 times table | ☆ | 153 | Mixed tables | ☆ |
| 128 | Dividing by 2 | ☆ | 142 | Using the 10 times table | ☆ | 154 | Mixed tables | ☆ |
| 129 | Using the 2 times table | ☆ | 143 | Using the 10 times table | ☆ | 155 | Mixed tables | ☆ |
| 130 | Using the 2 times table | ☆ | 144 | 3 times table | ☆ | 156 | Mixed tables | ☆ |
| 131 | Using the 2 times table | ☆ | | | | | | |
| 132 | 5 times table | ☆ | | | | | | |

**When you have completed the progress chart in this book, fill in the certificate at the back.**

# Math
## made easy

Grade 2
ages 7-8

Workbook

**Author and Consultant**
Sean McArdle

# Counting by 1s, 10s, and 100s

Finish each row.

| | | | | | | |
|---|---|---|---|---|---|---|
| Count by 1s. | 24 | 25 | 26 | 27 | 28 | 29 |
| Count by 10s. | 31 | 41 | 51 | 61 | 71 | 81 |
| Count by 100s. | 134 | 234 | 334 | 434 | 534 | 634 |

Finish each row. Count by 1s.

| | | | | | | | |
|---|---|---|---|---|---|---|---|
| 17 | 18 | 19 | 20 | 21 | 22 | 23 | 24 |
| 36 | 37 | 38 | 39 | 40 | 41 | 42 | 43 |
| 69 | 70 | 71 | 72 | 73 | 74 | 75 | 76 |
| 45 | 46 | 47 | 48 | 49 | 50 | 51 | 52 |
| 85 | 86 | 87 | 88 | 89 | 90 | 91 | 92 |

Finish each row. Count by 10s.

| | | | | | | | |
|---|---|---|---|---|---|---|---|
| 34 | 44 | 54 | 64 | 74 | 84 | 94 | 104 |
| 47 | 57 | 67 | 77 | 87 | 97 | 107 | 207 |
| 78 | 88 | 98 | 108 | 208 | 308 | 408 | 508 |
| 9 | 19 | 29 | 39 | 49 | 59 | 69 | 79 |
| 167 | 177 | 187 | 197 | 207 | 217 | 227 | 237 |
| 305 | 315 | 325 | 335 | 345 | 355 | 365 | 375 |

Finish each row. Count by 100s.

| | | | | | | | |
|---|---|---|---|---|---|---|---|
| 146 | 246 | 346 | 446 | 546 | 646 | 746 | 846 |
| 312 | 412 | 512 | 612 | 712 | 812 | 912 | 1,012 |
| 508 | 608 | 708 | 808 | 908 | 1,008 | 1,108 | 1,208 |
| 757 | 857 | 957 | 1,057 | 1,157 | 1,257 | 1,357 | 1,457 |
| 274 | 374 | 474 | 574 | 674 | 774 | 874 | 974 |

# Counting by 2s

| Count by 2s. | 12 | 14 | 16 | 18 | 20 | 22 |
|---|---|---|---|---|---|---|
| Count by 2s. | 31 | 33 | 35 | 37 | 39 | 41 |

**Finish each row. Count by 2s.**

| 17 | 19 | 21 | 23 | 25 | 27 | 29 | 31 |
|---|---|---|---|---|---|---|---|
| 36 | 38 | 40 | 42 | 44 | 46 | 48 | 50 |
| 72 | 74 | 76 | 78 | 80 | 82 | 84 | 86 |
| 43 | 45 | 47 | 49 | 51 | 53 | 55 | 57 |
| 14 | 16 | 18 | 20 | 22 | 24 | 26 | 28 |
| 39 | 41 | 43 | 45 | 47 | 49 | 51 | 53 |

**Finish each row. Count by 2s.**

| 20 | 22 | 24 | 26 | 28 | 30 | 32 | 34 |
|---|---|---|---|---|---|---|---|
| 75 | 77 | 79 | 81 | 83 | 85 | 87 | 89 |
| 44 | 46 | 48 | 50 | 52 | 54 | 56 | 58 |
| 69 | 71 | 73 | 75 | 77 | 79 | 81 | 83 |
| 31 | 33 | 35 | 37 | 39 | 41 | 43 | 45 |
| 88 | 90 | 92 | 94 | 96 | 98 | 100 | 102 |

**Continue each row. Count by 2s.**

| 20 | 22 | 24 | 26 | 28 | 30 | 32 | 34 |
|---|---|---|---|---|---|---|---|
| 47 | 49 | 51 | 53 | 55 | 57 | 59 | 61 |
| 75 | 77 | 81 | 83 | 85 | 87 | 89 | 91 |
| 40 | 48 | 50 | 52 | 54 | 56 | 58 | 60 |
| 85 | 89 | 91 | 93 | 95 | 97 | 99 | 101 |
| 45 | 47 | 50 | 52 | 54 | 56 | 58 | 60 |

# Odd and even

Numbers ending in    0    2    4    6    8    are called even numbers.

Numbers ending in    1    3    5    7    9    are called odd numbers.

Circle the numbers that are even.

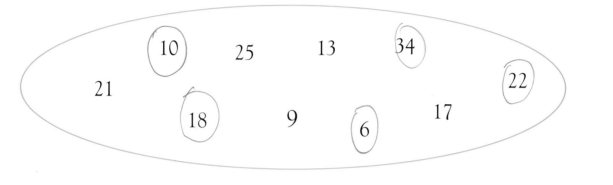

Circle the numbers that are odd.

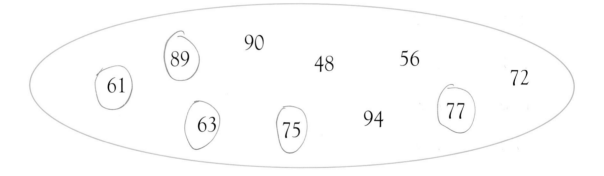

Write the odd numbers between 30 and 50.

31, 32, 33, 34, 35, 36, 37, 38, 39, 20, 21, 22, 23, 24 25, 26, 27, 28, 29, 30, 31, 32, 33, 34, 35, 36, 37, 38, 39, 40, 41, 42, 43, 44, 45, 46, 47, 48, 49, 50

Write the even numbers between 71 and 91.

72, 73, 74, 75, 76, 77, 78, 79, 80, 81, 82, 83, 84, 85, 86, 87, 88, 89, 90, 91

# Reading and writing numbers

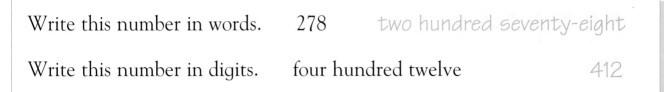

Write this number in words.     278     two hundred seventy-eight

Write this number in digits.     four hundred twelve     412

Write each of these numbers in words.

624   six hundred twenty four

175   one hundered seventy-five

392   three

926

852

Write each of these numbers in digits.

three hundred eighty-four

four hundred sixty-one

nine hundred forty-five

seven hundred twenty-six

Write each of these numbers in words.

340

407

870

Write each of these numbers in digits.

two hundred eight

six hundred nine

eight hundred seventy

five hundred one

# Place value

Write the correct number in the box.    426 = 400 + 20 + *6*

Write the number that is the same as ...
   4 hundreds 2 tens 6 ones.    *4    2    6*

---

Write the correct number in the box.

634 = 600 + 30 +               285 = 200 +            + 5

539 = 500 +         + 9        497 =          + 90 + 7

825 = 800 + 20 +              738 = 700 + 30 +

698 =          + 90 + 8        715 =          + 10 + 5

579 = 500 +         + 9        953 = 900 +            + 3

---

Write the correct number in the box.

307 = 300 +         + 7        850 = 800 + 50 +

601 = 600 +         + 1        503 = 500 +            + 3

---

Write the number that is the same as the word:

two hundreds, seven tens, three ones.

four hundreds, six tens, nine ones.

eight hundreds, five tens, three ones.

seven hundreds, six tens, eight ones.

nine hundreds, four tens, six ones.

---

Look at the cards.

Make the
greatest number
you can from
the digits.

Make the
smallest number
you can from
the digits.

# More and less

Write the number that is 1 more than each of these.

35 _36_     78 _79_     69 _70_     53 _54_     9 _10_     654 _655_

41 _42_     124 _125_     167 _168_     40 _41_     236 _237_     473 _474_

Write the number that is 1 less than each of these.

52 _51_     18 _17_     20 _19_     76 _77_     37 _38_     150 _149_

50          154          423          100          531          483

Write the number that is 10 more than each of these.

46          21          86          153          216

185          298          399          538          490

601          990          590          323          480

Write the number that is 10 less than each of these.

56          75          86          185          230

680          451          503          407          805

600          902          605          702          908

| Write the number that is 100 more than each of these. | | Write the number that is 100 less than each of these. | |
|---|---|---|---|
| 365 | 76 | 502 | 100 |
| 960 | 601 | 809 | 750 |

7

# Fact families

Finish the fact family for this group of numbers.

9

5          4

$5 + 4 = 9$
$4 + 5 = 9$
$9 - 4 = 5$
$9 - 5 = 4$

Finish the fact family for each group of numbers.

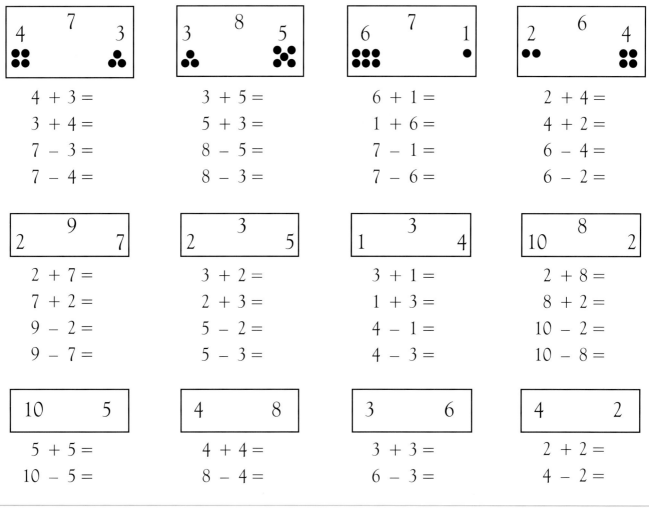

| 7 | | 8 | | 7 | | 6 | |
| 4 | 3 | 3 | 5 | 6 | 1 | 2 | 4 |

$4 + 3 =$        $3 + 5 =$        $6 + 1 =$        $2 + 4 =$
$3 + 4 =$        $5 + 3 =$        $1 + 6 =$        $4 + 2 =$
$7 - 3 =$        $8 - 5 =$        $7 - 1 =$        $6 - 4 =$
$7 - 4 =$        $8 - 3 =$        $7 - 6 =$        $6 - 2 =$

| 9 | | 3 | | 3 | | 8 | |
| 2 | 7 | 2 | 5 | 1 | 4 | 10 | 2 |

$2 + 7 =$        $3 + 2 =$        $3 + 1 =$        $2 + 8 =$
$7 + 2 =$        $2 + 3 =$        $1 + 3 =$        $8 + 2 =$
$9 - 2 =$        $5 - 2 =$        $4 - 1 =$        $10 - 2 =$
$9 - 7 =$        $5 - 3 =$        $4 - 3 =$        $10 - 8 =$

| 10 | 5 | 4 | 8 | 3 | 6 | 4 | 2 |

$5 + 5 =$        $4 + 4 =$        $3 + 3 =$        $2 + 2 =$
$10 - 5 =$        $8 - 4 =$        $6 - 3 =$        $4 - 2 =$

Finish the fact family for each group of numbers.

| 3 | | 9 | | 8 | | 7 | |
| 10 | 7 | 3 | 6 | 6 | 2 | 5 | 2 |

# Fractions

Color one-third ($\frac{1}{3}$) of each shape.

Color one-half ($\frac{1}{2}$) of each shape.

Color one-fourth ($\frac{1}{4}$) of each shape.

Color one-third ($\frac{1}{3}$) of each shape.

Color one-eighth ($\frac{1}{8}$) of each shape.

Color one-tenth ($\frac{1}{10}$) of each shape.

# Money

Change each amount into dollars and cents.

| | | |
|---|---|---|
| 153¢ | 428¢ | 392¢ |
| 372¢ | 563¢ | 290¢ |
| 827¢ | 526¢ | 483¢ |
| 460¢ | 729¢ | 926¢ |

Change each amount into cents.

| | | |
|---|---|---|
| $3.27 | $7.28 | $5.17 |
| $6.72 | $4.15 | $8.35 |
| $9.38 | $6.20 | $4.63 |
| $7.20 | $6.50 | $4.31 |

Change each amount into dollars and cents.

| | | |
|---|---|---|
| 150¢ | 208¢ | 480¢ |
| 410¢ | 706¢ | 302¢ |
| 205¢ | 620¢ | 950¢ |
| 609¢ | 204¢ | 606¢ |

Change each amount into cents.

| | | |
|---|---|---|
| $3.50 | $2.07 | $7.50 |
| $6.01 | $3.06 | $10.00 |
| $4.90 | $5.00 | $4.06 |
| $1.01 | $0.40 | $5.05 |

# Adding

Write the answer in the box.   25 + 30 = 55

Write the answer in the box.

| | | |
|---|---|---|
| 39 + 40 = | 28 + 60 = | 53 + 70 = |
| 27 + 30 = | 73 + 30 = | 46 + 50 = |
| 42 + 60 = | 74 + 50 = | 84 + 40 = |
| 30 + 45 = | 60 + 38 = | 90 + 17 = |

Write the answer in the box.

| | |
|---|---|
| 20 + 30 + 12 = | 50 + 20 + 18 = |
| 45 + 10 + 20 = | 60 + 20 + 7 = |
| 30 + 40 + 18 = | 30 + 50 + 12 = |
| 60 + 20 + 30 = | 46 + 30 + 20 = |
| 52 + 40 + 20 = | 30 + 45 + 20 = |
| 17 + 30 + 3 = | 28 + 50 + 2 = |

Write the answer in the box.

| | | |
|---|---|---|
| 63¢ + 20¢ = | 48¢ + 30¢ = | 65¢ + 20¢ = |
| 50¢ + 37¢ = | 39¢ + 60¢ = | 40¢ + 56¢ = |
| 12¢ + 15¢ = | 18¢ + 32¢ = | 34¢ + 16¢ = |
| 44¢ + 14¢ = | 63¢ + 24¢ = | 38¢ + 22¢ = |

Write the answer in the box.

| | |
|---|---|
| 12 ft + 20 ft + 60 ft = | 17 ft + 40 ft + 40 ft = |
| 10 ft + 15 ft + 20 ft = | 30 ft + 15 ft + 40 ft = |

# Adding

$$35 + 16 = \underline{51}$$

$$17 + 9 = \underline{26}$$

$$24 + 8 = \underline{32}$$

Write the answers between the lines.

| 24 + 9 | 43 + 6 | 21 + 7 | 46 + 5 |
|--------|--------|--------|--------|
| 43 + 7 | 72 + 5 | 64 + 7 | 38 + 8 |
| 46 + 10 | 37 + 11 | 53 + 12 | 49 + 9 |

Write the answers between the lines.

| 9 7 + 9 | 8 9 + 7 | 7 9 + 6 | 8 8 + 9 |
|---------|---------|---------|---------|
| 12¢ 6¢ +10¢ | 18¢ 7¢ +10¢ | 8¢ 11¢ + 6¢ | 13¢ 9¢ + 6¢ |
| 20¢ 7¢ +10¢ | 15¢ 10¢ + 2¢ | 8¢ 10¢ + 4¢ | 10¢ 8¢ +10¢ |

# Subtracting

Write the answers in the boxes.

$16 - 9 =$ 7     $23 - 12 =$ 11

Write the answers in the boxes.

$15 - 8 =$     $13 - 8 =$     $26 - 5 =$     $18 - 4 =$

$22 - 11 =$     $28 - 13 =$     $14 - 12 =$     $15 - 6 =$

$24 - 10 =$     $30 - 20 =$     $18 - 12 =$     $8 - 0 =$

$14 - 6 =$     $17 - 9 =$     $25 - 13 =$     $12 - 9 =$

$29 - 13 =$     $28 - 14 =$     $19 - 11 =$     $36 - 14 =$

Write the answers in the boxes.

$45¢ - 20¢ =$     $35¢ - 12¢ =$     $25¢ - 10¢ =$     $40¢ - 25¢ =$

$38¢ - 16¢ =$     $25¢ - 15¢ =$     $39¢ - 18¢ =$     $50¢ - 35¢ =$

$34¢ - 14¢ =$     $28¢ - 16¢ =$     $42¢ - 12¢ =$     $24¢ - 12¢ =$

$45¢ - 25¢ =$     $50¢ - 15¢ =$     $27¢ - 16¢ =$     $45¢ - 35¢ =$

$55¢ - 22¢ =$     $33¢ - 21¢ =$     $49¢ - 8¢ =$     $35¢ - 14¢ =$

Write the answers in the boxes.

How much less than
24¢ is 17¢?

Take 14¢ away from 30¢.

How much is 50¢ minus 14¢?

Take away 18¢ from 34¢.

What is the difference
between 60¢ and 25¢?

How much less than
40 in. is 16 in.?

Mandy has 50¢. She spends
26¢ on ice cream. How
much does she have left?

What is the difference
between 90 in. and 35 in.?

# Subtracting

Write the answers between the lines.

```
  28        2 11        3 10
- 16        3̷1̷         4̷0̷
  __       - 14        - 17
  12         __          __
             17          23
```

Write the answers between the lines.

```
    27          41          60          53
  - 14        - 25        - 37        - 38
  ____        ____        ____        ____


    32          45          33          50
  - 14        - 26        - 20        - 27
  ____        ____        ____        ____


    47          25          63          36
  - 28        -  6        - 44        - 28
  ____        ____        ____        ____


   28¢         43¢         50¢         48¢
 - 16¢       - 35¢       - 26¢       - 37¢
 _____       _____       _____       _____


   53¢         37¢         70¢         45¢
 - 35¢       - 28¢       - 47¢       - 38¢
 _____       _____       _____       _____


   40¢         60¢         41¢         54¢
 -  8¢       - 26¢       - 14¢       - 36¢
 _____       _____       _____       _____
```

# Estimating length

Circle the longest string.

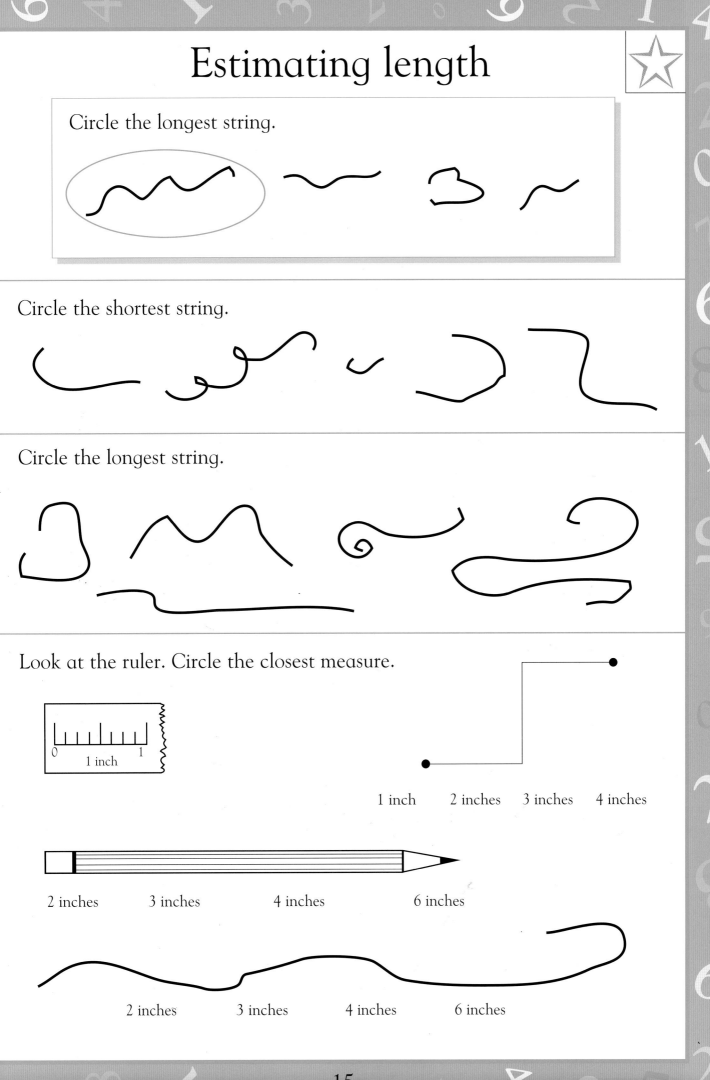

Circle the shortest string.

Circle the longest string.

Look at the ruler. Circle the closest measure.

0    1 inch    1

1 inch    2 inches    3 inches    4 inches

2 inches    3 inches    4 inches    6 inches

2 inches    3 inches    4 inches    6 inches

# Addition properties

Circle the number that makes the sentence true.

___ + 7 = 7                    43 + 21 = 21 + ___

1    (0)    14              22    64    (43)

Circle the number that makes the sentence true.

___ + 3 = 3                            15 + ___ = 15

0    3    6                            30    0    5

___ + 23 = 23 + 16                    25 + 41 = 41 + ___

16    23    46                         16    66    25

___ + 45 = 45                         70 + 0 = 0 + ___

45    0    1                           70    0    700

Complete the number sentences.

___ + 27 = 27          90 + 0 = ___          13 + 28 = 28 + ___

52 + 3 = ___ + 52      ___ + 0 = 67          56 + 43 = 43 + ___

2 + 83 = ___ + 2       ___ + 12 = 12         ___ + 64 = 64 + 28

55 + ___ = 55          ___ + 0 = 10          200 + 800 = 800 + ___

___ + 0 = 647          8 + 0 = ___           345 + 871 = ___ + 345

# Add or subtract?

Write + or − in the box.

$12 + 7 = 19$      $20 − 8 = 12$      $15 + 7 = 22$

Write + or − in the box.

| | | | |
|---|---|---|---|
| 6   7 = 13 | 9   3 = 12 | 8   6 = 14 | 5   9 = 14 |
| 13   6 = 7 | 10   6 = 4 | 3   8 = 11 | 15   7 = 8 |
| 8   6 = 2 | 12   6 = 18 | 9   6 = 15 | 12   3 = 9 |
| 17   10 = 7 | 14   5 = 9 | 15   8 = 7 | 18   10 = 8 |

Write the answer in the box.

I add 4 to a number and the answer is 7.
What number did I start with?

7 added to a number gives a total of 12.
What is the number?

I take 5 from a number and have 6 left.
What number did I start with?

9 added to a number makes 16.
What is the number?

I subtract 7 from a number and the answer
is 12. What number did I start with?

Two numbers add up to 17. One of the
numbers is 8. What is the other number?

Write + or − in the box.

| | | | |
|---|---|---|---|
| 15   10 = 25 | 20   5 = 15 | 28   15 = 13 | 40   22 = 18 |
| 35   15 = 20 | 34   14 = 48 | 18   12 = 30 | 45   17 = 28 |
| 37   6 = 43 | 65   4 = 61 | 50   26 = 24 | 84   34 = 50 |
| 43   17 = 60 | 62   17 = 45 | 31   14 = 17 | 17   6 = 11 |

# Subtracting

Write the answer between the lines.

```
    9 7 6          5 7 4          $3.8 4
  – 5 5 3        – 2 6 2        – $2.5 1
  ─────────      ─────────      ─────────
    4 2 3          3 1 2          $1.33
```

Write the answer between the lines.

```
    4 8 7          6 4 8          7 6 8          5 5 6          8 4 5
  – 3 4 5        – 1 3 6        – 4 2 7        – 3 3 3        – 7 1 4
  ─────────      ─────────      ─────────      ─────────      ─────────

  ─────────      ─────────      ─────────      ─────────      ─────────


    9 5 6          2 9 8          3 7 9          4 5 6          8 8 5
  – 3 3 1        – 1 5 7        – 2 2 6        – 3 1 4        – 3 6 3
  ─────────      ─────────      ─────────      ─────────      ─────────

  ─────────      ─────────      ─────────      ─────────      ─────────


    2 7 7          4 9 7          5 7 5          6 9 2          9 5 7
  – 1 1 3        – 2 5 5        – 3 2 1        – 5 3 1        – 4 2 5
  ─────────      ─────────      ─────────      ─────────      ─────────

  ─────────      ─────────      ─────────      ─────────      ─────────


    8 5 3          5 8 9          6 7 3          3 6 7          7 2 5
  – 6 4 2        – 4 3 5        – 5 4 2        – 2 3 2        – 3 1 3
  ─────────      ─────────      ─────────      ─────────      ─────────

  ─────────      ─────────      ─────────      ─────────      ─────────
```

Write the answer between the lines.

```
    $9.64          $8.97          $4.57          $6.71          $5.99
  – $4.32        – $5.71        – $1.25        – $5.50        – $3.76
  ─────────      ─────────      ─────────      ─────────      ─────────

  ─────────      ─────────      ─────────      ─────────      ─────────
```

# Working with coins

Write the answers in the boxes.

Sarah has  🪙 🪙 🪙 🪙 🪙

Jane has  🪙

How much more does
Jane have than Sarah?

50¢ – 33¢ =    17¢

---

Write the answers in the boxes.

Paul has these coins.  🪙 🪙 🪙   How much more does Paul
need to have $1?

Janine wants to buy a toy for 🪙 .   She has these coins.  🪙 🪙 🪙

🪙 🪙 🪙

How much more does Janine need?

Ricki gives the shopkeeper $1.00.
He buys treats that cost 94¢.
Ricki has two coins in his change.
Which two coins does he have?

Mark has three coins that add up to 36¢.
Which three coins does Mark have?

Jane is given these coins by her mother.

🪙 🪙 🪙 🪙 🪙 🪙 🪙 🪙 🪙

How much more than one dollar does Jane have?

Paul has three coins which total 40¢.
Which coins does Paul have?

Alex has these coins.  🪙 🪙 🪙 🪙

Raj has these coins.  🪙 🪙 🪙 🪙

How much more does Alex have than Raj?

# Money problems

Look at these coins.

How much more is needed to make 75¢?    35¢

How much is 15¢ and 19¢?    34¢

---

Write the answers in the boxes.

What is the total of 20¢ and 70¢?

What is 35¢ less 20¢?

Jasmine collects nickels and has 45¢ worth.
How many nickels does Jasmine have?

Don has these coins.
Which coin does he need to make $1.00?

Jim starts out with 80¢ but loses 35¢.  How much does he have left?

Mary has four coins that add up to 17¢.
Which coins does Mary have?

Which four of the these
coins add up to $0.86?

60¢ is shared equally by 4 children. How much do they each get?

How much is four groups of coins
with 1 dime and 1 nickel in each group?

These coins are shared equally by
two children. How much does each child get?

---

Write the answers in the boxes.

5¢ + 40¢ =          10¢ + 46¢ =          21¢ + 8¢ =

20¢ – 10¢ =          49¢ – 5¢ =          18¢ – 12¢ =

35¢ + 45¢ =          62¢ + 17¢ =          80¢ + 18¢ =

# Measurement problems

yardstick

measuring wheel

tape measure

ruler

Which measuring tool would be best to measure a garden?    *measuring wheel*

Write which measuring tool would be best for measuring each item.

pencil

the side of a
soccer field

trash can lid

table top

finger

round pond

soccer ball

curvy garden path

foot

swimming pool

front door

toy snake

21

# Telling time

## What time is shown on the clock?

*twenty after seven*          7:20

---

## What time is shown on each clock?

---

## Draw the hands on each clock face to show the time.

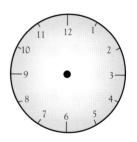

twenty-five after seven          ten after four          quarter to five

---

## Write each of these times on the digital watch faces.

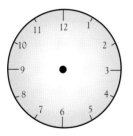          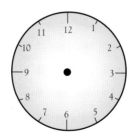

# Simple tally charts
# and bar graphs

Look at the tally chart and then answer the question.

| blue | ‖‖‖ ‖‖‖ ‖‖‖ ||| |
|------|------------------|
| red | ‖‖‖ || |

How many votes did
blue receive?     18

---

Look at the tally chart and then answer the questions.

**Favorite ice cream flavors**

| vanilla | ‖‖‖ ‖‖‖ | |
|---------|-------------|
| chocolate | ‖‖‖ ‖‖‖ ‖‖‖ ‖‖‖ ‖‖‖ |
| strawberry | ‖‖‖ ‖‖‖ ‖‖‖ ||| |

Which flavor had the most votes?

Which flavor had 11 votes?

What was the difference in votes between
the most popular flavor and strawberry?

---

Look at the bar graph and then answer the questions.

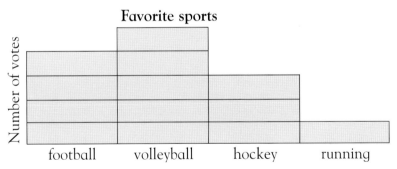

**Favorite sports**

Number of votes

football   volleyball   hockey   running

Which sport did four children vote for?

How many votes did volleyball receive?

Which was the least popular sport?

How many children voted altogether?

How many more voted for football than for hockey?

# Naming 2-dimensional shapes

Write the name of each shape inside it.

circle    square

Write the name of each shape inside it. Use the words in the Word Box.

| Word Box | | |
| --- | --- | --- |
| rectangle | triangle | pentagon |
| square | hexagon | octagon |

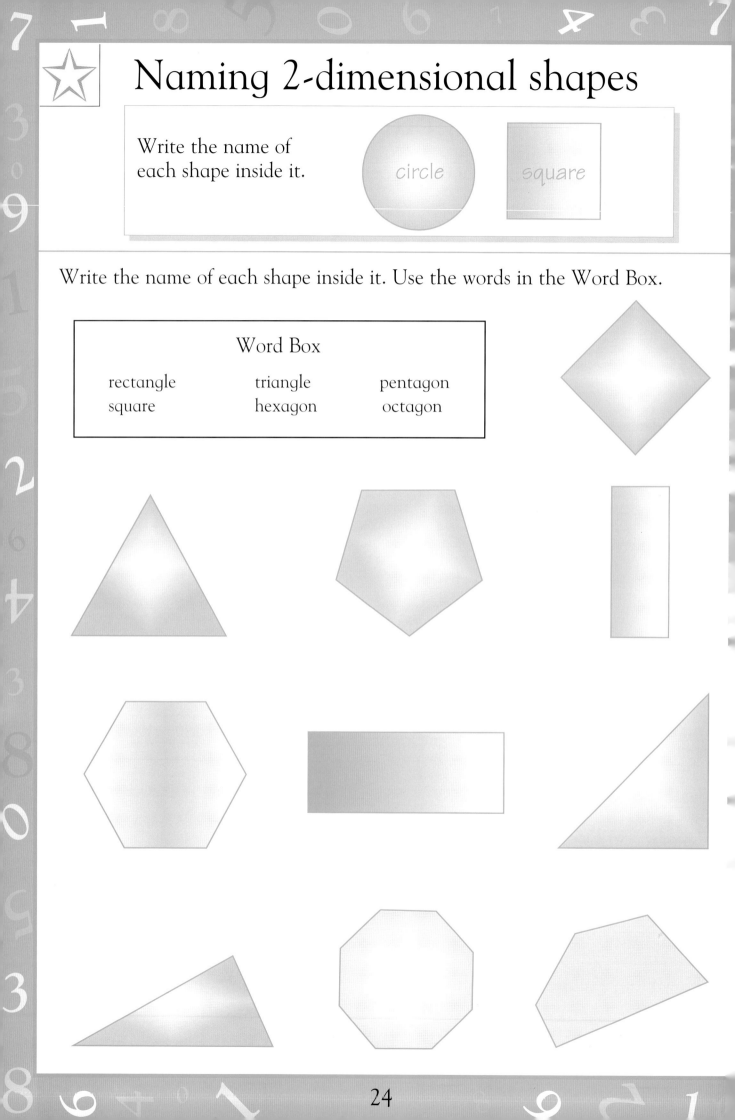

# Sorting 2-dimensional shapes

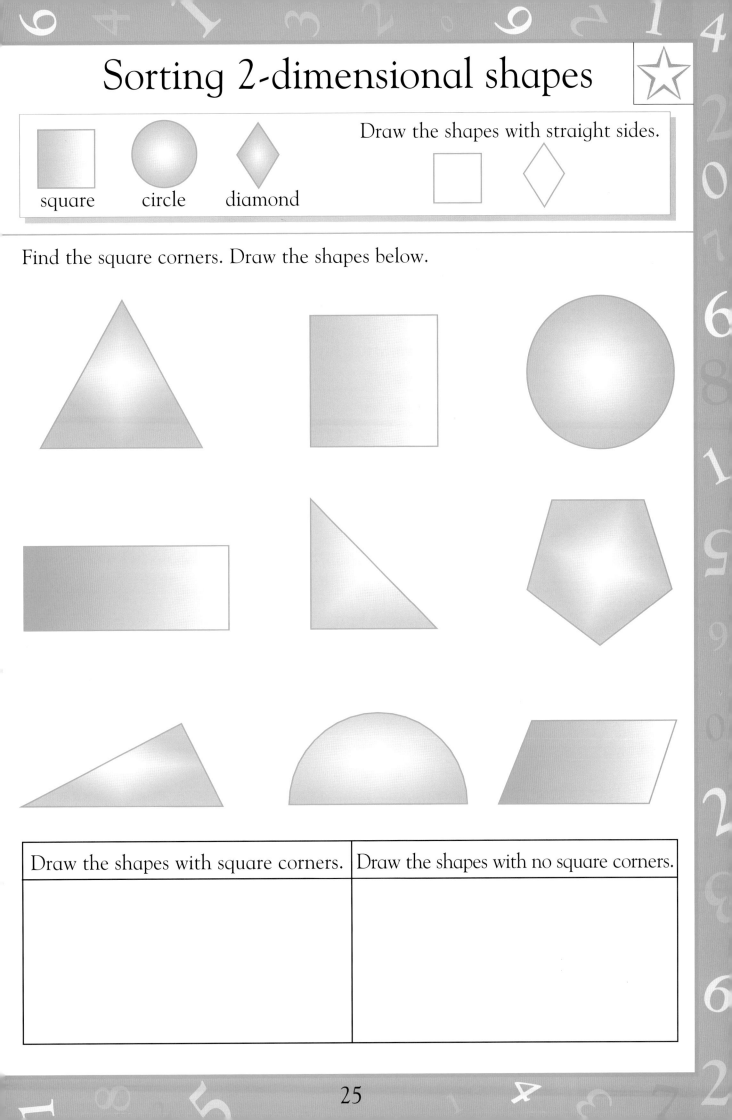

square   circle   diamond

Draw the shapes with straight sides.

Find the square corners. Draw the shapes below.

| Draw the shapes with square corners. | Draw the shapes with no square corners. |
|---|---|
|  |  |

# Picture graphs

Look at this picture graph. Then answer the questions.

### Mina's marbles

| | | | | | |
|---|---|---|---|---|---|
| Clear | ◐ | ◐ | ◐ | ◐ | ◐ |
| Blue | ◐ | ◐ | ◐ | | |
| Green | ◐ | ◐ | ◐ | ◐ | |
| Red | ◐ | ◐ | ◐ | | |
| Yellow | ◐ | | | | |

How many blue
marbles does Mina have?   *3*

Does Mina have more
green marbles or yellow marbles?   *green*

How many marbles
does Mina have in all?   *16*

Look at this picture graph. Then answer the questions.

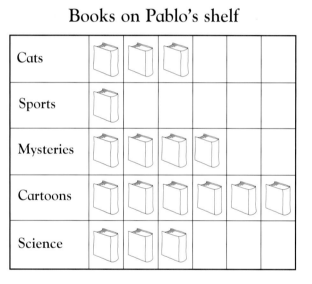

### Books on Pablo's shelf

How many science
books does Pablo have?

Does he have more books
about cats than mysteries?

How many more cartoon books
does he have than mysteries?

How many books about
cats and science does he have?

Look at this picture graph. Then answer the questions.

### Pets on Redmond Road

| | | | | | | |
|---|---|---|---|---|---|---|
| Cats | 🐱 | 🐱 | 🐱 | 🐱 | | | |
| Dogs | 🐶 | 🐶 | 🐶 | 🐶 | 🐶 | | |
| Fish | 🐟 | 🐟 | 🐟 | 🐟 | 🐟 | 🐟 | |
| Birds | 🐦 | 🐦 | 🐦 | | | | |

On Redmond Road,
are there more cats or dogs?

How many more
fish are there than dogs?

How many cats
and dogs are there?

How many pets are there in all?

# Equations

Circle the correct number sentence.

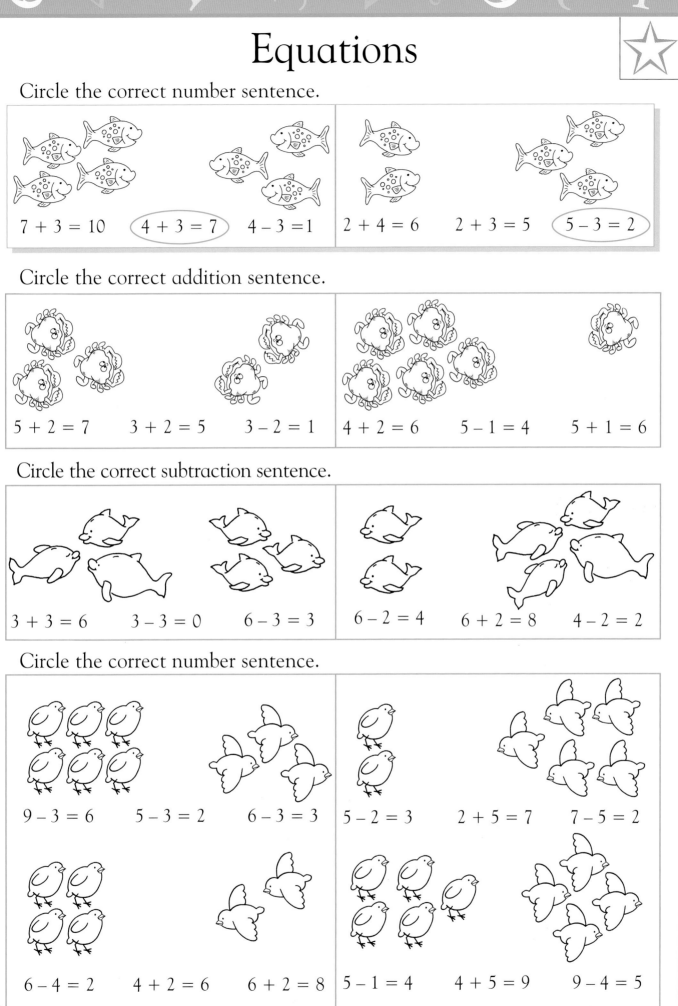

$7 + 3 = 10$    $4 + 3 = 7$    $4 - 3 = 1$      $2 + 4 = 6$    $2 + 3 = 5$    $5 - 3 = 2$

Circle the correct addition sentence.

$5 + 2 = 7$    $3 + 2 = 5$    $3 - 2 = 1$      $4 + 2 = 6$    $5 - 1 = 4$    $5 + 1 = 6$

Circle the correct subtraction sentence.

$3 + 3 = 6$    $3 - 3 = 0$    $6 - 3 = 3$      $6 - 2 = 4$    $6 + 2 = 8$    $4 - 2 = 2$

Circle the correct number sentence.

$9 - 3 = 6$    $5 - 3 = 2$    $6 - 3 = 3$      $5 - 2 = 3$    $2 + 5 = 7$    $7 - 5 = 2$

$6 - 4 = 2$    $4 + 2 = 6$    $6 + 2 = 8$      $5 - 1 = 4$    $4 + 5 = 9$    $9 - 4 = 5$

# 3-dimensional shapes

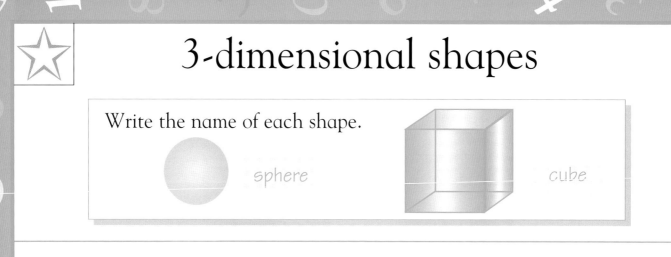

Write the name of each shape.

sphere

cube

Write the name of each shape. Use the words in the word box.

| Word Box |
| --- |
| sphere    prism    cone    cube    cylinder    pyramid |

prism

# Sorting 3-dimensional shapes

Look at the shape. Then answer the questions.

How many curved surfaces ?    1

How many flat surfaces ?    0

Look at each shape. Then answer the questions below.

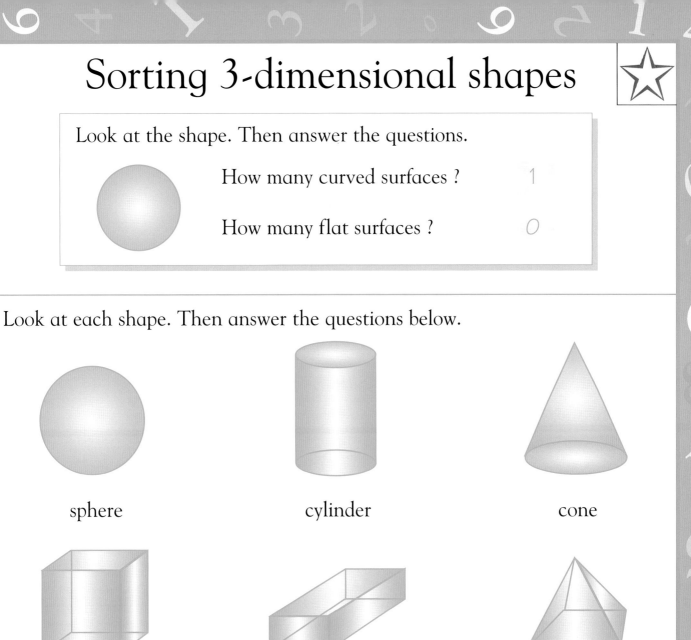

sphere

cylinder

cone

cube

prism

pyramid

| Shape | How many curved surfaces? | How many flat surfaces? |
|---|---|---|
| sphere | | |
| cylinder | | |
| cone | | |
| cube | | |
| prism | | |
| pyramid | | |

# Location on a grid

Look at the grid and then answer the question.

Which box is the bird in?     B, 2

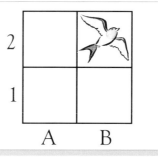

2

1

A     B

---

Look at the grid and then answer the questions below.

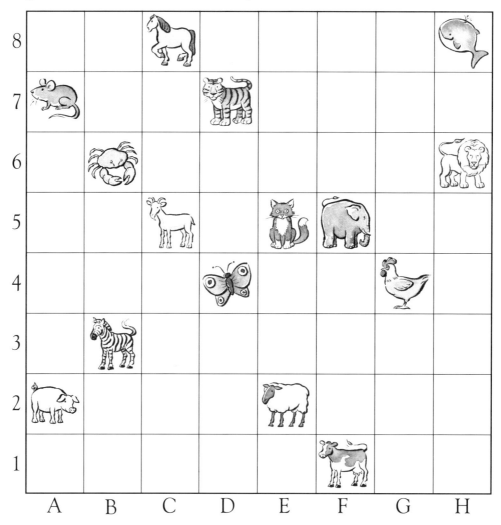

Write where each of the animals can be found.

| | | |
|---|---|---|
| mouse | elephant | horse |
| lion | zebra | tiger |
| cat | chicken | pig |
| cow | goat | whale |
| crab | butterfly | sheep |

# Placing on a grid

Draw each picture in the correct box.

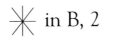 in B, 2

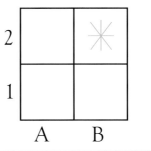

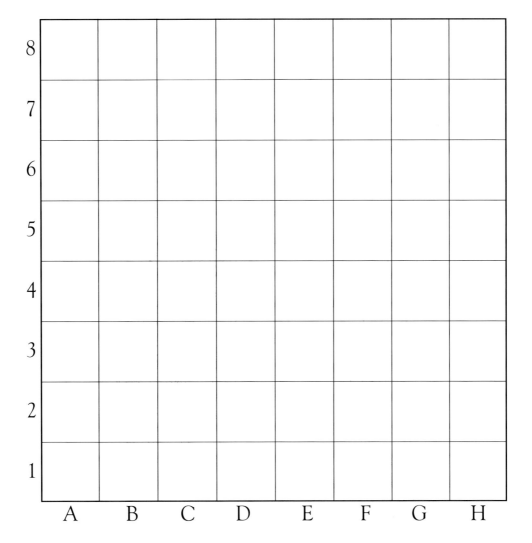

Draw each picture in the correct box on the grid.

△ in  B, 4          ○ in  H, 7          ▲ in  D, 5          ⬛ in  A, 6

☐ in  C, 3          ⬜ in  E, 8          ■ in  F, 2          ◉ in  G, 1

◎ in  B, 7          ◡ in  H, 4          ● in  D, 8          ◡ in  A, 2

# Counting by 3s, 4s, and 5s

Find the pattern. Continue each row.

| Count by 3s. | | 9 | 12 | 15 | 18 | 21 | 24 | 27 |
| --- | --- | --- | --- | --- | --- | --- | --- | --- |
| Count by 4s. | | 8 | 12 | 16 | 20 | 24 | 28 | 32 |
| Count by 5s. | 55 | 50 | 45 | 40 | 35 | 30 | 25 |

Find the pattern. Continue each row.

| 0 | 3 | 6 | | | | | |
| --- | --- | --- | --- | --- | --- | --- | --- |
| 8 | 12 | 16 | | | | | |
| 38 | 41 | 44 | | | | | |
| 40 | 45 | 50 | | | | | |
| 63 | 67 | 71 | | | | | |
| 85 | 90 | 95 | | | | | |
| 6 | 10 | 14 | | | | | |
| 21 | 18 | 15 | | | | | |
| 68 | 65 | 62 | | | | | |
| 85 | 80 | 75 | | | | | 50 |
| 43 | 40 | 37 | | | | | |
| 49 | 45 | 41 | | | | | |
| 71 | 67 | 63 | | | | | |
| 83 | 78 | 73 | | | | | |
| 39 | 34 | | | | | | 4 |

# Adding

Write the answer between the lines.

| 500 | 200 | 300 | 100 | 600 |
| + 300 | + 400 | + 400 | + 700 | + 300 |

| 240 | 110 | 540 | 320 | 860 |
| + 430 | + 830 | + 220 | + 510 | + 130 |

| 204 | 402 | 554 | 701 | 324 |
| + 163 | + 283 | + 304 | + 108 | + 601 |

| 284 | 621 | 507 | 417 | 105 |
| + 100 | + 261 | + 170 | + 280 | + 802 |

Write the answer between the lines.

| $5.72 | $9.07 | $5.50 | $3.09 | $5.80 |
| +$0.22 | +$1.21 | +$3.45 | +$4.80 | +$1.07 |

# Comparing and ordering

Write these numbers in order, starting with the smallest.

431     678     273     586     273   431   586   678

Write these numbers in order, starting with the smallest.

267     931     374     740

734     218     625     389

836     590     374     669

572     197     469     533

948     385     846     289

406     560     460     650

738     837     378     783

582     285     528     852

206     620     602     260

634     436     364     463

47     740     74     704

501     150     51     105

290     92     209     29

803     380     83     38

504     450     54     45

# Comparing and ordering

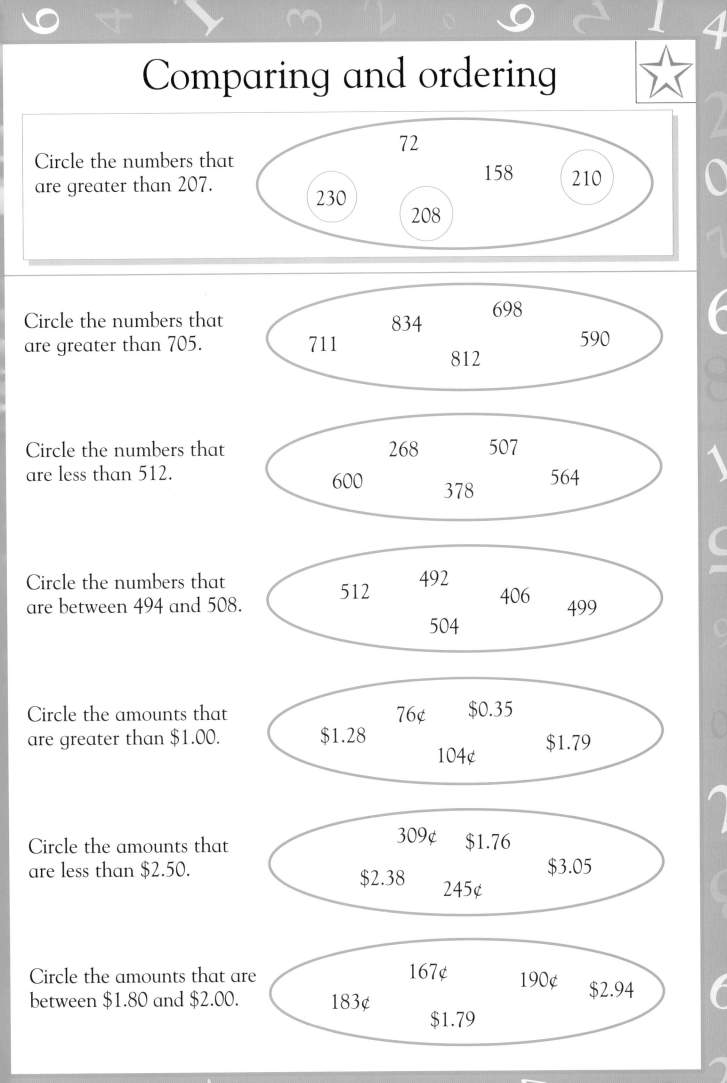

Circle the numbers that are greater than 207.

72

158    210

230

208

Circle the numbers that are greater than 705.

698

834

711    590

812

Circle the numbers that are less than 512.

268    507

600    564

378

Circle the numbers that are between 494 and 508.

492

512    406    499

504

Circle the amounts that are greater than $1.00.

76¢    $0.35

$1.28    $1.79

104¢

Circle the amounts that are less than $2.50.

309¢    $1.76

$2.38    $3.05

245¢

Circle the amounts that are between $1.80 and $2.00.

167¢    190¢    $2.94

183¢

$1.79

# Missing addends

Write the missing addend.

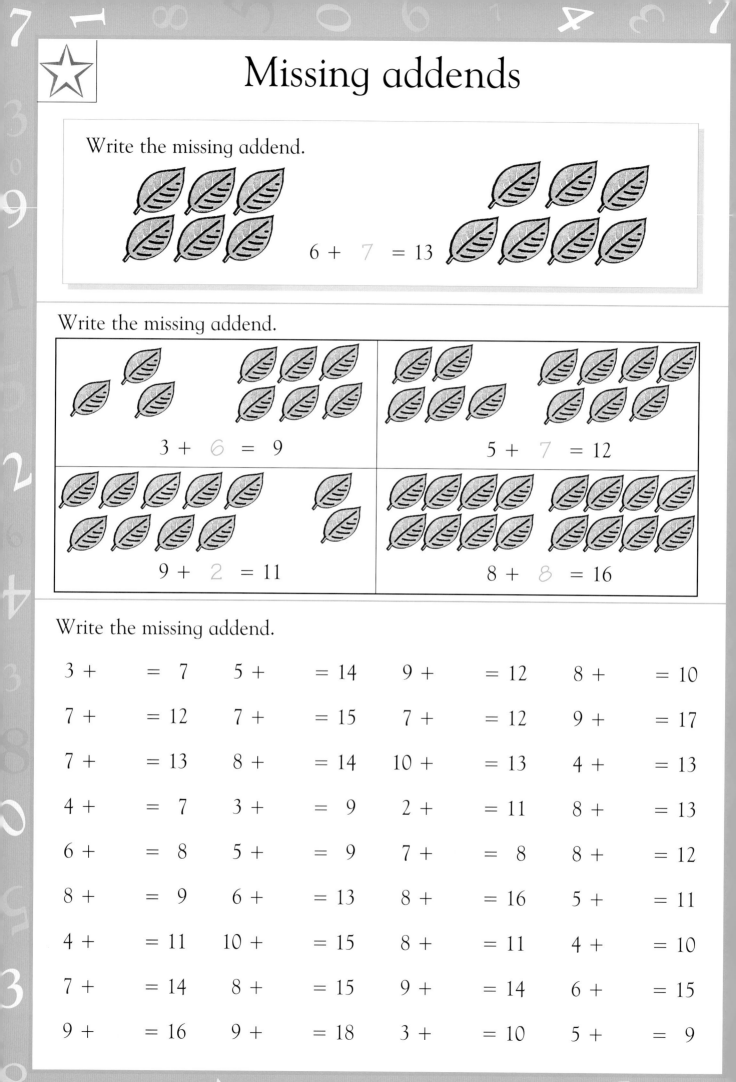

6 + 7 = 13

Write the missing addend.

3 + 6 = 9

5 + 7 = 12

9 + 2 = 11

8 + 8 = 16

Write the missing addend.

| 3 + | = 7 | 5 + | = 14 | 9 + | = 12 | 8 + | = 10 |
| 7 + | = 12 | 7 + | = 15 | 7 + | = 12 | 9 + | = 17 |
| 7 + | = 13 | 8 + | = 14 | 10 + | = 13 | 4 + | = 13 |
| 4 + | = 7 | 3 + | = 9 | 2 + | = 11 | 8 + | = 13 |
| 6 + | = 8 | 5 + | = 9 | 7 + | = 8 | 8 + | = 12 |
| 8 + | = 9 | 6 + | = 13 | 8 + | = 16 | 5 + | = 11 |
| 4 + | = 11 | 10 + | = 15 | 8 + | = 11 | 4 + | = 10 |
| 7 + | = 14 | 8 + | = 15 | 9 + | = 14 | 6 + | = 15 |
| 9 + | = 16 | 9 + | = 18 | 3 + | = 10 | 5 + | = 9 |

# Reading tables

Read the table. Then answer the questions.

**Ages of cousins**

| NAME | AGE |
|------|-----|
| Kinta | 8 |
| Paul | 7 |
| Clara | 9 |
| Meg | 7 |
| Lee | 6 |

How old is Paul?

Who is older than Kinta?

Who is the same age as Meg?

Who is the youngest?

---

Read the table. Then answer the questions.

**Favorite juice**

| Apple | 6 |
|-------|---|
| Cranberry | 2 |
| Grape | 3 |
| Cherry | 1 |
| Orange | 9 |

How many people chose orange juice?

Which juice did 2 people choose?

How many more people like orange juice than apple juice?

Did more people choose grape juice or cranberry juice?

---

Read the table. Then answer the questions.

**Weight of dogs**

| NAME | Bear | Mike | Perry | Spike | Marca |
|------|------|------|-------|-------|-------|
| POUNDS | 64 | 13 | 20 | 11 | 6 |

Which dog weighs more than 50 pounds?

Which dog weighs less than 10 pounds?

How much more does Perry weigh than Mike?

How much less does Spike weigh than Mike?

# Extending geometric patterns

Circle the next three squares in the pattern.

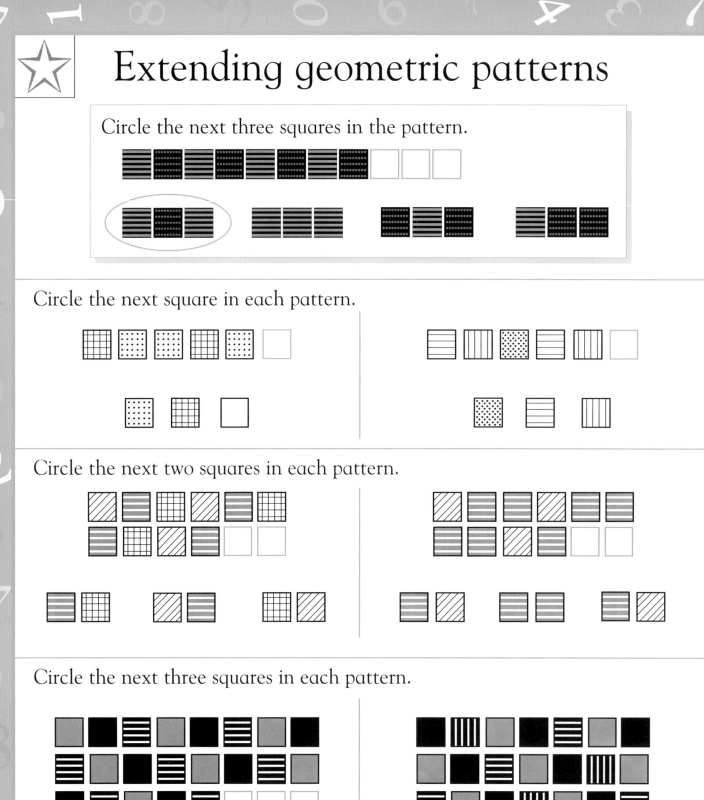

Circle the next square in each pattern.

Circle the next two squares in each pattern.

Circle the next three squares in each pattern.

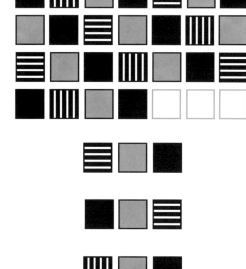

# Adding

Write the answer in each box.

| | | |
|---|---|---|
| $25 + 30 + 20 =$ | $60 + 25 + 15 =$ | $14 + 14 + 30 =$ |
| $72 + 12 + 10 =$ | $35 + 15 + 30 =$ | $30 + 13 + 14 =$ |
| $23 + 24 + 30 =$ | $42 + 16 + 20 =$ | $21 + 40 + 34 =$ |
| $32 + 10 + 45 =$ | $30 + 34 + 21 =$ | $15 + 15 + 60 =$ |
| $12 + 13 + 14 =$ | $10 + 11 + 12 =$ | $12 + 14 + 13 =$ |
| $15 + 21 + 32 =$ | $25 + 35 + 7 =$ | $20 + 14 + 5 =$ |
| $41 + 22 + 6 =$ | $42 + 13 + 4 =$ | $32 + 40 + 7 =$ |
| $62 + 8 + 11 =$ | $45 + 21 + 12 =$ | $31 + 51 + 6 =$ |
| $40 + 30 + 20 =$ | $50 + 40 + 20 =$ | $30 + 40 + 50 =$ |
| $8 + 11 + 80 =$ | $25 + 41 + 13 =$ | $43 + 30 + 6 =$ |
| $22 + 33 + 44 =$ | $13 + 70 + 11 =$ | $11 + 14 + 60 =$ |
| $17 + 12 + 60 =$ | $24 + 26 + 50 =$ | $31 + 8 + 20 =$ |

Write the answer in each box.

| | |
|---|---|
| $6 + 7 + 8 + 9 =$ | $4 + 6 + 8 + 10 =$ |
| $3 + 5 + 7 + 9 =$ | $8 + 9 + 10 + 11 =$ |
| $1 + 4 + 7 + 11 =$ | $8 + 6 + 4 + 2 =$ |
| $10 + 7 + 5 + 2 =$ | $9 + 7 + 5 + 3 =$ |

# Adding

Write the answer in the box.

$$\begin{array}{r} 34 \\ + \ 13 \\ \hline 47 \end{array} \qquad \begin{array}{r} {\scriptstyle 1} \\ 26 \\ + \ 15 \\ \hline 41 \end{array} \qquad \begin{array}{r} {\scriptstyle 1} \\ 73 \\ + \ 27 \\ \hline 100 \end{array}$$

Write the answer in the box.

$$\begin{array}{r} 45 \\ + \ 24 \\ \hline \end{array} \qquad \begin{array}{r} 31 \\ + \ 18 \\ \hline \end{array} \qquad \begin{array}{r} 53 \\ + \ 26 \\ \hline \end{array} \qquad \begin{array}{r} 62 \\ + \ 16 \\ \hline \end{array}$$

$$\begin{array}{r} 37 \\ + \ 10 \\ \hline \end{array} \qquad \begin{array}{r} 26 \\ + \ 13 \\ \hline \end{array} \qquad \begin{array}{r} 72 \\ + \ 15 \\ \hline \end{array} \qquad \begin{array}{r} 45 \\ + \ 24 \\ \hline \end{array}$$

$$\begin{array}{r} 39 \\ + \ 10 \\ \hline \end{array} \qquad \begin{array}{r} 24 \\ + \ 15 \\ \hline \end{array} \qquad \begin{array}{r} 52 \\ + \ 17 \\ \hline \end{array} \qquad \begin{array}{r} 36 \\ + \ 13 \\ \hline \end{array}$$

$$\begin{array}{r} 56 \\ + \ 14 \\ \hline \end{array} \qquad \begin{array}{r} 12 \\ + \ 16 \\ \hline \end{array} \qquad \begin{array}{r} 67 \\ + \ 11 \\ \hline \end{array} \qquad \begin{array}{r} 54 \\ + \ 16 \\ \hline \end{array}$$

$$\begin{array}{r} 48 \\ + \ 12 \\ \hline \end{array} \qquad \begin{array}{r} 64 \\ + \ 14 \\ \hline \end{array} \qquad \begin{array}{r} 36 \\ + \ 13 \\ \hline \end{array} \qquad \begin{array}{r} 55 \\ + \ 15 \\ \hline \end{array}$$

$$\begin{array}{r} 26 \\ + \ 17 \\ \hline \end{array} \qquad \begin{array}{r} 37 \\ + \ 14 \\ \hline \end{array} \qquad \begin{array}{r} 48 \\ + \ 19 \\ \hline \end{array} \qquad \begin{array}{r} 56 \\ + \ 17 \\ \hline \end{array}$$

$$\begin{array}{r} 28 \\ + \ 16 \\ \hline \end{array} \qquad \begin{array}{r} 64 \\ + \ 26 \\ \hline \end{array} \qquad \begin{array}{r} 56 \\ + \ 27 \\ \hline \end{array} \qquad \begin{array}{r} 38 \\ + \ 23 \\ \hline \end{array}$$

$$\begin{array}{r} 29 \\ + \ 24 \\ \hline \end{array} \qquad \begin{array}{r} 37 \\ + \ 27 \\ \hline \end{array} \qquad \begin{array}{r} 28 \\ + \ 17 \\ \hline \end{array} \qquad \begin{array}{r} 19 \\ + \ 26 \\ \hline \end{array}$$

$$\begin{array}{r} 26 \\ + \ 38 \\ \hline \end{array} \qquad \begin{array}{r} 36 \\ + \ 76 \\ \hline \end{array} \qquad \begin{array}{r} 46 \\ + \ 44 \\ \hline \end{array} \qquad \begin{array}{r} 34 \\ + \ 66 \\ \hline \end{array}$$

# Subtracting

> Write the answer in the box.
>
> 54 – 12 =  42        51 – 21 =  30

Write the answer in the box.

| | | | |
|---|---|---|---|
| 39 – 17 = | 48 – 16 = | 53 – 21 = | 57 – 33 = |
| 78 – 26 = | 47 – 24 = | 67 – 25 = | 79 – 27 = |
| 64 – 33 = | 73 – 23 = | 48 – 26 = | 77 – 34 = |
| 47 – 26 = | 66 – 26 = | 35 – 13 = | 98 – 36 = |
| 69 – 48 = | 57 – 34 = | 63 – 41 = | 76 – 53 = |

Write the answer in the box.

| | | | |
|---|---|---|---|
| 77¢ – 36¢ = | 47¢ – 23¢ = | 58¢ – 46¢ = | 69¢ – 46¢ = |
| 79¢ – 39¢ = | 76¢ – 34¢ = | 89¢ – 36¢ = | 91¢ – 41¢ = |
| 75¢ – 35¢ = | 68¢ – 26¢ = | 78¢ – 43¢ = | 45¢ – 35¢ = |
| 87¢ – 63¢ = | 49¢ – 34¢ = | 58¢ – 38¢ = | 47¢ – 34¢ = |
| 98¢ – 26¢ = | 79¢ – 29¢ = | 59¢ – 26¢ = | 67¢ – 35¢ = |

Write the answer in the box.

How much is 70¢ minus 23¢?

Take 46¢ away from $1.00.

How much is 85¢ minus 46¢?

Take away 47¢ from 94¢.

What is the difference between 56¢ and $1.00?

How much less than 72 in. is 36 in.?

Mia has 60¢. She spends 32¢ on candy. How much does she have left?

Take away 48 in. from 94 in.

# Subtracting

Write the answer in the box.

| $\begin{array}{r} {}^{6\ 13} \\ 7\!\!\!/3 \\ -\ 48 \\ \hline 25 \end{array}$ | $\begin{array}{r} {}^{3\ 15} \\ 4\!\!\!/5 \\ -\ 26 \\ \hline 19 \end{array}$ | $\begin{array}{r} {}^{6\ 12} \\ 7\!\!\!/2 \\ -\ 36 \\ \hline 36 \end{array}$ |

Write the answer in the box.

| 67 | 43 | 63 | 72 |
|----|----|----|----|
| − 48 | − 26 | − 46 | − 45 |

| 71 | 82 | 63 | 90 |
|----|----|----|----|
| − 47 | − 36 | − 44 | − 47 |

| 80 | 90 | 65 | 81 |
|----|----|----|----|
| − 46 | − 63 | − 37 | − 47 |

Write the answer in the box.

| 46 in. | 59 in. | 74 in. | 60 in. |
|--------|--------|--------|--------|
| − 18 in. | − 36 in. | − 27 in. | − 44 in. |

| 70 in. | 54 in. | 39 in. | 91 in. |
|--------|--------|--------|--------|
| − 47 in. | − 26 in. | − 4 in. | − 47 in. |

Write the answer in the box.

| 43¢ | 61¢ | 73¢ | 71¢ |
|-----|-----|-----|-----|
| − 17¢ | − 24¢ | − 36¢ | − 46¢ |

| 70¢ | 81¢ | 63¢ | 74¢ |
|-----|-----|-----|-----|
| − 44¢ | − 37¢ | − 46¢ | − 44¢ |

| 90 in. | 94 in. | 96 in. | 98¢ |
|--------|--------|--------|-----|
| − 34 in. | − 47 in. | −78 in. | − 45¢ |

# Reading a calendar

Look at this calendar. Then answer the questions.

**September**

| S | M | T | W | T | F | S |
|---|---|---|---|---|---|---|
|   | 1 | 2 | 3 | 4 | 5 | 6 |
| 7 | 8 | 9 | 10 | 11 | 12 | 13 |
| 14 | 15 | 16 | 17 | 18 | 19 | 20 |
| 21 | 22 | 23 | 24 | 25 | 26 | 27 |
| 28 | 29 | 30 |   |   |   |   |

What day of the week is the first day of September on this calendar?

What date is the last Tuesday in September?

---

Look at this calendar. Then answer the questions.

How many days are in the month of July?

**July**

| S | M | T | W | T | F | S |
|---|---|---|---|---|---|---|
|   |   |   |   | 1 | 2 | 3 |
| 4 | 5 | 6 | 7 | 8 | 9 | 10 |
| 11 | 12 | 13 | 14 | 15 | 16 | 17 |
| 18 | 19 | 20 | 21 | 22 | 23 | 24 |
| 25 | 26 | 27 | 28 | 29 | 30 | 31 |

What day of the week is the last day of July on this calendar?

A camp starts on July 5 and ends on July 9. How many camp days are there?

The campers go swimming on Tuesday and Thursday. On which dates will they swim?

---

Look at this calendar. Then answer the questions.

What date is the first Sunday of November?

**November**

| S | M | T | W | T | F | S |
|---|---|---|---|---|---|---|
|   |   |   |   |   |   | 1 |
| 2 | 3 | 4 | 5 | 6 | 7 | 8 |
| 9 | 10 | 11 | 12 | 13 | 14 | 15 |
| 16 | 17 | 18 | 19 | 20 | 21 | 22 |
| 23 | 24 | 25 | 26 | 27 | 28 | 29 |
| 30 |   |   |   |   |   |   |

What day of the week is November 14?

How many Saturdays are shown in November?

Jenna's birthday is November 23. What day of the week is it?

# ⭐ Multiplication as repeated addition

Write how many.

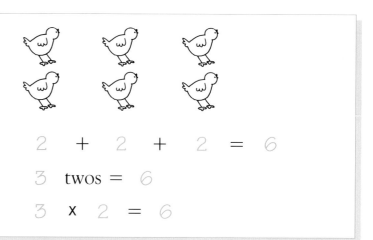

There are  3  groups.

There are  2  in each group.

You can add.

You can multiply.

2  +  2  +  2  =  6

3  twos =  6

3  x  2  =  6

---

Write how many.

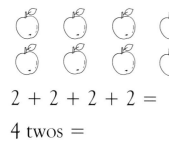

2 + 2 + 2 + 2 =

4 twos =

+  =

twos =

+  +  +  +  =

twos =

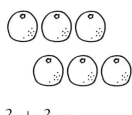

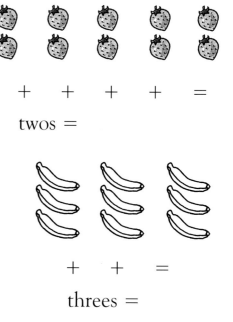

3 + 3 =

2 threes =

+  +  +  =

threes =

+  +  =

threes =

---

Write how many.

How many groups?

How many in each group?

Write as addition.

+  +  =

Write as multiplication.

x  =

How many groups?

How many in each group?

Write as addition.

+  +  +  =

Write as multiplication.

x  =

# Choose the operation

Put either + or − in the box to make each answer correct.

20 **+** 13 = 33          24 **−** 18 = 6          17 **+** 14 = 31

---

Put either + or − in the box to make each answer correct.

| | | | |
|---|---|---|---|
| 15 ___ 19 = 34 | 21 ___ 9 = 12 | 16 ___ 11 = 5 | 29 ___ 23 = 52 |
| 60 ___ 25 = 35 | 45 ___ 18 = 63 | 65 ___ 30 = 35 | 42 ___ 18 = 60 |
| 71 ___ 36 = 107 | 60 ___ 37 = 23 | 57 ___ 12 = 45 | 66 ___ 16 = 82 |
| 59 ___ 20 = 39 | 72 ___ 40 = 32 | 84 ___ 32 = 52 | 38 ___ 38 = 76 |
| 29 ___ 29 = 0 | 45 ___ 45 = 90 | 29 ___ 45 = 74 | 73 ___ 16 = 57 |

---

Write the answer in the box.

I add 26 to a number and the answer is 50. What number did I start with?

36 added to a number gives a total of 64. What is the number?

I take 22 away from a number and have 15 left. What number did I start with?

Two numbers are added together and the total is 84. One of the numbers is 66. What is the other number?

67 added to a number makes 80. What is the number?

I subtract 18 from a number and the result is 24. What number did I start with?

Two numbers add up to 55. One of the numbers is 25. What is the other number?

After spending 34¢, I have 65¢ left. How much did I start with?

---

Write + or − in the box.

| | | |
|---|---|---|
| 17¢ ___ 35¢ = 52¢ | 46¢ ___ 37¢ = 9¢ | 72¢ ___ 31¢ = 41¢ |
| 68¢ ___ 68¢ = 0¢ | 25¢ ___ 3¢ = 22¢ | 80¢ ___ 46¢ = 34¢ |
| 74¢ ___ 20¢ = 94¢ | 28¢ ___ 14¢ = 42¢ | 52¢ ___ 17¢ = 35¢ |
| 53¢ ___ 24¢ = 77¢ | 63¢ ___ 27¢ = 36¢ | 56¢ ___ 23¢ = 79¢ |

# Venn diagrams

Read the clues to find the secret number.

1 2 3 4 5

3
5    7

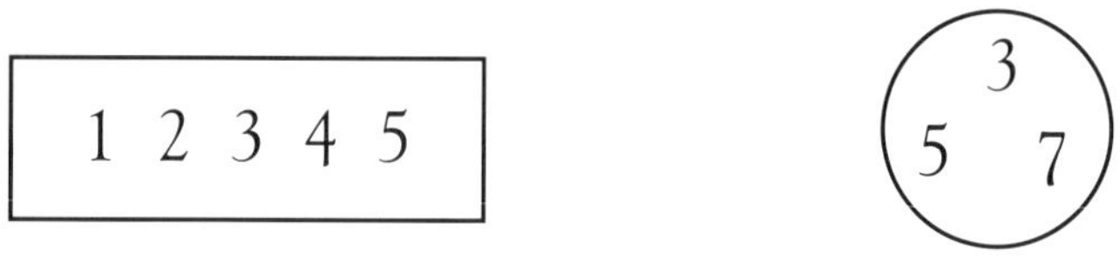

It is in both the rectangle and the circle.

It is greater than 3.

What number is it?    5

Read the clues to find the secret number.

10
12   13
16       14

12       15

11       14

13

It is not in the square.
It is an even number.
It is less than 12.

What number is it?

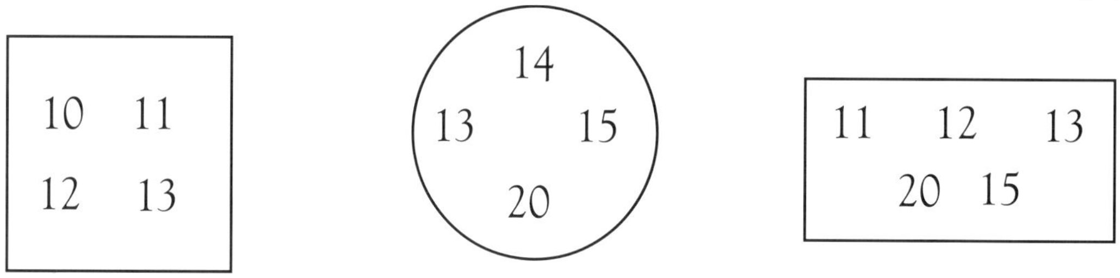

10   11

12   13

14
13        15

20

11    12    13
20   15

It is in the rectangle and the circle.
It is greater than 13 and less than 20.
It is an odd number.

What number is it?

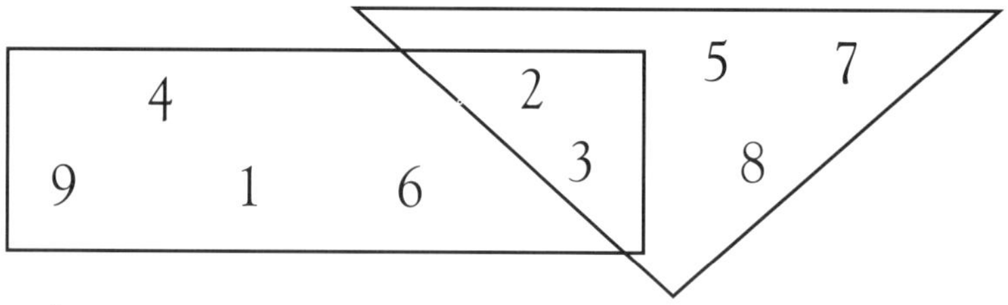

4

9        1        6

2        5    7

3        8

It is not an even number.
It is in the triangle.
It is in the rectangle.

What number is it?

# Working with coins

Write the answer in the box.

Annie has these coins.

How much does Annie
have altogether?

Ian has three coins
that total 51¢. Which
coins does he have?

Doris is given three coins in her change.
The coins add up to 65¢.
Which coins does
Doris have?

How much less than $1.00 is the total of
these coins?

Which coin is smaller in
size than a penny?

What is the total of these coins?

Steve has these coins.

Rashid has these coins.

How much more money
does Steve have than Rashid?

Which three coins
add up to 36¢?

Bill has 68¢. Which three
coins could he be given to
make his money total 80¢?

Jan has these coins.

Jose has these coins.

How much more does
Jan have than Jose?

# Money problems

Write the answer in the box.

How much needs to be added to 65¢ to make $1.00?          35¢

What is the total of           0

---

Write the answer in the box.

How many 5¢ coins are needed to make a total of 50¢?

One dollar is shared equally by four children. How much will they each get?

How much do three dimes make?

How many groups of $2.50 are needed to make $10.00?

Andrea spends $1.63 and gives the storekeeper $2.00. How much change does she get?

After spending $1.50, Andrew has 90¢ left. How much did Andrew start with?

How many 25¢ coins are equal to $1.00?

Julie has $2.60 and is given $2.40. How much does Julie have now?

Wendy needs $5.00 for a T-shirt but only has $1.60. How much more does Wendy need?

Sean has $2.05 but needs $4.00 to buy a toy. How much more does Sean need?

---

Write the answer in the box.

$1.10 − $0.60 =          $2.50 + $2.50 =          $1.50 + $0.65 =

$1.20 − $0.90 =          $5.00 + $2.35 =          75¢  −  35¢  =

65¢  −  45¢  =          $2.27 + $3.33 =          56¢  −  45¢  =

50¢  +  60¢  =          80¢  −  30¢  =          $1.60 + $4.50 =

$1.80 − $0.50 =          $2.00 − $0.50 =          $2.60 + $2.35 =

# Measurement problems

Write the answer in the box.

How many grams are equal to 1 kilogram?    1000 g

How many milliliters are the same as 1 liter?    1000 ml

Write the answer in the box. Use the information above.

How many grams are equal to half a kilogram?

How many milliliters are the same as 2 liters?

Is 800 ml more or less than half a liter?

How many 100 g weights are equal to 1 kilogram?

Is 300 ml more or less than half a liter?

How many grams are the same as 3 kg?

How many 200 ml glasses are equal to one liter?

How many milliliters are the same as 0.5 liters?

How many grams are the same as 3 kg?

How many 250 ml jars are equal to one liter?

Which unit of measurement would you use for each of these? Choose from meter, gram, milliliter, liter, kilometer and kilogram.

To measure the mass of a dog.

To measure the capacity of a spoon.

To measure the distance from France to England.

To measure the capacity of a bucket.

To measure the mass of a caterpillar.

To measure the length of a short fence.

# Telling time

What time does each clock or watch show?

20 to 6

quarter after 9

What time does each clock or watch show?

Join each clock to the watch that shows the same time.

# Telling time

Draw the hands on the clock
to show 5:20.

Draw the hands on each clock to show the time.

3:20

5:30

8:35

7:45

9:25

11:15

10:05

6:10

9:45

12:15

1:40

12:05

2:10

6:30

8:05

# Telling time

Show twenty after seven on the watch.    Show half past four on the watch.

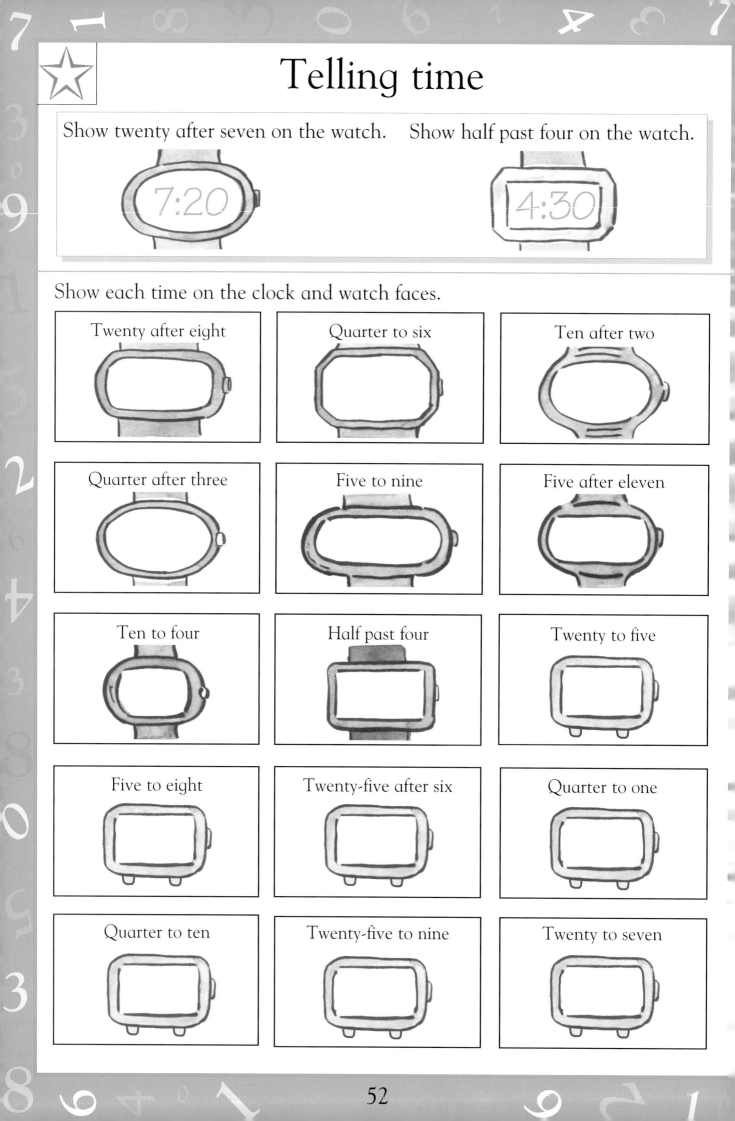

7:20

4:30

Show each time on the clock and watch faces.

Twenty after eight

Quarter to six

Ten after two

Quarter after three

Five to nine

Five after eleven

Ten to four

Half past four

Twenty to five

Five to eight

Twenty-five after six

Quarter to one

Quarter to ten

Twenty-five to nine

Twenty to seven

# Bar graphs

Look at the bar graph. Then answer the question.

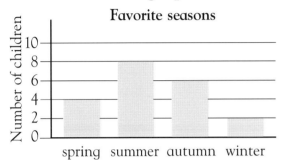

How many cherries does Robbie have?

6

Look at the bar graph. Then answer the questions.

This graph shows the favorite seasons of a group of children. How many children were asked which season they liked best?

How many children liked autumn best?

Which season did 4 children like?

Which was the favorite season?

How many more children liked autumn than liked winter?

Look at the bar graph. Then answer the questions.

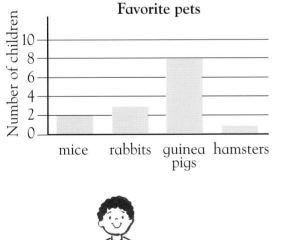

This graph shows the favorite pets of a group of children. How many children were asked about which pets they liked?

Which pet did 8 children like?

How many children liked rabbits?

How many children liked hamsters?

How many more children liked rabbits than liked hamsters?

# 2-dimensional shapes

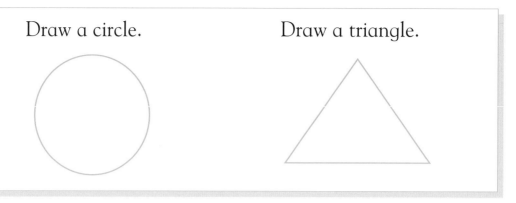

Draw a circle.

Draw a triangle.

Draw each shape.

| Rectangle | Circle | Square |
|---|---|---|
|  |  |  |

| Pentagon | Hexagon | Octagon |
|---|---|---|
|  |  |  |

| Triangle with three equal sides | Triangle with two equal sides | Triangle with no equal sides |
|---|---|---|
|  |  |  |

# Properties of polygons

Circle the polygon that has the same number of sides.

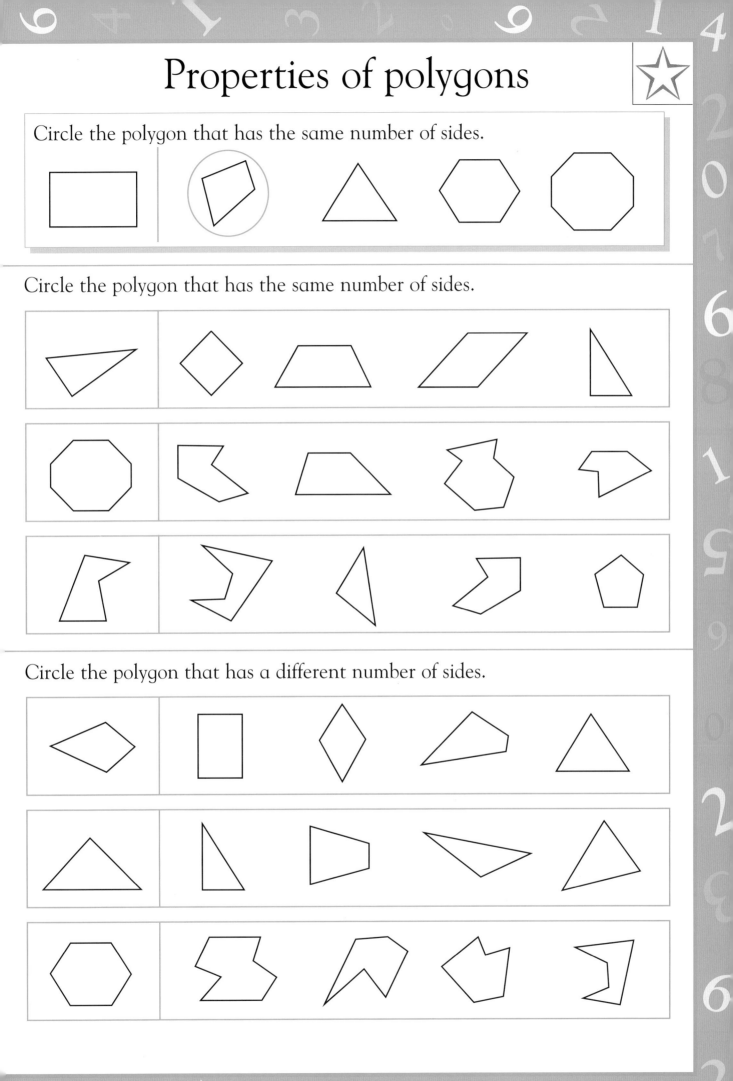

Circle the polygon that has the same number of sides.

Circle the polygon that has a different number of sides.

55

# Pictographs

Look at this pictograph. Then answer the questions.

**People using the puppet theater**

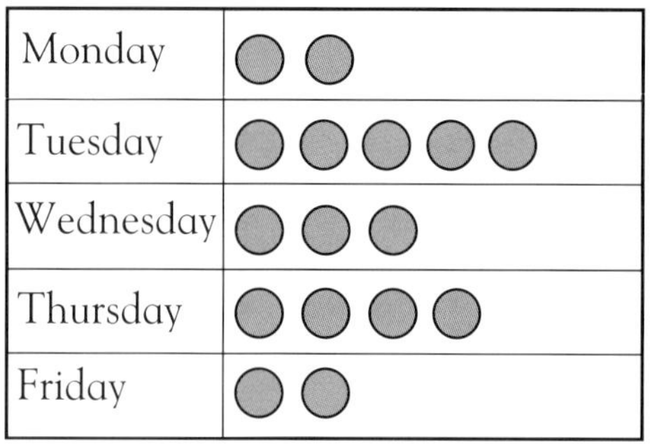

| Monday | ● ● |
|---|---|
| Tuesday | ● ● ● ● ● |
| Wednesday | ● ● ● |
| Thursday | ● ● ● ● |
| Friday | ● ● |

Three people can use the
puppet theater at a time
● = 3 people

How many people used
the puppet theater on Friday?            6

Did more people use the theater on
Wednesday or Monday?            Wednesday

How many more people used the
theater on Tuesday than Friday?            9 more

How many people used the
theater on Monday and Tuesday?            21

Look at this pictograph. Then answer the questions.

**Favorite way of traveling**

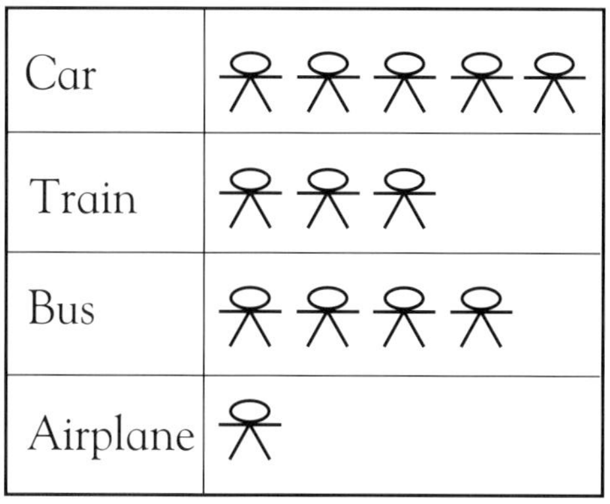

| Car | ⟨⟨⟨⟨⟨ |
|---|---|
| Train | ⟨⟨⟨ |
| Bus | ⟨⟨⟨⟨ |
| Airplane | ⟨ |

⟨ = 5 people

How many people
like to travel by bus?

Do more people like to
travel by bus or by airplane?

Which way to travel
did the least people choose?

How many more people like
to travel by car than by train?

How many people
chose train and bus?

How many people
were included in the graph?

Look at this pictograph. Then answer the questions.

**Number of cookies sold**

| Carmen | ▥ ▥ ▥ ▥ ▥ |
|---|---|
| Dino | ▥ ▥ |
| Peter | ▥ ▥ ▥ ▥ |
| Kathy | ▥ ▥ ▥ |

▥ = 10 people

Who sold the most cookies?

Who sold the fewest cookies?

How many more cookies
did Peter sell than Dino?

How many cookies did
Carmen and Kathy sell together?

How many cookies were sold in all?

# Most likely/least likely

Look at the marbles. Then answer the questions.

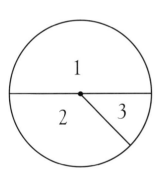

Which kind of marble would you be least likely to pick without looking?

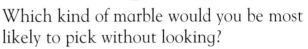

Which kind of marble would you be most likely to pick without looking?

Look at the spinner. Then answer the questions.

Is the spinner more likely to land on 1 or 2?

Is the spinner more likely to land on 2 or 3?

Which number is the spinner most likely to land on?

Which number is the spinner least likely to land on?

Look at the tally chart. Then answer the questions.

Imagine that each time you shake the bag, one coin falls out.

**Tally of coins in the bag**

| COLOR | TALLIES |
|---|---|
| Pennies | IIII |
| Dimes | II |
| Nickels | ЖⅡ |
| Quarters | Ж |

Is a penny or a dime more likely to fall out?

Is a quarter or a nickel more likely to fall out?

Which coin is most likely to fall out?

Which coin is least likely to fall out?

# 3-dimensional shapes

Write the name of each shape.

Sphere                    Cube

Write the name of each shape. Use the names in the Word Box.

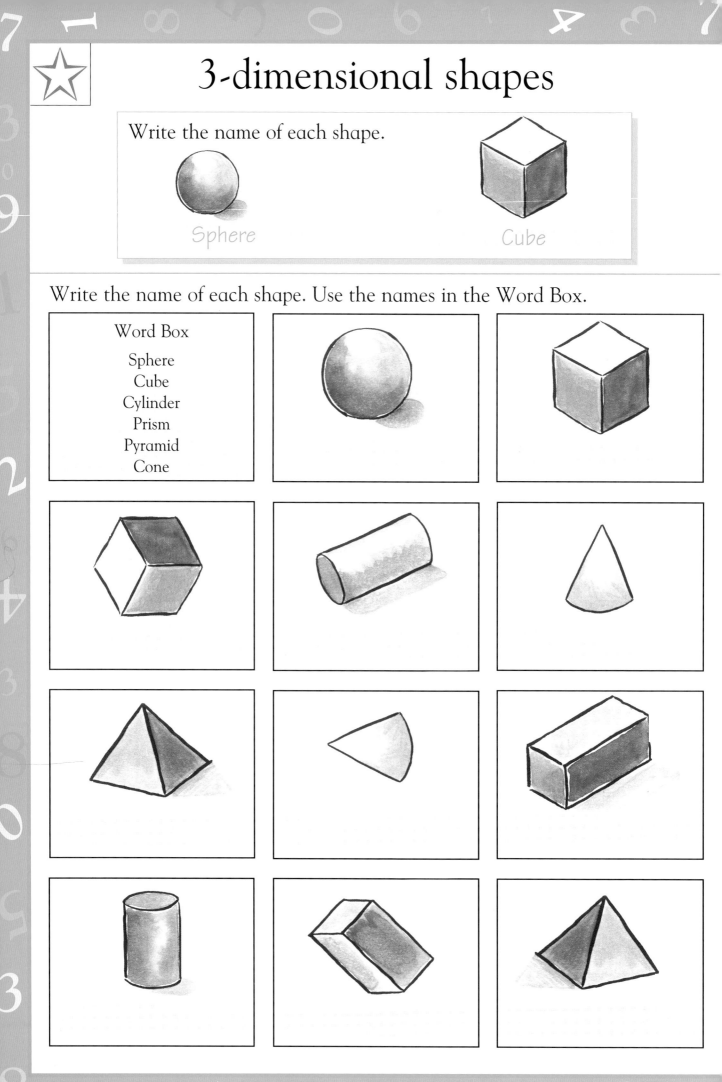

Word Box

Sphere
Cube
Cylinder
Prism
Pyramid
Cone

# Sorting 3-dimensional shapes

Look at these shapes.

Which shape has corners?     *prism*

Which shape has no corners?     *sphere*

Sphere          Prism

Look at these shapes.

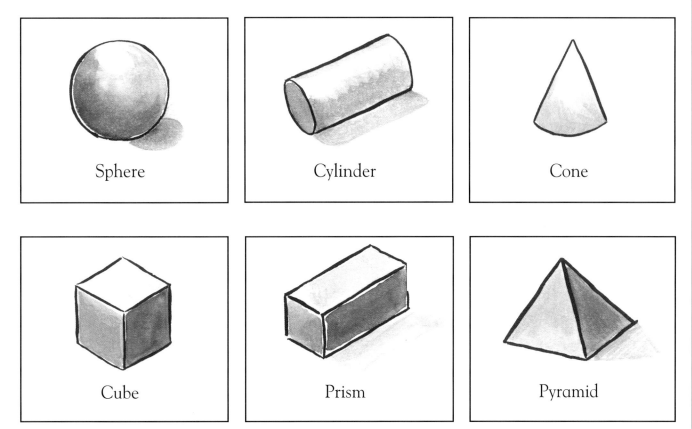

Sphere          Cylinder          Cone

Cube          Prism          Pyramid

Now complete this table by writing the name of each shape in the correct box.

| Shapes that have corners | Shapes that have no corners |
|---|---|
|  |  |

# Location on a grid

Look at the grid. Write where the * can be found.

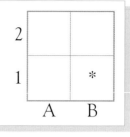

B, 1

Look at the grid. Then follow the directions below.

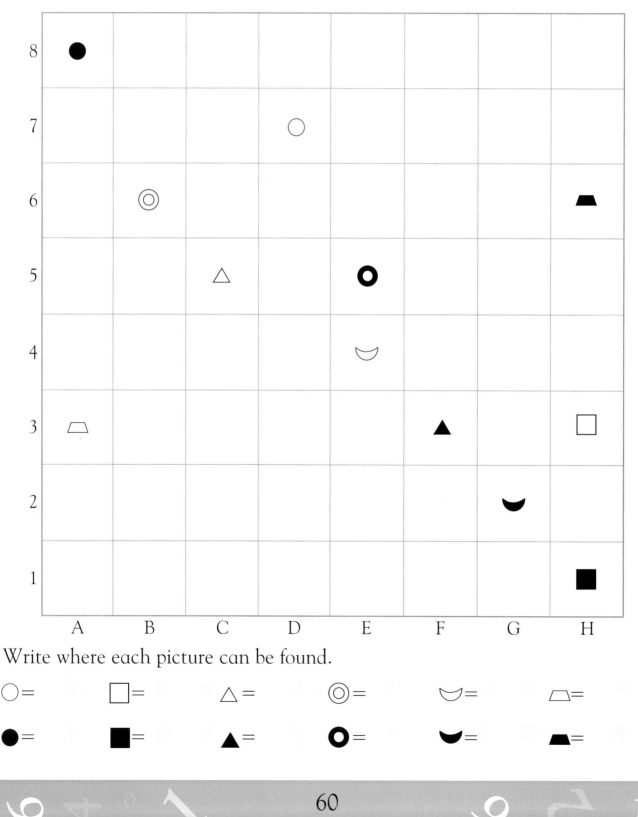

Write where each picture can be found.

◯ =        ☐ =        △ =        ◎ =        ⌣ =        ⬭ =

⬤ =        ■ =        ▲ =        ◯ =        ⌣ =        ◣ =

# Location on a grid

Color B, 2 on the grid.

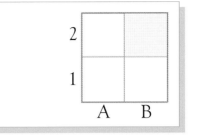

Mark each box on the grid with the correct color.

yellow at E, 2    green at A, 6    yellow at C, 1    green at H, 4
purple at D, 6    red at E, 7    red at F, 3    purple at B, 5
orange at G, 8    blue at D, 2    orange at C, 5    blue at F, 7

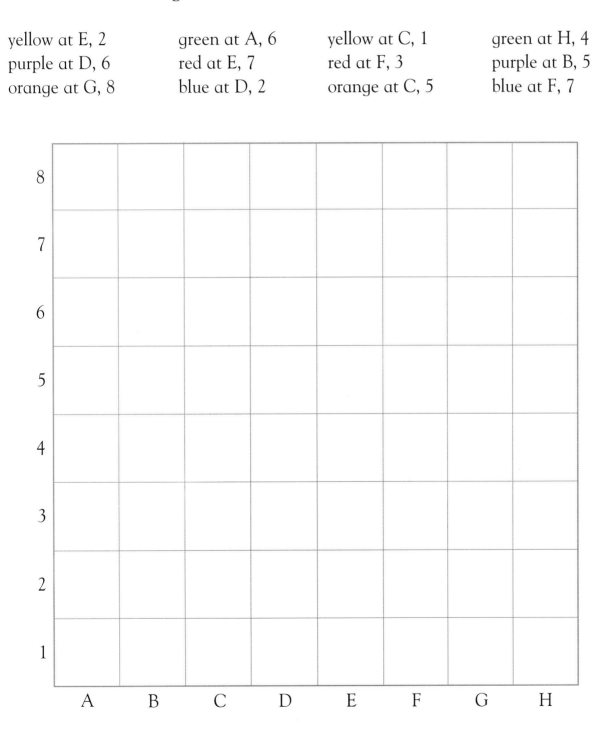

# Square corners

Circle the square corners on each shape.

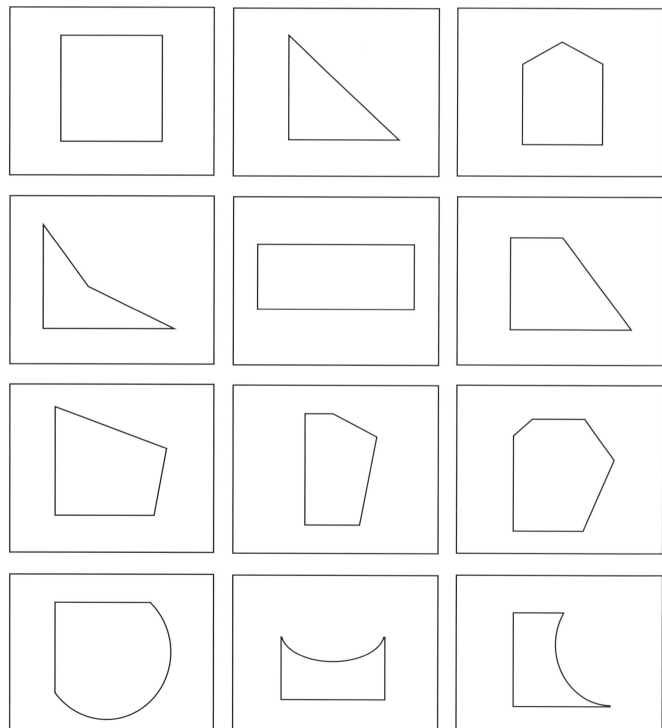

Circle the square corners on each shape.

# Square corners

Circle the square corners on these shapes.

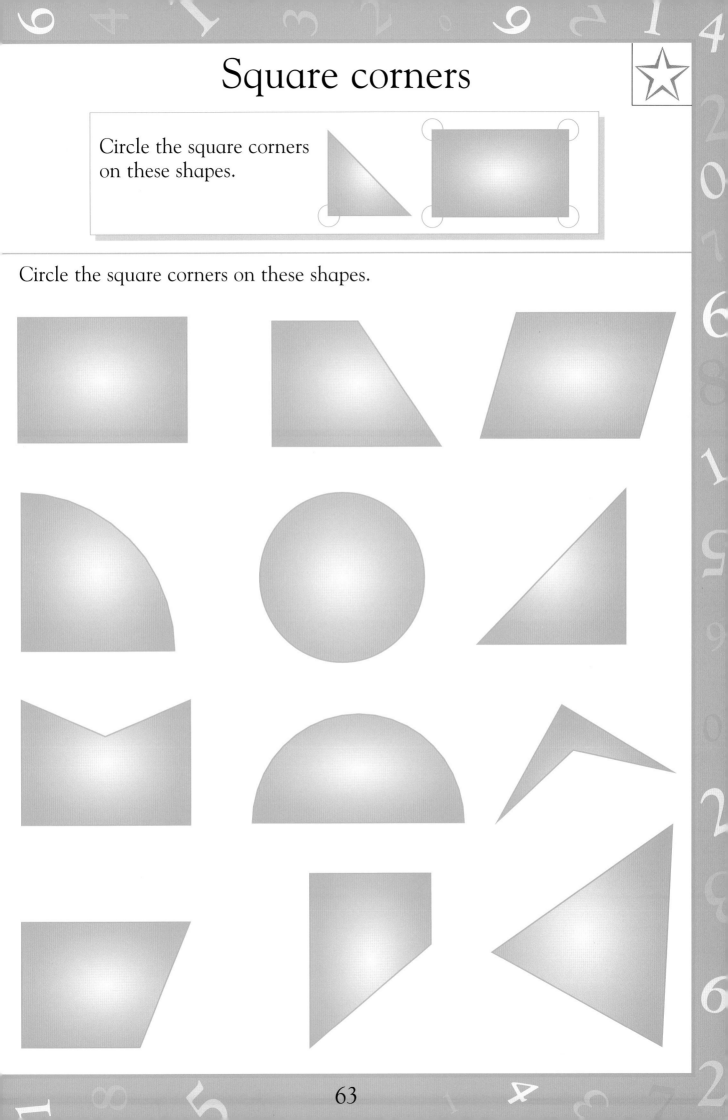

Circle the square corners on these shapes.

# Adding

Write the answer between the lines.

```
   721          1 1            502
        646
+   35      +   98      +   25
   756         744           527
```

Write the answer between the lines.

```
   220        491        560        709        312
+   36      +   50      +   64      +   53      +   30
_____       _____       _____       _____       _____
```

```
   203        970        348        470        662
+   41      +   12      +   25      +   10      +   49
_____       _____       _____       _____       _____
```

```
   241        371        437        421        752
+   12      +   83      +   45      + 168      +   67
_____       _____       _____       _____       _____
```

```
   792        534        615        185        658
+   38      +   99      +   25      +   87      +   17
_____       _____       _____       _____       _____
```

Write the answer between the lines.

```
  $9.45      $5.60      $8.35      $6.50      $1.65
+ $0.68    + $0.43    + $0.89    + $0.70    + $0.95
_____     _____     _____     _____     _____
```

```
  $7.29      $4.82     $10.19      $3.78      $9.12
+ $0.12    + $0.18    +$ 0.94    + $0.47    + $0.74
_____     _____     _____     _____     _____
```

# Ordering

Write these numbers in order starting with the smallest.

| 270 | 720 | 207 | 702 |
|---|---|---|---|

| 870 | 780 | 807 | 708 |
|---|---|---|---|

| 906 | 690 | 960 | 609 |
|---|---|---|---|

| 106 | 610 | 601 | 160 |
|---|---|---|---|

| 560 | 506 | 650 | 605 |
|---|---|---|---|

| 849 | 489 | 948 | 984 |
|---|---|---|---|

| 890 | 980 | 809 | 908 |
|---|---|---|---|

| 486 | 684 | 864 | 648 |
|---|---|---|---|

| 405 | 450 | 540 | 504 |
|---|---|---|---|

| 746 | 647 | 764 | 674 |
|---|---|---|---|

| 570 | 586 | 490 | 92 |
|---|---|---|---|

| 76 | 104 | 200 | 92 |
|---|---|---|---|

| 440 | 66 | 781 | 177 |
|---|---|---|---|

| 632 | 236 | 77 | 407 |
|---|---|---|---|

| 842 | 587 | 99 | 88 |
|---|---|---|---|

| 74 | 101 | 12 | 800 |
|---|---|---|---|

| 500 | 468 | 395 | 288 |
|---|---|---|---|

| 600 | 304 | 403 | 89 |
|---|---|---|---|

| 78 | 9 | 302 | 470 |
|---|---|---|---|

| 345 | 543 | 53 | 34 |
|---|---|---|---|

# Adding

Write the answer between the lines.

```
   324        537         608
 + 152      + 164       + 549
 ─────      ─────       ─────
   476        701        1157
```

Write the answer between the lines.

```
   560        342        329        253        607
 + 361      + 450      + 624      + 553      + 349
 ─────      ─────      ─────      ─────      ─────

 ─────      ─────      ─────      ─────      ─────
```

```
   273        117        721        308        822
 + 265      + 483      + 195      + 500      + 103
 ─────      ─────      ─────      ─────      ─────

 ─────      ─────      ─────      ─────      ─────
```

```
   220        491        560        709        312
 + 163      + 299      + 340      + 168      + 312
 ─────      ─────      ─────      ─────      ─────

 ─────      ─────      ─────      ─────      ─────
```

```
   805        380        160        626        725
 + 191      + 461      + 175      + 302      + 125
 ─────      ─────      ─────      ─────      ─────

 ─────      ─────      ─────      ─────      ─────
```

Write the answer between the lines.

```
   738        607        826        591        450
 + 480      + 523      + 372      + 537      + 935
 ─────      ─────      ─────      ─────      ─────

 ─────      ─────      ─────      ─────      ─────
```

# Counting

Write the missing numbers above each ↑.

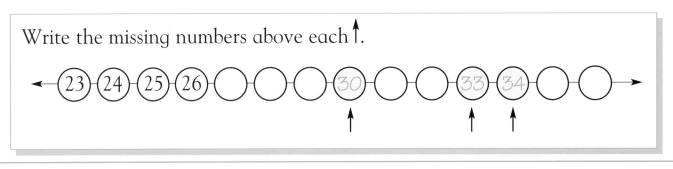

Write the missing numbers above each ↑.

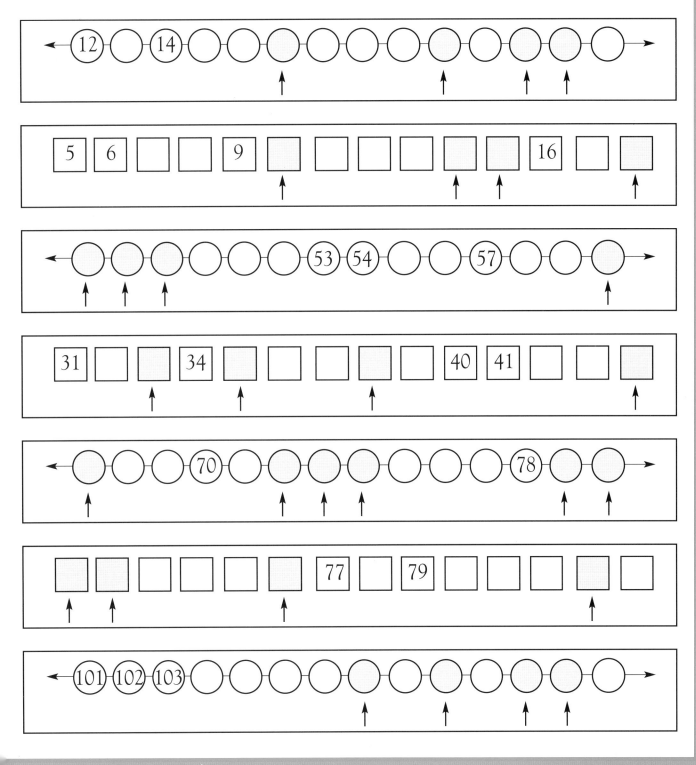

67

# Place value

The value of 5 in <u>5</u>23 is    500    or    five hundred

The value of 2 in 5<u>2</u>3 is    20    or    twenty

The value of 3 in 52<u>3</u> is    3    or    three

Change the 2 in 24 to 3.    34    The number is greater by    10

What is the value of 5 in these numbers?
Write each value with a number and with a word.

| 35 | 152 | 905 | 512 |

| 65 | 547 | 57 | 950 |

Circle each number that has a 3 with the value of thirty.

632      953      13      534      38      355

Circle each number that has a 4 with the value of four hundred.

482      954      434      544      444      104

Circle each number that has an 8 with the value of eight.

38      83      813      85      638      888

Write the new number. Then write the value.

Change the 6 in 86 to 9.      The number is greater by

Change the 1 in 17 to 4.      The number is greater by

Change the 3 in 305 to 5.      The number is greater by

Change the 6 in 86 to 5.      The number is less by

Change the 4 in 42 to 2.      The number is less by

Change the 7 in 704 to 2.      The number is less by

# Fractions of shapes

Shade half of each shape.

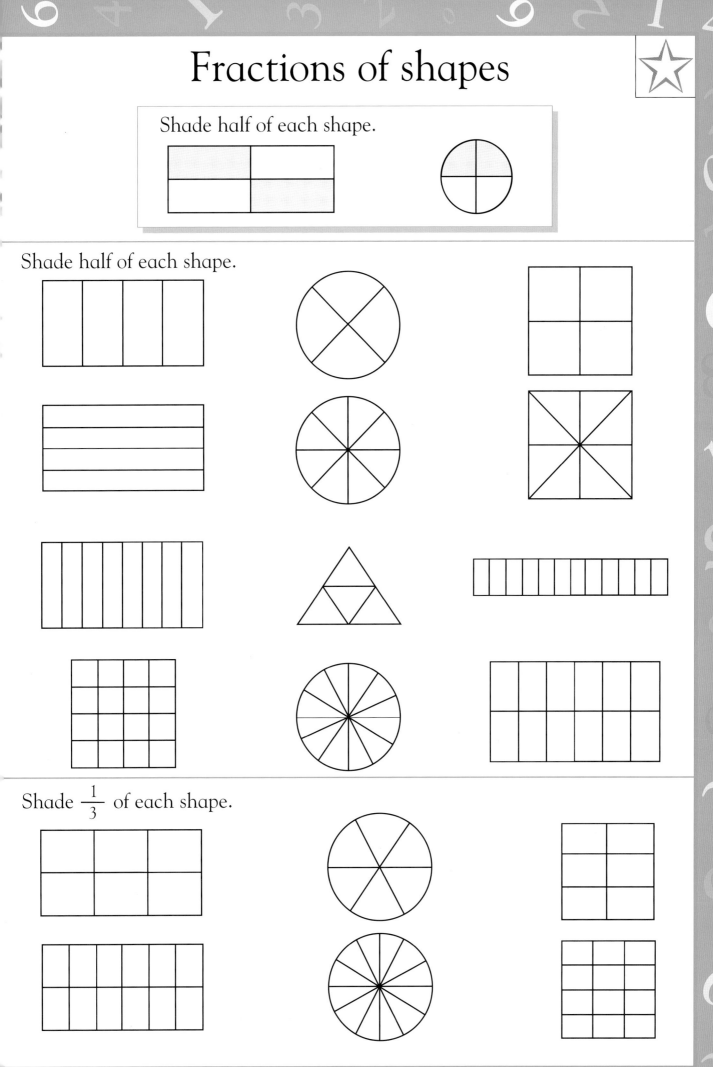

Shade half of each shape.

Shade $\frac{1}{3}$ of each shape.

# Finding patterns

Find the counting pattern. Write the missing numbers.

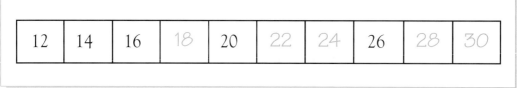

| 12 | 14 | 16 | 18 | 20 | 22 | 24 | 26 | 28 | 30 |

Find the counting pattern. Write the missing numbers.

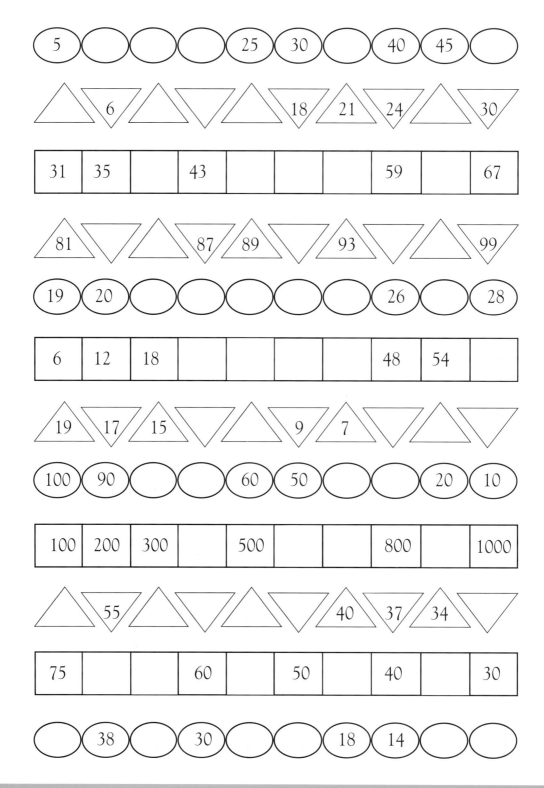

5 ◯ ◯ ◯ 25 30 ◯ 40 45 ◯

△ 6 ▽ △ ▽ △ 18 21 24 ▽ △ 30

| 31 | 35 | | 43 | | | | 59 | | 67 |

81 ▽ △ 87 89 ▽ △ 93 ▽ △ 99

19 20 ◯ ◯ ◯ ◯ ◯ 26 ◯ 28

| 6 | 12 | 18 | | | | 48 | 54 | |

19 17 15 ▽ △ 9 7 ▽ △ ▽

100 90 ◯ ◯ 60 50 ◯ ◯ 20 10

| 100 | 200 | 300 | | 500 | | | 800 | | 1000 |

△ 55 ▽ △ ▽ △ 40 37 34 ▽

| 75 | | | 60 | | 50 | | 40 | | 30 |

◯ 38 ◯ 30 ◯ ◯ 18 14 ◯ ◯

# Adding

Write the answer in the box.

One child has 46 jacks. Another child has 35 jacks.
How many jacks do the children have altogether?

*81*

Write the answer in the box.

Scott has 47¢ and Mira has 36¢. How much do they have in all?

David has 29¢ and Katie has 62¢. How much do they have altogether?

Penny skips for 24 seconds and then Bob skips for 54 seconds. For how many seconds did they skip in total?

Dan finds 44¢ in one pocket and 38¢ in his other pocket. How much does he have altogether?

A line is 45 inches long. Peta continues it for another 25 inches. How long is the line now?

What is the sum when 17 is added to 38?

Three girls add their money together. They have $26, $24, and $20. How much do they have altogether?

A pencil 11 cm long is put end to end with another pencil 12 cm long. What is the total length of the two pencils?

What is the total when 34 is added to 46?

One child has 47 football cards. Another has 48 football cards. How many cards do they have altogether?

One bag of candy has 26 toffee bars. A second bag has 19 bars. How many toffee bars are there altogether?

Abel spends 48¢ on candy and then 38¢ on an ice cream. How much has Abel spent altogether?

Martha has 45 marbles in one hand and 56 in the other hand. How many marbles does Martha have altogether?

A bag of cherries has 43 ripe ones and 17 rotten ones. How many cherries are in the bag?

There are 34 children in one class and 36 in another. How many children are there in total?

# Adding

Write the answer in the box.

What is the total of 13, 17,
and 20?

Joanne is given some money at
Christmas. She is given $5.00 by
Uncle Eddie, $2.50 by Aunt Jo,
and $3.50 by her sister. How
much is she given in all?

A child collects 32 birthday cards
and 77 Christmas cards. How
many cards does she have?

How much do these coins add
up to: 25¢, 50¢, 10¢, and 5¢?

Add together 50¢, 20¢,
and 50¢.

What is the sum of 23, 24,
and 25?

Jane has three piggy banks.
One has $1.20, the second has
$0.80, and the third has $3.00.
How much does Jane have
altogether?

How much is 50¢ plus 70¢
plus 80¢?

One bag holds 24 grapes,
another bag holds 34 grapes,
and the third bag holds
30 grapes. What is the total
number of grapes?

Bill collects comics. He has
120 and is given 60 more by a
friend. How many comics does
Bill have now?

Jill buys three bars of chocolate.
One costs 30¢, another costs 28¢,
and the third costs 32¢. What is
the total cost of the chocolate?

What is the total of 60, 70,
and 80?

Three loads of sand are delivered
to a building site. They weigh
70 lb, 90 lb, and 100 lb. How
much do they weigh altogether?

Add together 12, 24, and 36.

A teacher gives out 33 stars on
Monday, 25 on Tuesday, and 35 on
Wednesday. How many stars has
she given out altogether?

# Subtracting

Write the answer in the box.

Doris had 40 marbles but then lost 17 in a game.
How many marbles does Doris have left?

23

---

Write the answer in the box.

I have 35 jelly beans. Then I eat 12. How many are left?

Two numbers add up to 30. One of the numbers is 18. What is the other number?

A piece of wood is 60 inches long. A section 28 inches long is cut off. How long is the remaining piece of wood?

Two numbers add up to 80. One of the numbers is 45. What is the other number?

A class has 33 children. 15 of the class are boys. How many of the class are girls?

Out of 46 squirrels, 38 are gray and the rest are red. How many squirrels are red?

What is 56 less than 100?

A bag contains 60 cherries. 12 of the cherries are rotten. How many cherries are not rotten?

Two numbers total 65. One of the numbers is 32. What is the other number?

A number added to 15 makes a total of 40. What number has been added?

Mary goes shopping with $5.00. She spends $1.80. How much does Mary have left?

Dick goes shopping with $5.00. He returns home with $1.30. How much has Dick spent?

The sum of two numbers is 80. One of the numbers is 43. What is the other number?

A child has 50¢ to spend. She gives 24¢ to a friend. How much does she have left?

# Subtracting

Write the answer in the box.

A road is 35 miles long. A section 13 miles long
has to be repaired. What length of road does not need repair?

*22 miles*

Write the answer in the box.

Shane has to run 100 meters.
After running 74 meters he trips.
How far did he have left to run?

Samantha has to swim for one
hour at a swim meet. How much
longer must she swim if she has
already swum for 38 minutes?

Two numbers add up to 80. One
of the numbers is 44. What is the
other number?

I add 37 to a number and have
a total of 66. What is the
number?

A school dentist sees 84 children
in a day. If she sees 37 in the
morning, how many will she see
in the afternoon?

What is the difference when I
take away 33 from 70?

A box has 60 chocolates. 29 have
nuts. The rest are plain. How
many chocolates are plain?

A number has been taken away
from 90 and the difference is 26.
What number has been
taken away?

How much money is left if I start
with 95¢ and then spend 67¢?

A lady grows 100 roses in her
garden. 58 of the roses are red and
the rest are white. How many of
the roses are white?

There are 520 spectators at a
football game. 320 are adults and
the rest are children. How many
are children?

How much money is left if I start
with $1.00 and then spend 65¢?

Out of 70 sailors, 34 are women.
How many are men?

A bag contains 80 marbles.
45 marbles are clear. The rest are
colored. How many are colored?

A piece of wood is 30 inches long.
It is cut into two sections. One
section is 12 inches long. How
long is the other section?

# Reading tally charts

Look at the tally chart. Then answer the questions.

**Winners at Tag**

| Kelly | Mark | Sandy | Rita | Brad |
|---|---|---|---|---|
| ||||| || | ||| | ||||| | | ||||| | ||||| |||| |

Who won the most games?  Brad

Who won more games, Sandy or Kelly?  Kelly

How many more games did Rita win than Mark?  2 more

---

Look at the tally chart. Then answer the questions.

**Colors of T-Shirts sold**

| | |
|---|---|
| Blue | ||||| ||||| | |
| White | ||||| ||| |
| Green | ||||| |||| |
| Black | ||||| ||||| || |

Which color shirt was sold most?

How many green shirts were sold?

Which color sold more, blue or green?

How many black shirts were sold?

How many more green shirts were sold than white shirts?

How many more black shirts were sold than green shirts?

How many T-shirts were sold in all?

---

Look at the tally chart. Then answer the questions.

**Snack choices**

| Chips | Cherries | Cheese | Cookie | Apple |
|---|---|---|---|---|
| ||||| |||| | ||||| | ||||| ||||| | | ||||| ||| | ||||| || |

How many people chose chips?

Which snack did 7 people choose?

Did more people choose chips or cookies?

Which snack did the fewest people choose?

How many more people chose cheese than chips?

How many people chose apples and cherries?

75

# Same shape and size

Which figure has same shape and size?

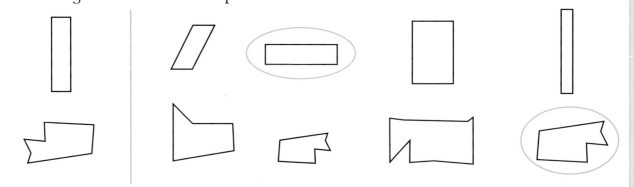

Circle the figure that has same shape and size.

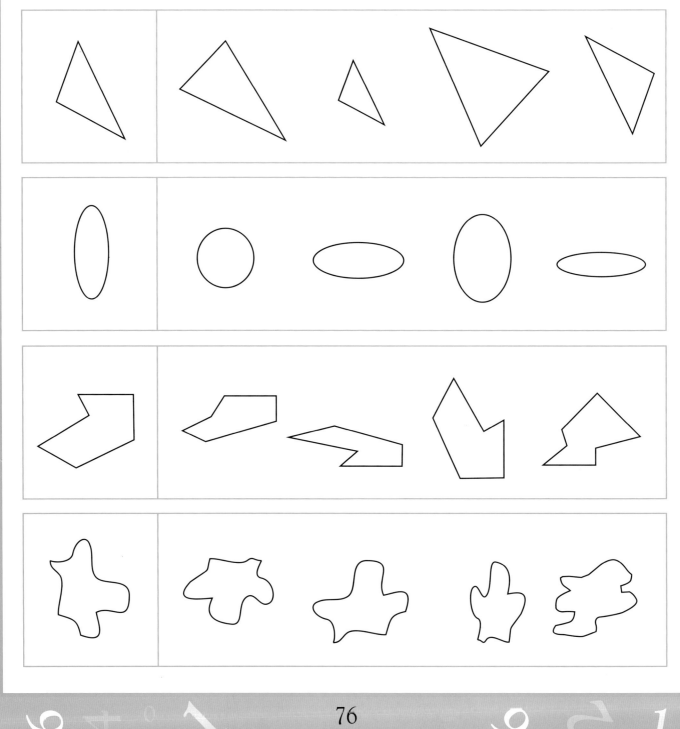

# Subtracting

Write the answer between the lines.

```
  4 13            4 11           4 11 13
  3 5̸ 3̸          5̸ 1̸ 7          5̸ 2̸ 3̸
-  1 1 7         -  2 8 6        -  1 7 5
  ───────        ───────        ───────
  2 3 6            2 3 1          3 4 8
```

Write the answer between the lines.

```
   4 8 2        2 5 4        9 8 6        3 7 1        8 4 2
-  3 5 8     -  1 1 9     -  4 5 8     -  1 3 6     -  7 2 5
  ───────      ───────      ───────      ───────      ───────
```

```
   5 5 5        8 4 2        9 8 4        9 7 8        7 5 6
-  3 7 2     -  4 8 1     -  5 9 2     -  2 9 3     -  3 2 8
  ───────      ───────      ───────      ───────      ───────
```

```
   3 2 5        5 1 9        7 3 2        6 7 1        9 1 2
-  1 5 8     -  3 4 9     -  5 8 7     -  2 9 8     -  2 5 6
  ───────      ───────      ───────      ───────      ───────
```

```
   5 5 1        6 7 3        8 2 4        7 1 1        9 1 5
-  3 7 5     -  1 8 5     -  3 6 7     -  4 8 5     -  5 3 6
  ───────      ───────      ───────      ───────      ───────
```

Write the answer between the lines.

```
  $6.15         $8.45        $5.55        $8.13        $9.12
- $5.00       - $3.28      - $2.95      - $2.46      - $1.65
  ───────      ───────      ───────      ───────      ───────
```

# Subtracting

Write the answer between the lines.

$$
\begin{array}{r} 359 \\ -\phantom{0}35 \\ \hline 324 \end{array}
\qquad
\begin{array}{r} 4\,\overset{6}{7}\,\overset{12}{2} \\ -\phantom{0}34 \\ \hline 438 \end{array}
\qquad
\begin{array}{r} \overset{4}{5}\,\overset{11}{2}\,\overset{10}{0} \\ -\phantom{0}25 \\ \hline 495 \end{array}
$$

Write the answer between the lines.

$$
\begin{array}{r} 957 \\ -\phantom{0}32 \\ \hline \phantom{000} \end{array}
\qquad
\begin{array}{r} 569 \\ -\phantom{0}50 \\ \hline \phantom{000} \end{array}
\qquad
\begin{array}{r} 468 \\ -\phantom{0}24 \\ \hline \phantom{000} \end{array}
\qquad
\begin{array}{r} 295 \\ -\phantom{0}83 \\ \hline \phantom{000} \end{array}
\qquad
\begin{array}{r} 729 \\ -\phantom{0}16 \\ \hline \phantom{000} \end{array}
$$

$$
\begin{array}{r} 692 \\ -\phantom{0}43 \\ \hline \phantom{000} \end{array}
\qquad
\begin{array}{r} 850 \\ -\phantom{0}36 \\ \hline \phantom{000} \end{array}
\qquad
\begin{array}{r} 274 \\ -\phantom{0}17 \\ \hline \phantom{000} \end{array}
\qquad
\begin{array}{r} 387 \\ -\phantom{0}57 \\ \hline \phantom{000} \end{array}
\qquad
\begin{array}{r} 163 \\ -\phantom{0}49 \\ \hline \phantom{000} \end{array}
$$

$$
\begin{array}{r} 641 \\ -\phantom{0}52 \\ \hline \phantom{000} \end{array}
\qquad
\begin{array}{r} 523 \\ -\phantom{0}76 \\ \hline \phantom{000} \end{array}
\qquad
\begin{array}{r} 318 \\ -\phantom{0}79 \\ \hline \phantom{000} \end{array}
\qquad
\begin{array}{r} 424 \\ -\phantom{0}68 \\ \hline \phantom{000} \end{array}
\qquad
\begin{array}{r} 257 \\ -\phantom{0}89 \\ \hline \phantom{000} \end{array}
$$

$$
\begin{array}{r} 912 \\ -\phantom{0}28 \\ \hline \phantom{000} \end{array}
\qquad
\begin{array}{r} 450 \\ -\phantom{0}75 \\ \hline \phantom{000} \end{array}
\qquad
\begin{array}{r} 990 \\ -\phantom{0}65 \\ \hline \phantom{000} \end{array}
\qquad
\begin{array}{r} 380 \\ -\phantom{0}54 \\ \hline \phantom{000} \end{array}
\qquad
\begin{array}{r} 739 \\ -\phantom{0}41 \\ \hline \phantom{000} \end{array}
$$

Write the answer between the lines.

$$
\begin{array}{r} \$5.52 \\ -\ \$0.38 \\ \hline \phantom{000} \end{array}
\qquad
\begin{array}{r} \$8.09 \\ -\ \$0.51 \\ \hline \phantom{000} \end{array}
\qquad
\begin{array}{r} \$4.82 \\ -\ \$0.60 \\ \hline \phantom{000} \end{array}
\qquad
\begin{array}{r} \$3.93 \\ -\ \$0.17 \\ \hline \phantom{000} \end{array}
\qquad
\begin{array}{r} \$5.70 \\ -\ \$0.95 \\ \hline \phantom{000} \end{array}
$$

# Choosing the operation

Write the answer in the box.

I add 25 to a number and the sum is 40. What number did I start with?    15

I subtract 13 and have 24 left. What number did I start with?    37

Write the answer in the box.

22 is added to a number and the sum is 30. What number did I begin with?

I subtract 14 from a number and end up with 17. What number did I start with?

I add 16 to a number and the total of the two numbers is 30. What number did I begin with?

When 26 is subtracted from a number, the difference is 14. What is the number?

After adding 22 to a number the total is 45. What is the number?

What number must you subtract from 19 to find a difference of 7?

I start with 29 and take away a number. The difference is 14. What number did I subtract?

35 is added to a number and the total is 60. What is the number?

I increase a number by 14 and the total is 30. What number did I start with?

After taking 17 away from a number I am left with 3. What number did I start with?

Paul starts with 50¢ but spends some money in a shop. He goes home with 18¢. How much did Paul spend?

Sue starts out with 23¢ but is given some money by her aunt. Sue then has 50¢. How much was she given?

Alice gives 20¢ to charity. If she started with 95¢, how much has she have left?

Jane has a 32-ounce bottle of orange soda. She drinks 12 ounces. How many ounces does she have left?

A box contains 60 pins and then some are added so that the new total is 85. How many pins have been added?

A tower is made up of 30 blocks. 45 more are put on the top. How many blocks are in the tower now?

# Subtracting

Write the answer between the lines.

```
    3 10              3 10              9
  8 4̶ 0̶            4̶ 0 5          6̶ 1̶0̶10
- 5 0 6          - 1 6 2          7̶ 0̶ 0̶
  ─────            ─────          - 1 7 5
   334              243            ─────
                                    525
```

Write the answer between the lines.

```
   3 5 0          5 6 0          8 6 0          7 7 0          4 8 0
 - 1 2 7        - 1 4 5        - 4 3 2        - 3 3 6        - 1 2 3
 ───────        ───────        ───────        ───────        ───────

 ───────        ───────        ───────        ───────        ───────


   5 0 6          4 0 2          6 0 8          7 0 5          9 0 3
 - 3 7 3        - 2 8 1        - 3 7 1        - 4 5 2        - 6 9 2
 ───────        ───────        ───────        ───────        ───────

 ───────        ───────        ───────        ───────        ───────


   3 0 0          5 1 0          4 0 7          6 3 0          7 0 2
 - 1 8 3        - 2 6 7        - 1 6 8        - 3 9 8        - 4 6 3
 ───────        ───────        ───────        ───────        ───────

 ───────        ───────        ───────        ───────        ───────


   9 0 1          8 0 0          2 0 7          7 0 9          9 0 4
 - 2 7 5        - 3 5 0        - 1 0 7        - 3 2 9        - 5 3 6
 ───────        ───────        ───────        ───────        ───────

 ───────        ───────        ───────        ───────        ───────
```

Write the answer between the lines.

```
  $6.00          $6.05          $9.00          $8.30          $7.00
- $5.00        - $2.82        - $8.56        - $2.06        - $5.62
───────        ───────        ───────        ───────        ───────

───────        ───────        ───────        ───────        ───────
```

# Working with money

Write the total in the box. $5 $1 HALF DOLLAR $6.50

Write the total in the box.

# Money problems

Write the answer in the box.

Rick goes shopping with a five dollar bill. He spends $2.30. How much does Rick have left?

$2.70

Write the answer in the box.

John has three bills. The total value of the bills is $35. Which three bills does he have?

Patrick has a $5 bill and a 50¢ coin. How much more does he need to have $8.00?

After spending $5.50, Ann still has $2.40 left. How much did Ann start with?

A package of pens costs $3.45. If Mac pays for them with a $5 bill, how much change will he get?

A man buys a Chinese meal that costs $7.80. He pays for the food with a $10 bill. How much change will he get?

Three pineapples cost a total of $5.10. A lady pays for the pineapples with a $5 bill and a $1 bill. How much change will she get?

Apples cost 60¢ a pound. How much will 4 pounds cost?

How much change will you get if you buy food for $8.35 and pay for it with a $10 bill?

Jan saves 50¢ a week for 10 weeks. How much does she have after the ten weeks?

Rob buys a new coat for $34.50 and pays for it with a $50 bill. How much change will he get?

The change given to a woman is $1.50. She bought a bag for $8.50. How much had she given the clerk?

What is the change from $20.00 when a hat is bought for $14.50?

The change from $5.00 is $0.80. How much was spent?

After spending $3.20 on food, a man is given $6.80 in change. How much had he given to the storekeeper?

A box of chocolates costs $6.28. It is paid for with a $5 bill and two $1 bills. How much extra has been paid?

# Measurement problems

Write the measurement shown by the arrow.

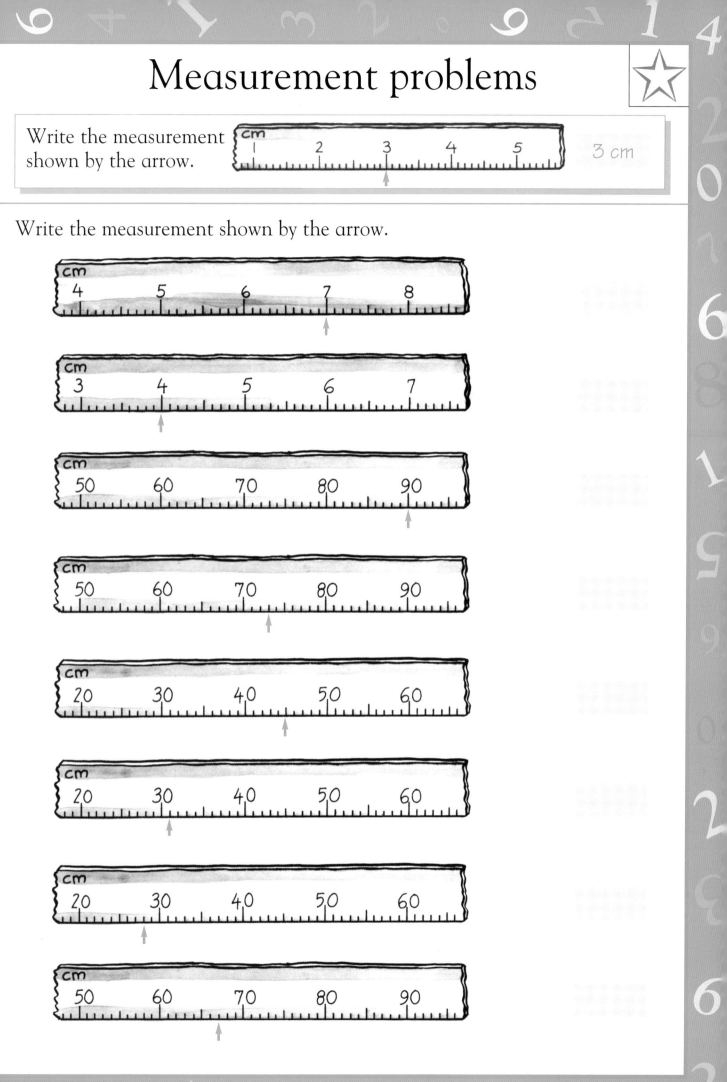

**cm**
1  2  3  4  5

3 cm

Write the measurement shown by the arrow.

**cm**
4  5  6  7  8

**cm**
3  4  5  6  7

**cm**
50  60  70  80  90

**cm**
50  60  70  80  90

**cm**
20  30  40  50  60

**cm**
20  30  40  50  60

**cm**
20  30  40  50  60

**cm**
50  60  70  80  90

# Parts of a set

Write the fraction that shows the shaded part of the set.
How many of the fish are shaded?

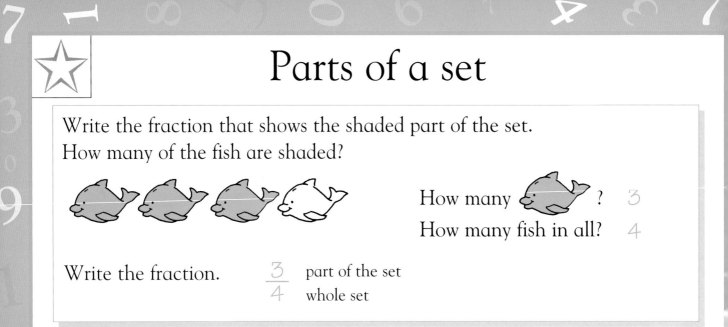

How many  🐟  ?    3

How many fish in all?    4

Write the fraction.    $\dfrac{3}{4}$   part of the set / whole set

Circle the fraction that shows the shaded part of the set.

$\dfrac{1}{3}$    $\dfrac{2}{3}$    $\dfrac{3}{2}$

$\dfrac{2}{3}$    $\dfrac{3}{5}$    $\dfrac{2}{5}$

$\dfrac{1}{4}$    $\dfrac{3}{4}$    $\dfrac{2}{4}$

$\dfrac{4}{5}$    $\dfrac{1}{5}$    $\dfrac{1}{4}$

Write the fraction that shows the shaded part of the set.

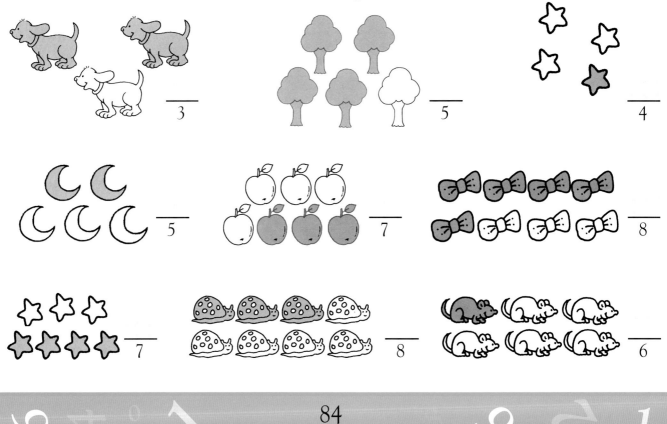

$\dfrac{}{3}$     $\dfrac{}{5}$     $\dfrac{}{4}$

$\dfrac{}{5}$     $\dfrac{}{7}$     $\dfrac{}{8}$

$\dfrac{}{7}$     $\dfrac{}{8}$     $\dfrac{}{6}$

# Bar graphs and pictographs

Look at the bar graph and answer the question.

Number of pets

Sarah  Paul

Which child has three pets?   Paul

Look at the bar graph and answer the questions.

**Vacation choices**

Number of children

Farm   Camp   Beach   City   Theme park

How many children went to camp on vacation?

Which place did three children go to?

Which place did fewer children go to than to the city?

Which was the most popular place for vacations?

How many children altogether went on vacation?

Look at the pictograph and answer the questions.

**Children's favorite hobbies**

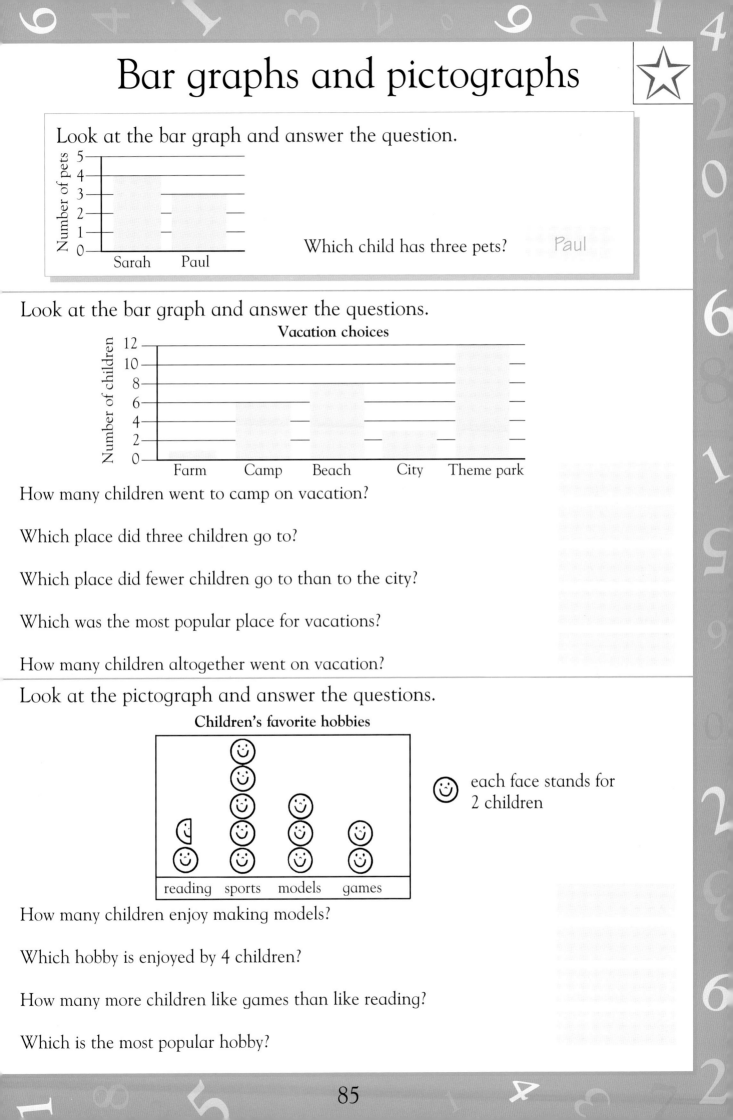

each face stands for 2 children

reading   sports   models   games

How many children enjoy making models?

Which hobby is enjoyed by 4 children?

How many more children like games than like reading?

Which is the most popular hobby?

# 2-dimensional shapes

Name each of the shapes.

square    circle

Name each of the shapes. Use the names in the word box.

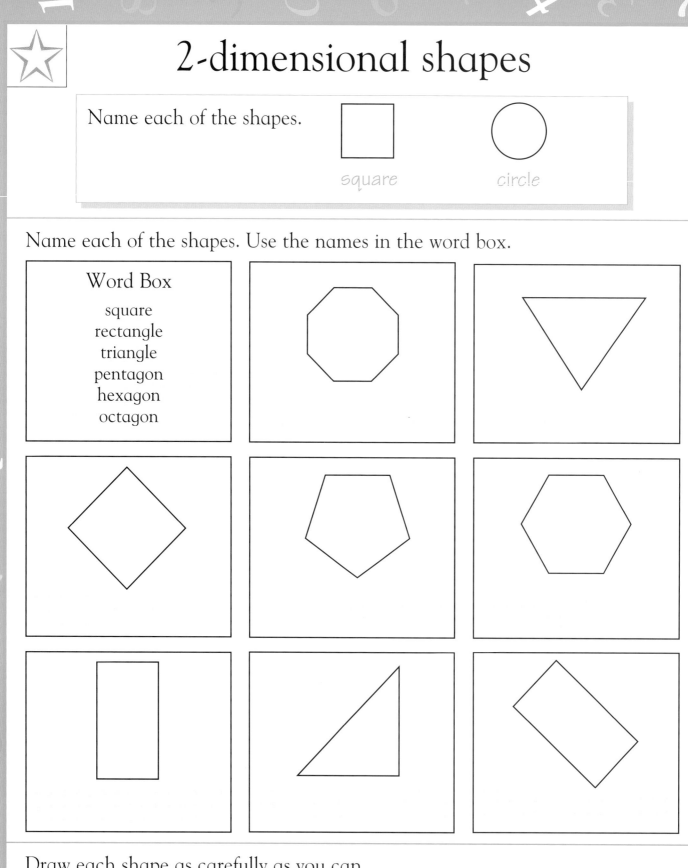

Word Box

square
rectangle
triangle
pentagon
hexagon
octagon

Draw each shape as carefully as you can.

pentagon

hexagon

# Sorting 2-dimensional shapes

Which shapes have square corners?
Mark each square corner.

1 and 3

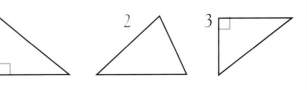

Look at the shapes. Mark each square corner.

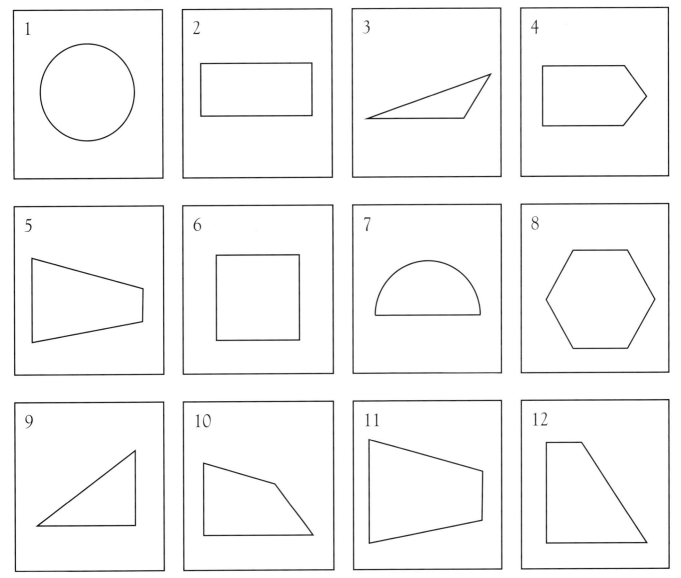

Write the numbers of the shapes in the correct part of the table below.

| Shapes with square corners | Shapes with no square corners |
|---|---|
|  |  |

# Symmetry

Hold a mirror along the dotted line. Does it show a line of symmetry?

yes                    no                    yes

Does the dotted line show a line of symmetry? Write yes or no.

# Symmetry

Complete each drawing. The dotted line is the line of symmetry.

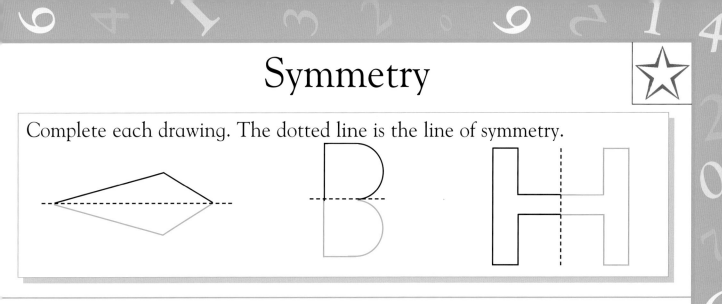

Complete each drawing. The dotted line is the line of symmetry.

# Symmetry

Complete each drawing. The dotted line is the line of symmetry.

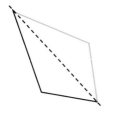 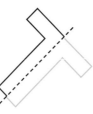 

Complete each drawing. The dotted line is the line of symmetry.

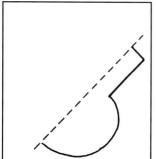 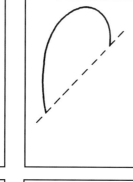 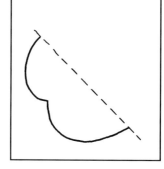 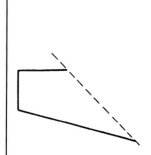

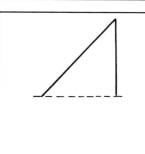 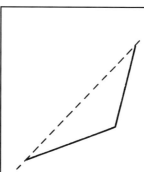 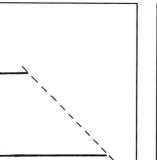 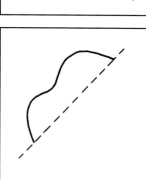

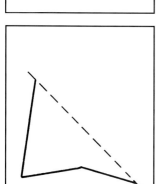 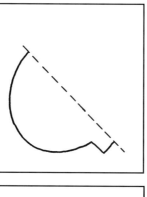 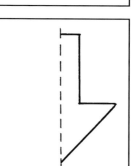 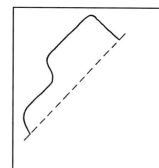

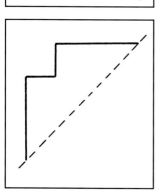 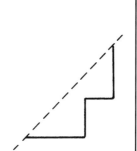 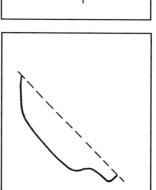 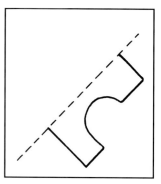

# Square corners

Are these corners greater than or less than a square corner? Write greater, less or square corner.

less          greater          square corner

Are these corners greater than or less than a square corner?
Write greater, less, or square corner in the box.

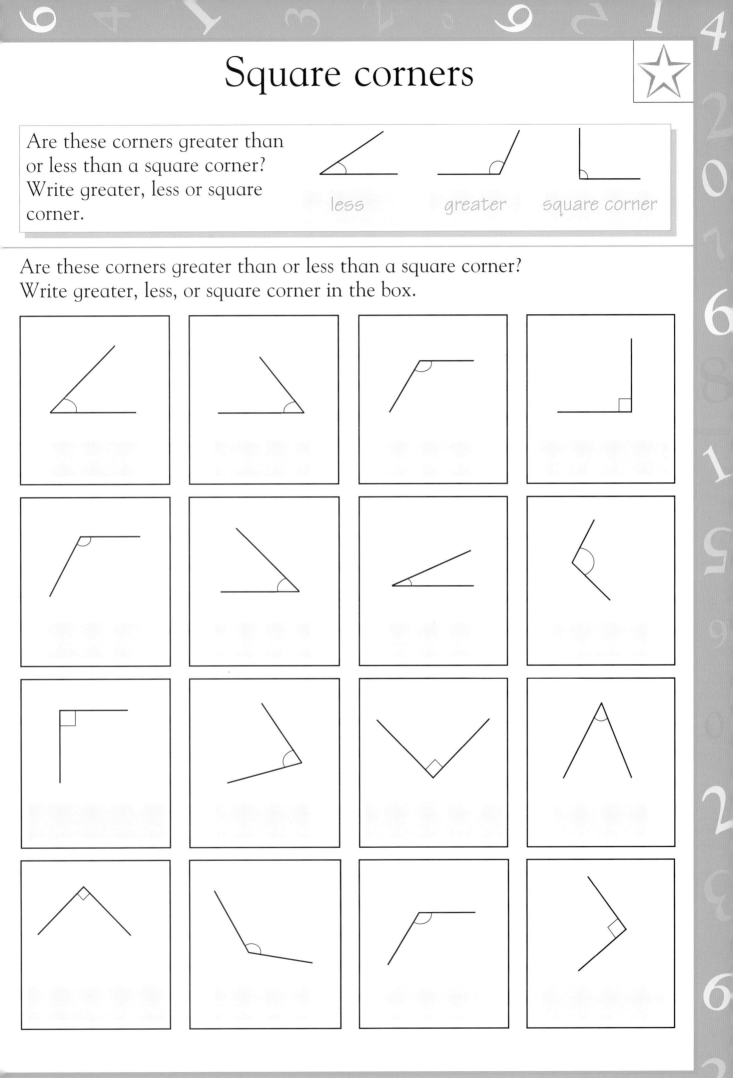

# 3-dimensional shapes

Write the name of each shape in the box.

prism

sphere

Write the name of each shape in the box.

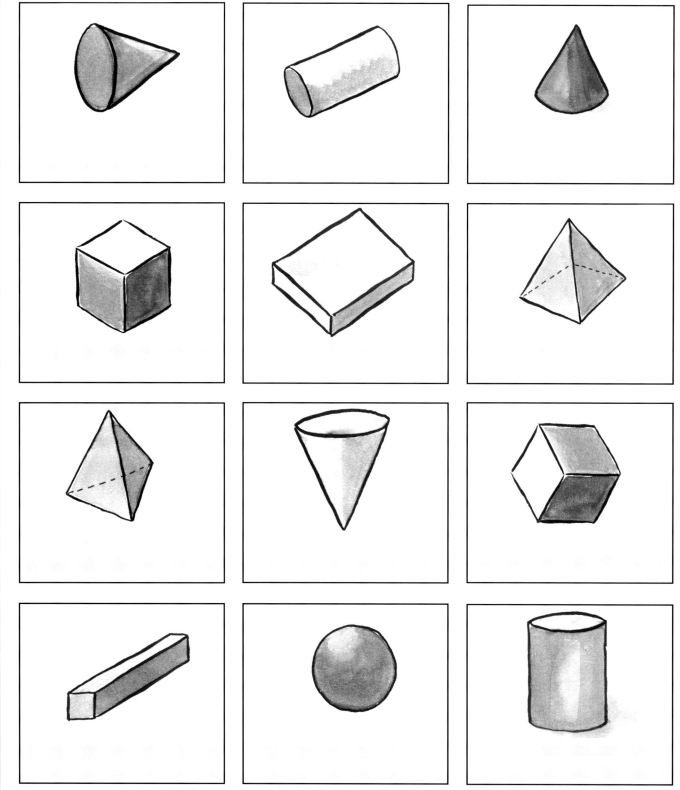

# Sorting 3-dimensional shapes

Does the shape have a curved surface?

yes          no

Does each shape have a curved surface? Write yes or no.

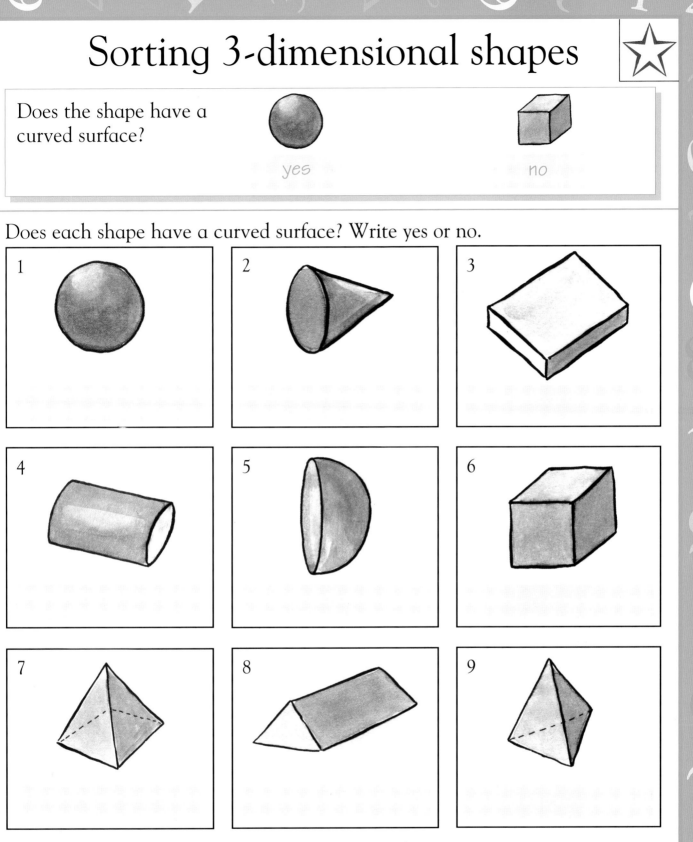

| 1 | 2 | 3 |
| 4 | 5 | 6 |
| 7 | 8 | 9 |

Write the numbers of the shapes in the correct box.

| Shapes with curved surfaces | Shapes with no curved surfaces |
|---|---|
|  |  |

# Location on a grid

Mark C, 2 on the grid and color it.

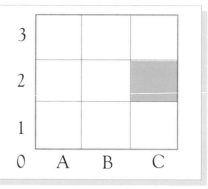

Mark each box on the grid with the correct color.

| | | | |
|---|---|---|---|
| red at D, 7 | purple at C, 5 | red at D, 3 | purple at G, 5 |
| green at H, 1 | yellow at B, 7 | green at D, 2 | yellow at H, 4 |
| blue at A, 4 | black at E, 8 | blue at B, 1 | black at F, 4 |

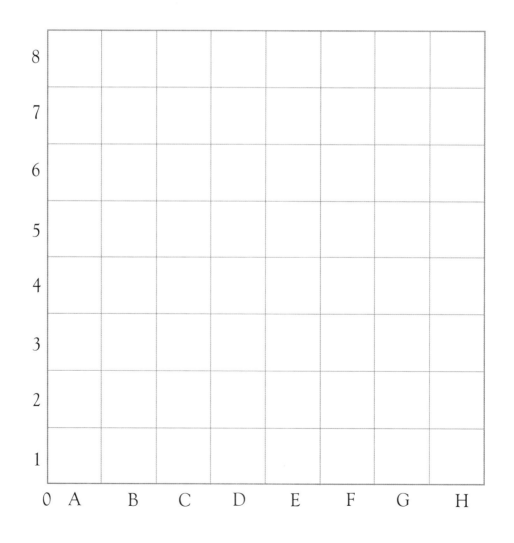

# Counting by 2s

Draw the "hops" and write the numbers. Do you need to add or subtract?

# Counting by 3s, 4s, and 5s

Draw the arrows and write the numbers. Do you need to add or subtract?

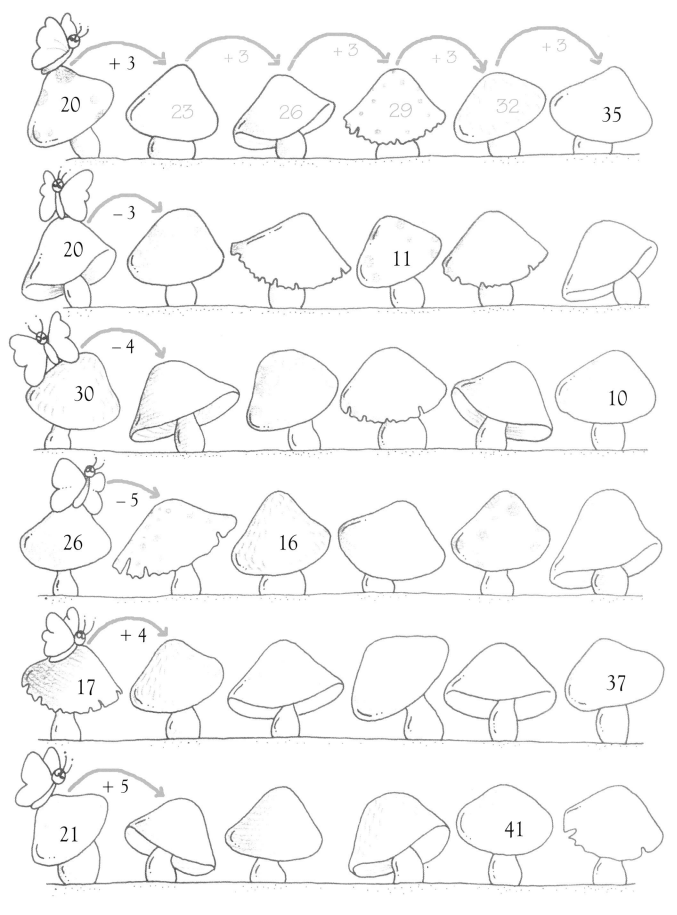

+ 3    +3    +3    +3    +3

20    23    26    29    32    35

− 3

20              11

− 4

30                          10

− 5

26        16

+ 4

17                          37

+ 5

21                    41

# Patterns of 2, 5, and 10

Count, color, and find a pattern.

Count by 2s and color them green.

| 1 | 2 | 3 | 4 | 5 | 6 | 7 | 8 | 9 | 10 |
|---|---|---|---|---|---|---|---|---|----|
| 11 | 12 | 13 | 14 | 15 | 16 | 17 | 18 | 19 | 20 |
| 21 | 22 | 23 | 24 | 25 | 26 | 27 | 28 | 29 | 30 |
| 31 | 32 | 33 | 34 | 35 | 36 | 37 | 38 | 39 | 40 |
| 41 | 42 | 43 | 44 | 45 | 46 | 47 | 48 | 49 | 50 |

Count by 5s and color them purple.

| 1 | 2 | 3 | 4 | 5 | 6 | 7 | 8 | 9 | 10 |
|---|---|---|---|---|---|---|---|---|----|
| 11 | 12 | 13 | 14 | 15 | 16 | 17 | 18 | 19 | 20 |
| 21 | 22 | 23 | 24 | 25 | 26 | 27 | 28 | 29 | 30 |
| 31 | 32 | 33 | 34 | 35 | 36 | 37 | 38 | 39 | 40 |
| 41 | 42 | 43 | 44 | 45 | 46 | 47 | 48 | 49 | 50 |

Count by 10s and color them yellow.

| 1 | 2 | 3 | 4 | 5 | 6 | 7 | 8 | 9 | 10 |
|---|---|---|---|---|---|---|---|---|----|
| 11 | 12 | 13 | 14 | 15 | 16 | 17 | 18 | 19 | 20 |
| 21 | 22 | 23 | 24 | 25 | 26 | 27 | 28 | 29 | 30 |
| 31 | 32 | 33 | 34 | 35 | 36 | 37 | 38 | 39 | 40 |
| 41 | 42 | 43 | 44 | 45 | 46 | 47 | 48 | 49 | 50 |

# Fractions of shapes

Color one third $\left(\frac{1}{3}\right)$.

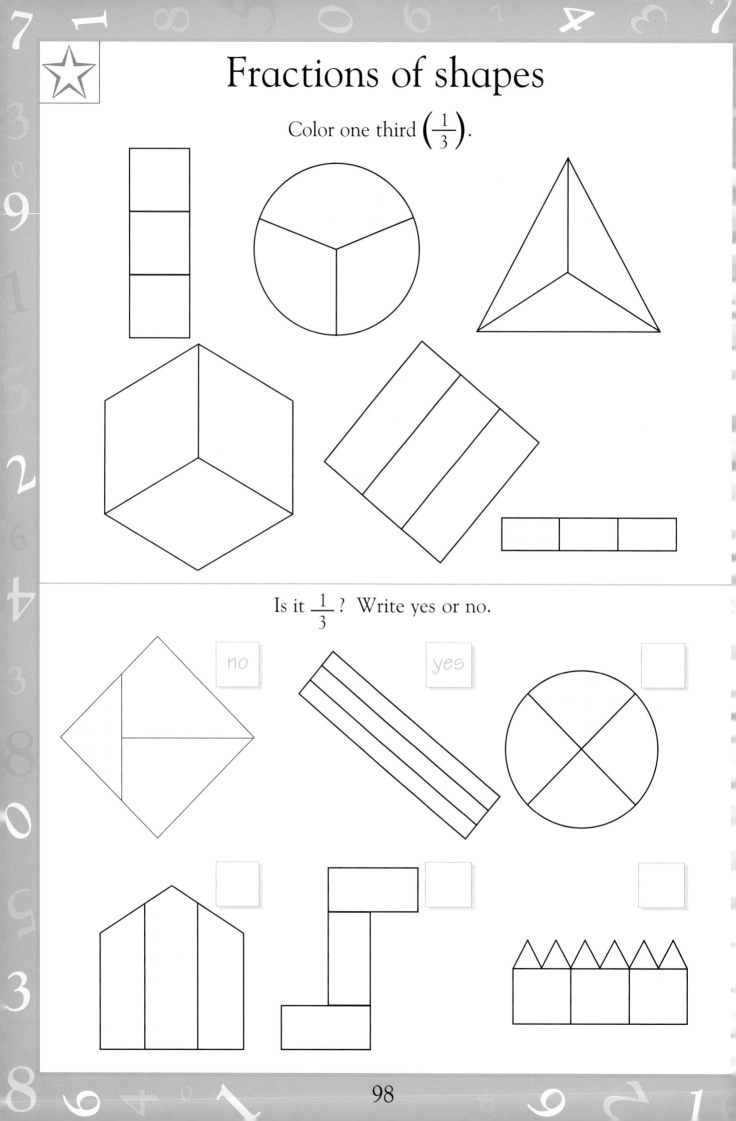

Is it $\frac{1}{3}$ ? Write yes or no.

no

yes

# Ordering

Write the numbers in order.

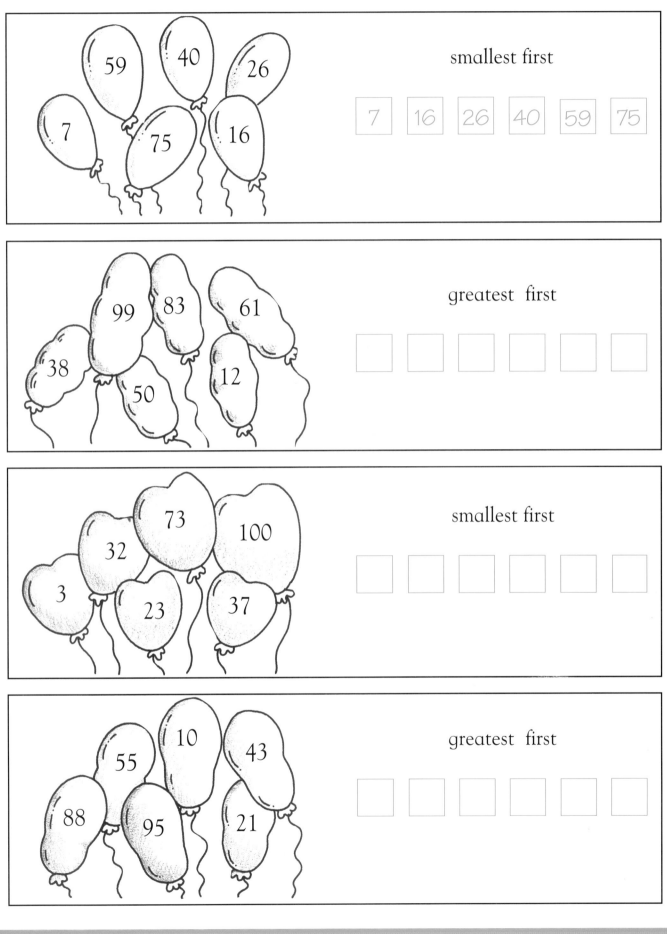

smallest first

| 7 | 16 | 26 | 40 | 59 | 75 |

greatest first

smallest first

greatest first

# Doubles

Write the missing numbers.

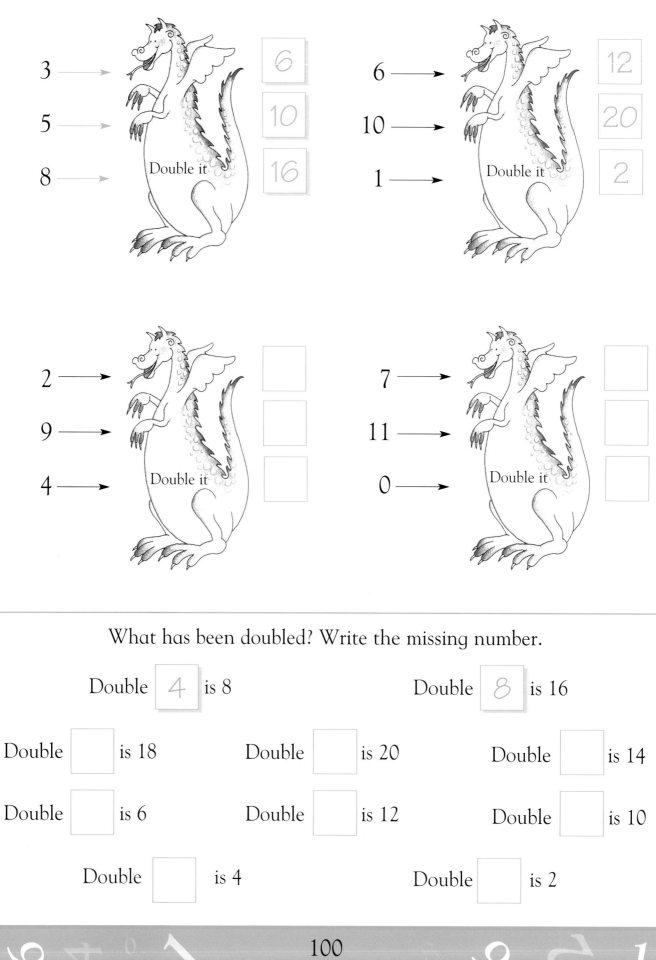

3 → Double it → 6
5 → → 10
8 → → 16

6 → Double it → 12
10 → → 20
1 → → 2

2 → Double it →
9 → →
4 → →

7 → Double it →
11 → →
0 → →

What has been doubled? Write the missing number.

Double 4 is 8          Double 8 is 16

Double ☐ is 18     Double ☐ is 20     Double ☐ is 14

Double ☐ is 6      Double ☐ is 12     Double ☐ is 10

Double ☐ is 4          Double ☐ is 2

# Addition grid

Draw rings around the pairs of numbers that add up to 20.

| | | | | | | |
|---|---|---|---|---|---|---|
| 15 | 5 | 3 | 10 | 10 | 4 | 19 |
| 8 | 6 | 20 | 0 | 9 | 1 | 10 |
| 12 | 13 | 7 | 12 | 0 | 16 | 1 |
| 4 | 5 | 10 | 16 | 4 | 5 | 10 |
| 9 | 2 | 18 | 7 | 20 | 3 | 10 |
| 11 | 3 | 3 | 1 | 0 | 11 | 9 |
| 17 | 1 | 1 | 19 | 3 | 18 | 11 |

# Number wall

Write all the odd numbers. ☐ ☐ ☐

Add them up and write the total. ☐

Write all the even numbers. ☐ ☐ ☐

Add them up and write the total. ☐

Find three numbers that add up to make 13. ☐ + ☐ + ☐

Write the smallest number. ☐     Double it. ☐

Write the largest number. ☐     Find $\frac{1}{2}$ of it. ☐

Find two ways of making 10. ☐ + ☐ = 10     ☐ + ☐ = 10

Add up all the numbers on the wall. ☐ + ☐ + ☐ + ☐ + ☐ + ☐ =

# Matching fractions

Color the matching squares.

Use yellow for halves.
Use orange for thirds.
Use green for fourths.

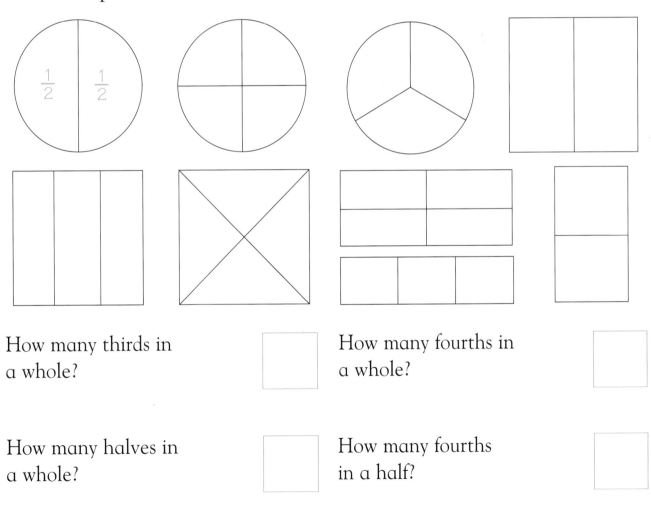

Label each part.

How many thirds in
a whole?

How many fourths in
a whole?

How many halves in
a whole?

How many fourths
in a half?

# Counting

Count on forward or backward by 10s. Write the missing numbers.

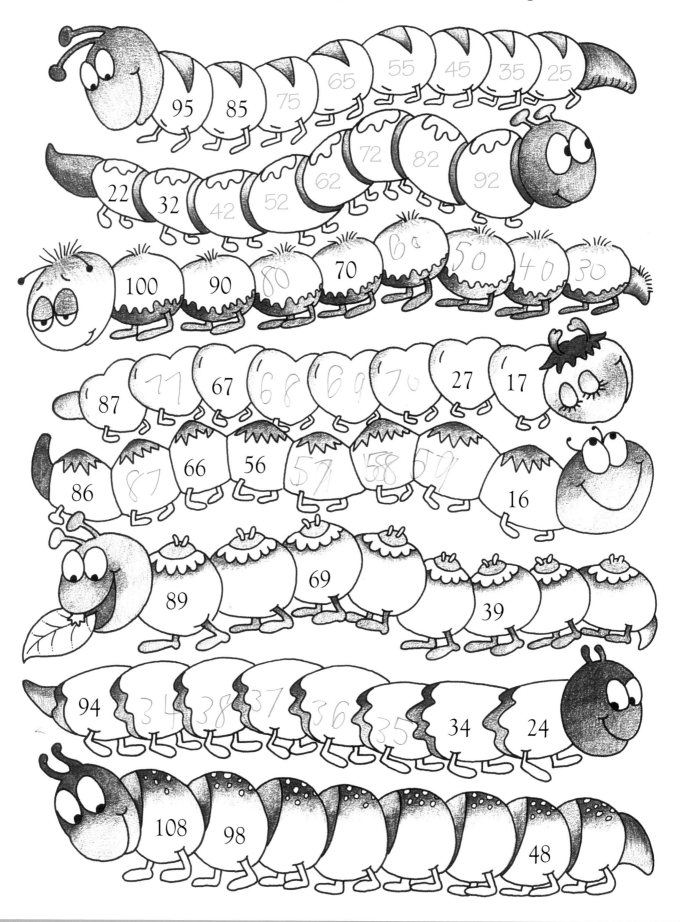

# Venn diagrams

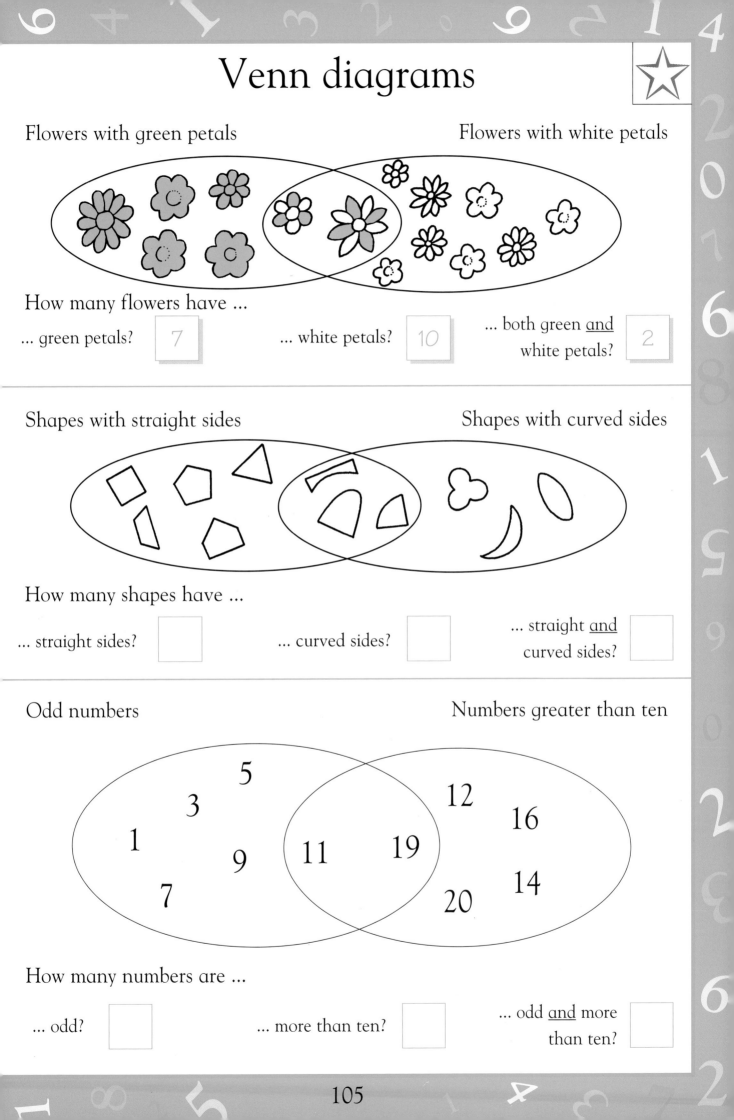

Flowers with green petals

Flowers with white petals

How many flowers have ...

... green petals? `7`

... white petals? `10`

... both green <u>and</u> white petals? `2`

Shapes with straight sides

Shapes with curved sides

How many shapes have ...

... straight sides?

... curved sides?

... straight <u>and</u> curved sides?

Odd numbers

Numbers greater than ten

How many numbers are ...

... odd?

... more than ten?

... odd <u>and</u> more than ten?

# Comparing

Complete the boxes.

| 2 less | number | 2 more |
|---|---|---|
| 51 | 53 | 55 |

| number | between | number |
|---|---|---|
| 96 | 97      98 | 99 |

| number | between | number |
|---|---|---|
| 20 | | 24 |

| 3 less | number | 3 more |
|---|---|---|
| | 30 | |

| 2 less | between | 2 more |
|---|---|---|
| | 29 | |

| number | between | number |
|---|---|---|
| 18 | | 22 |

| number | between | number |
|---|---|---|
| 131 | | 134 |

| 10 less | number | 10 more |
|---|---|---|
| | 119 | |

| 5 less | number | 5 more |
|---|---|---|
| | 85 | |

| number | between | number |
|---|---|---|
| 40 | | 45 |

| number | between | number |
|---|---|---|
| 99 | | 102 |

| 5 less | number | 5 more |
|---|---|---|
| | 156 | |

# Odd or even?

Add or subtract to find the answers.
Choose two colors. Color the odd houses one color
and the even houses another color.

32
+4
36
even

23
−4
19
odd

10
−5

11
+ 2

25
−6

20
+ 7

23
−7

35
−5

30
−6

16
+ 8

25
− 10

28
−8

17
+ 9

36
− 10

# Clocks

Write the times under the clocks.

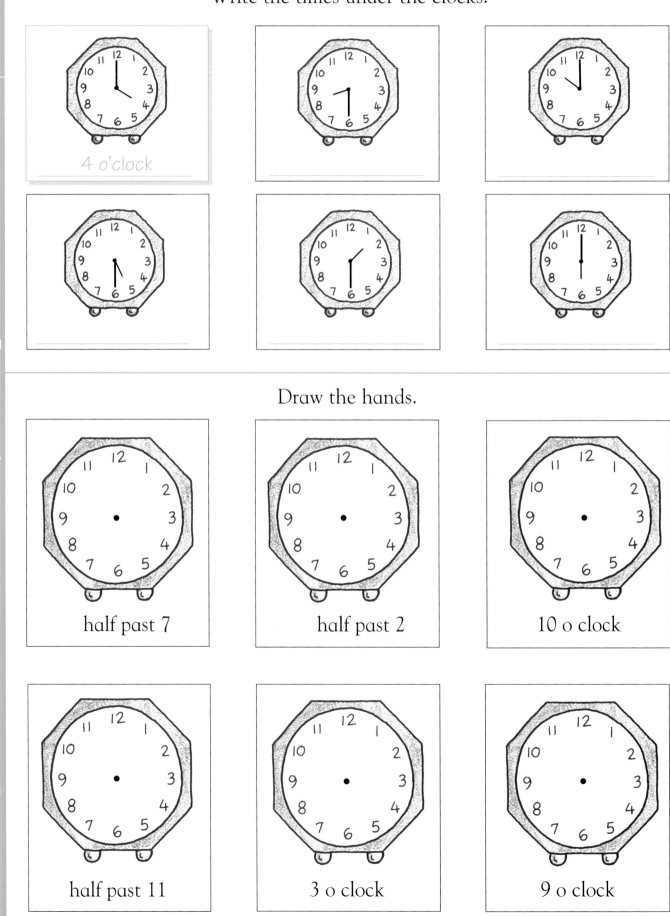

4 o'clock

Draw the hands.

half past 7

half past 2

10 o clock

half past 11

3 o clock

9 o clock

# Fact families

Use the 3 numbers to write 4 different facts.

| 6 + 7 = 13 | 7 + 6 = 13 | 13 – 7 = 6 | 13 – 6 = 7 |

| 16 + 4 = 20 | + = | – = | – = |

| 6    5    11 | | | |

| 7    8    15 | | | |

| 8    12    20 | | | |

| 10    8    18 | | | |

| 8    9    17 | | | |

| 9    7    16 | | | |

| 14    6    20 | | | |

| 11    8    19 | | | |

# Identifying patterns

Continue each pattern.

| | | | | | |
|---|---|---|---|---|---|
| 0 | 6 | 12 | 18 | 24 | 30 |
| 0 | 7 | 14 | 21 | 28 | 35 |
| 60 | 52 | 44 | 36 | 28 | 20 |

Continue each pattern.

| | | | |
|---|---|---|---|
| 3 | 9 | 15 | 21 |
| 2 | 9 | 16 | 23 |
| 1 | 9 | 17 | 25 |
| 7 | 15 | 23 | 31 |
| 7 | 13 | 19 | 25 |
| 7 | 12 | 17 | 22 |

Continue each pattern.

| | | | |
|---|---|---|---|
| 71 | 65 | 59 | 53 |
| 90 | 82 | 74 | 66 |
| 56 | 49 | 42 | 35 |
| 72 | 66 | 60 | 54 |
| 96 | 88 | 80 | 72 |
| 48 | 42 | 36 | 30 |

Continue each pattern.

| | | | | | | | |
|---|---|---|---|---|---|---|---|
| 36 | 43 | | | | | | 85 |
| 61 | 55 | | | | | | 19 |
| 0 | | | | | | | 49 |
| 7 | | | | | | | 56 |
| 4 | | | | 36 | | | |

110

# Real-life problems

Look at the picture. Answer the questions.

What time is it ? _6.4_

Today is Friday. What day was it yesterday? _Thursday_

How many cupcakes can each person have? _2_

If half of the apples were eaten, how many would be left? _3_

If each person had 2 drinks, how many drinks would there be altogether? _8_

How many more sandwiches are there than apples? _5_

If 13 candies were eaten, how many would be left? _6_

Each package contains 2 presents. How many presents are there altogether? _6_

What shape are the sandwiches? _△_

Is there an odd or an even number of chairs? _even_

# Addition fact families

Circle the number sentence that is in the same fact family.

| | | | |
|---|---|---|---|
| 12 − 5 = 7<br>5 + 7 = 12 | 12 − 4 = 8 | (7 + 5 = 12) | 12 + 12 = 24 |
| 10 − 8 = 2<br>8 + 2 = 10 | 8 − 6 = 2 | (2 + 8 = 10) | 8 − 2 = 6 |

Circle the number sentence that is in the same fact family.

| | | | |
|---|---|---|---|
| 7 − 8 = 15<br>8 + 7 = 15 | 7 + 5 = 12 | 15 − 8 = 7 | 8 − 7 = 1 |
| 17 − 6 = 11<br>11 + 6 = 17 | 17 − 11 = 6 | 17 + 6 = 12 | 5 + 6 = 11 |
| 14 − 5 = 9<br>14 − 9 = 5 | 9 − 3 = 6 | 14 + 9 = 23 | 5 + 9 = 14 |
| 9 + 7 = 16<br>7 + 9 = 16 | 16 − 9 = 7 | 16 + 7 = 23 | 9 − 7 = 2 |
| 19 − 9 = 10<br>19 − 10 = 9 | 9 + 3 = 12 | 9 + 10 = 19 | 18 − 8 = 10 |
| 4 + 7 = 11<br>11 − 4 = 7 | 11 + 4 = 15 | 7 + 4 = 11 | 7 + 7 = 14 |

Write the fact family for each group of numbers.

| | | |
|---|---|---|
| 5, 6, 11 | 6, 10, 4 | 5, 13, 8 |

# Real-life problems

Solve the problem and then write the answers.

Tuhil is reading a book that
has 72 pages. He has read 38 pages.
How many more pages does
Tuhil have to read?

34 pages

$$\begin{array}{r} 72 \\ -\ 38 \\ \hline 34 \end{array}$$

Solve the problem and then write the answer in the box.

Eric has 37 marbles and plays two
games. He wins another 24 marbles
in the first game but then loses 18 in
the second game. How many marbles
does Eric have now?

Angie has 70 felt-tip pens and gives
26 of them to Abir. She buys 12 new
pens to replace the ones she has
given away. How many pens does
Angie have now?

Edwin empties his trouser pockets
and finds 26¢ in one pocket, 13¢ in
another pocket, and 37¢ in another
one. How much money has Edwin
found altogether?

Isabelle has 64 french fries with her
burger. She eats 16 fries and gives 6
to her baby brother. How many fries
does Isabelle have left?

# Adding

Write the answer between the lines.

| 34 | 28 | 75 |
|----|----|----|
| + 42 | + 11 | + 14 |
| *76* | *39* | *89* |

Write the answer between the lines.

| 24 | 36 | 45 | 61 |
|----|----|----|----|
| + 14 | + 23 | + 13 | + 17 |

| 63 | 71 | 48 | 53 |
|----|----|----|----|
| + 14 | + 16 | + 10 | + 16 |

| 60 | 46 | 54 | 83 |
|----|----|----|----|
| + 36 | + 21 | + 33 | + 6 |

| 28 | 53 | 74 | 38 |
|----|----|----|----|
| + 31 | + 36 | + 25 | + 21 |

| 57 | 65 | 79 | 47 |
|----|----|----|----|
| + 22 | + 14 | + 10 | + 12 |

| 35 | 46 | 57 | 68 |
|----|----|----|----|
| + 13 | + 22 | + 31 | + 40 |

| 44 | 53 | 26 | 62 |
|----|----|----|----|
| + 25 | + 34 | + 33 | + 17 |

| 50 | 47 | 66 | 45 |
|----|----|----|----|
| + 37 | + 11 | + 22 | + 32 |

# Adding

Write the answer between the lines.

```
   15          25          55
+  20       + 40        +  5
 ___         ___         ___
  35          65          60
```

Write the answer between the lines.

```
   50          70          90          20
+  25       + 15        +  5        + 45
 ___         ___         ___         ___


   65          25          35          85
+  30       + 40        + 50        + 10
 ___         ___         ___         ___


   30          60          55          75
+  25       + 35        + 30        + 20
 ___         ___         ___         ___


   25          45          65          15
+  15       +  5        + 25        + 15
 ___         ___         ___         ___


   75          15          35          45
+  10       + 25        + 25        + 15
 ___         ___         ___         ___


   65          45           5          55
+  35       + 25        + 65        + 35
 ___         ___         ___         ___


   35          45          15          75
+  45       + 35        + 30        +  5
 ___         ___         ___         ___


    5          50          45          80
+  95       + 35        + 45        + 15
 ___         ___         ___         ___
```

# Subtracting

Write the answer between the lines.

$$\begin{array}{r} 36 \\ -\ 14 \\ \hline 22 \end{array} \qquad \begin{array}{r} 25 \\ -\ 13 \\ \hline 12 \end{array} \qquad \begin{array}{r} 57 \\ -\ 26 \\ \hline 31 \end{array}$$

Write the answer between the lines.

$$\begin{array}{r} 27 \\ -\ 14 \\ \hline \end{array} \qquad \begin{array}{r} 35 \\ -\ 12 \\ \hline \end{array} \qquad \begin{array}{r} 47 \\ -\ 32 \\ \hline \end{array} \qquad \begin{array}{r} 63 \\ -\ 20 \\ \hline \end{array}$$

$$\begin{array}{r} 54 \\ -\ 23 \\ \hline \end{array} \qquad \begin{array}{r} 38 \\ -\ 16 \\ \hline \end{array} \qquad \begin{array}{r} 47 \\ -\ 12 \\ \hline \end{array} \qquad \begin{array}{r} 56 \\ -\ 21 \\ \hline \end{array}$$

$$\begin{array}{r} 44 \\ -\ 32 \\ \hline \end{array} \qquad \begin{array}{r} 57 \\ -\ 24 \\ \hline \end{array} \qquad \begin{array}{r} 65 \\ -\ 32 \\ \hline \end{array} \qquad \begin{array}{r} 78 \\ -\ 35 \\ \hline \end{array}$$

$$\begin{array}{r} 66 \\ -\ 26 \\ \hline \end{array} \qquad \begin{array}{r} 75 \\ -\ 35 \\ \hline \end{array} \qquad \begin{array}{r} 84 \\ -\ 64 \\ \hline \end{array} \qquad \begin{array}{r} 93 \\ -\ 33 \\ \hline \end{array}$$

$$\begin{array}{r} 87 \\ -\ 34 \\ \hline \end{array} \qquad \begin{array}{r} 76 \\ -\ 45 \\ \hline \end{array} \qquad \begin{array}{r} 67 \\ -\ 33 \\ \hline \end{array} \qquad \begin{array}{r} 49 \\ -\ 28 \\ \hline \end{array}$$

$$\begin{array}{r} 56 \\ -\ 35 \\ \hline \end{array} \qquad \begin{array}{r} 73 \\ -\ 40 \\ \hline \end{array} \qquad \begin{array}{r} 47 \\ -\ 25 \\ \hline \end{array} \qquad \begin{array}{r} 54 \\ -\ 32 \\ \hline \end{array}$$

$$\begin{array}{r} 79 \\ -\ 38 \\ \hline \end{array} \qquad \begin{array}{r} 45 \\ -\ 21 \\ \hline \end{array} \qquad \begin{array}{r} 76 \\ -\ 43 \\ \hline \end{array} \qquad \begin{array}{r} 75 \\ -\ 12 \\ \hline \end{array}$$

$$\begin{array}{r} 43 \\ -\ 30 \\ \hline \end{array} \qquad \begin{array}{r} 55 \\ -\ 12 \\ \hline \end{array} \qquad \begin{array}{r} 67 \\ -\ 33 \\ \hline \end{array} \qquad \begin{array}{r} 53 \\ -\ 12 \\ \hline \end{array}$$

# Subtracting

Write the answer between the lines.

```
    1 13          2 14           3 13
    2̶3̶            3̶4̶            4̶3̶
  − 16          − 17          − 18
  _____        _____        _____
     7            17            25
```

Write the answer between the lines.

| | | | |
|---|---|---|---|
| 36 | 41 | 53 | 65 |
| − 28 | − 35 | − 46 | − 47 |
| | | | |
| 44 | 35 | 62 | 73 |
| − 27 | − 18 | − 24 | − 44 |
| | | | |
| 56 | 37 | 43 | 68 |
| − 46 | − 18 | − 26 | − 49 |
| | | | |
| 34 | 45 | 63 | 37 |
| − 12 | − 18 | − 46 | − 15 |
| | | | |
| 60 | 47 | 63 | 86 |
| − 43 | − 24 | − 40 | − 29 |
| | | | |
| 73 | 56 | 48 | 80 |
| − 34 | − 47 | − 36 | − 45 |
| | | | |
| 54 | 70 | 37 | 53 |
| − 38 | − 45 | − 18 | − 26 |
| | | | |
| 34 | 71 | 25 | 83 |
| − 18 | − 44 | − 17 | − 29 |

# Choosing the operation

Write either + or – in the box to make each problem correct.

15 + 25 = 40     30 – 8 = 22     50 – 25 = 25

Write either + or – in the box to make each problem correct.

| 45 | 12 = 33 | 48 | 14 = 34 | 31 | 15 = 46 |
|---|---|---|---|---|---|
| 17 | 13 = 30 | 60 | 35 = 25 | 70 | 35 = 35 |
| 27 | 15 = 12 | 26 | 18 = 44 | 50 | 12 = 62 |
| 65 | 25 = 40 | 80 | 35 = 45 | 63 | 23 = 40 |

Write either + or – in the box to make each problem correct.

| 12 yd | 5 yd = 27 yd | 34 ft | 18 ft = 16 ft |
|---|---|---|---|
| 29 cm | 17 cm = 12 cm | 42 in. | 20 in. = 62 in. |
| 28 in. | 28 in. = 56 in. | 60 cm | 15 cm = 45 cm |
| 40 ft | 8 ft = 32 ft | 90 cm | 35 cm = 55 cm |
| 28 cm | 15 cm = 43 cm | 70 yd | 29 yd = 41 yd |
| 90 in. | 12 in. = 78 in. | 28 m | 21 m = 49 m |

Write the answer in the box.

I start with 12 apples and end up with 18 apples. How many have I added or subtracted?

A number is added to 14 and the result is 20. What number has been added?

I start with 14 pens. I finish up with 9 pens. How many pens have I lost or gained?

I take a number away from 30 and have 12 left. What number did I take away?

# Tables and graphs

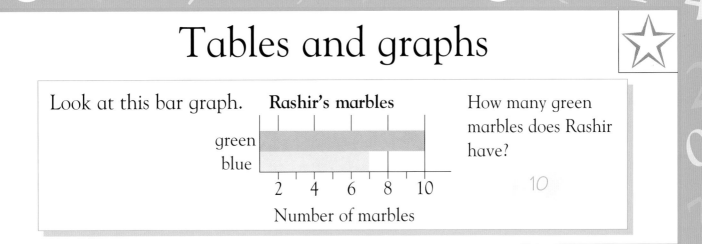

Look at this bar graph.

**Rashir's marbles**

green
blue

Number of marbles

How many green marbles does Rashir have?

*10*

Look at this bar graph.

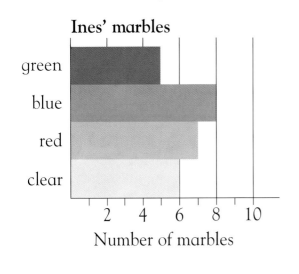

**Ines' marbles**

green
blue
red
clear

Number of marbles

How many green marbles does Ines have?

Ines has 7 marbles of which color?

How many clear marbles does Ines have?

Of which color does Ines have the most marbles?

How many marbles does Ines have altogether?

Complete the table.

**Favorite pets**

| Pets | tally marks | total |
|------|-------------|-------|
| hamsters | ⊬⊬⊬ l l | |
| mice | | 4 |
| gerbils | l l l | |
| rats | | 5 |

Number of children

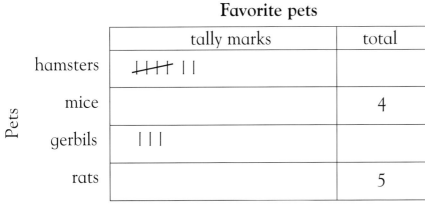

How many more children have hamsters than have rats?

Which animal is owned by 4 children?

# Identifying patterns

Complete each pattern.

| 48 | 42 | 36 | 30 | 24 | 18 | 12 | 6 |
|----|----|----|----|----|----|----|----|
| 44 | 41 | 38 | 35 | 32 | 29 | 26 | 23 |

Complete each pattern.

| 21 | 19 | 17 |
|----|----|----|
| 38 | 34 | 30 |
| 36 | 31 | 26 |
| 55 | 50 | 45 |
| 42 | 37 | 32 |
| 52 | 48 | 44 |
| 62 | 57 | 52 |
| 35 | 31 | 27 |
| 41 | 39 | 37 |
| 38 | 33 | 28 |
| 42 | 36 | 30 |
| 50 | 44 | 38 |
| 63 | 57 | 51 |
| 37 | 34 | 31 |
| 58 | 53 | 48 |
| 78 | 70 | 62 |
| 67 | 60 | 53 |

# Odds and evens

Write the answer in the box.

3 + 3 =   6         4 + 6 =   10         7 + 3 =   10         2 + 6 =   8

---

Add the even numbers to the even numbers.

| 4 + 8 = | 12 + 6 = | 10 + 6 = | 8 + 14 = |
|---|---|---|---|
| 20 + 14 = | 14 + 12 = | 16 + 10 = | 30 + 20 = |
| 14 + 16 = | 18 + 6 = | 22 + 8 = | 20 + 40 = |

What do you notice about each answer? _____

---

Add the odd numbers to the odd numbers.

| 7 + 9 = | 5 + 7 = | 11 + 5 = | 9 + 5 = |
|---|---|---|---|
| 7 + 7 = | 9 + 3 = | 15 + 5 = | 13 + 7 = |
| 11 + 3 = | 17 + 9 = | 15 + 9 = | 13 + 15 = |

What do you notice about each answer? _____

---

Add the odd numbers to the even numbers.

| 3 + 8 = | 9 + 12 = | 5 + 18 = | 7 + 14 = |
|---|---|---|---|
| 11 + 4 = | 13 + 10 = | 15 + 6 = | 21 + 4 = |
| 7 + 20 = | 13 + 30 = | 9 + 12 = | 17 + 6 = |

What do you notice about each answer? _____

---

Add the even numbers to the odd numbers.

| 6 + 7 = | 8 + 5 = | 10 + 9 = | 2 + 17 = |
|---|---|---|---|
| 10 + 29 = | 14 + 3 = | 8 + 13 = | 12 + 5 = |
| 14 + 7 = | 8 + 51 = | 16 + 9 = | 30 + 17 = |

What do you notice about each answer? _____

# Real-life problems

Write the answer in the box.

Sarah has eight wrenches and is given six more.
How many wrenches does she have now?

8 + 6 = 14

Write the answer in the box.

Karl has 20 marbles but loses 12 in a game of marbles.
How many marbles does he have left?

After buying some candies for 30¢, Naomi still has
65¢ left. How much did she have to begin with?

Billy takes 20 balls out of a barrel
and leaves 15 in the barrel.
How many balls are
there altogether?

June collected 150 stamps and her father gave her
60 more. How many stamps does June have now?

Angela puts 40 toys in a box that already has 35 toys in it.
How many toys are in the box now?

Patrick leaves 45¢ at home and takes 50¢ with him. How much
money does Patrick have altogether?

Don gives some of his allowance to his sister. He gives his sister
80¢ and has 60¢ left. How much allowance did Don have in the
first place?

Five letters of the alphabet are vowels. How many letters of the
alphabet are not vowels?

# Symmetry

The dotted line is a mirror line. Complete each shape.

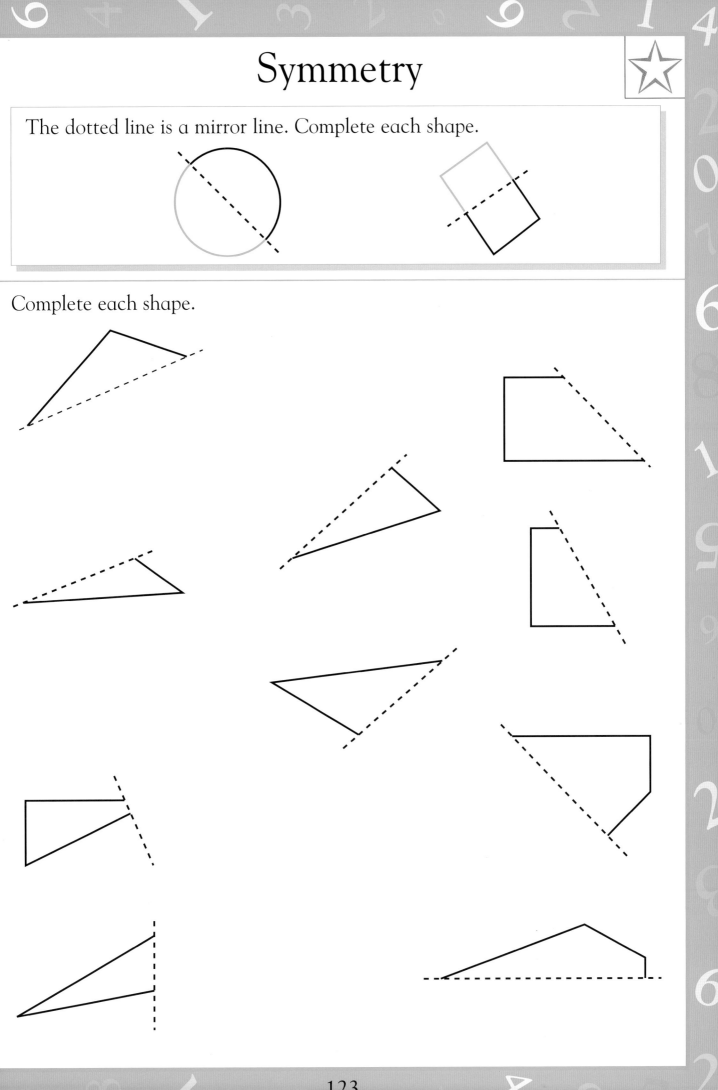

Complete each shape.

# Adding

Write the answer between the lines.

```
    12          17          15          12          18
    13          10          13          14          10
+   13      +   11      +   11      +   12      +   11
──────      ──────      ──────      ──────      ──────


    17          19          16          12          19
    26          13          21          25          32
+   12      +   14      +   31      +   33      +   12
──────      ──────      ──────      ──────      ──────


    20          30          40          50          60
    32          26          42          21          14
+   16      +   25      +   25      +   21      +    8
──────      ──────      ──────      ──────      ──────


    25          35          45          55          65
    15          25          15          35          15
+    5      +    5      +    5      +    5      +    5
──────      ──────      ──────      ──────      ──────


    23          34          45          56          67
    45          32          16          16          12
+   32      +   13      +    9      +    7      +    8
──────      ──────      ──────      ──────      ──────
```

# Subtracting

Write the answer between the lines.

```
   40        60        70        50        90
−  18     −  23     −  37     −  18     −  27
‾‾‾‾‾     ‾‾‾‾‾     ‾‾‾‾‾     ‾‾‾‾‾     ‾‾‾‾‾

‾‾‾‾‾     ‾‾‾‾‾     ‾‾‾‾‾     ‾‾‾‾‾     ‾‾‾‾‾


   41        62        85        64        71
−  14     −  15     −  37     −  45     −  36
‾‾‾‾‾     ‾‾‾‾‾     ‾‾‾‾‾     ‾‾‾‾‾     ‾‾‾‾‾

‾‾‾‾‾     ‾‾‾‾‾     ‾‾‾‾‾     ‾‾‾‾‾     ‾‾‾‾‾


   45        65        75        95        85
−  18     −  34     −  69     −  49     −  38
‾‾‾‾‾     ‾‾‾‾‾     ‾‾‾‾‾     ‾‾‾‾‾     ‾‾‾‾‾

‾‾‾‾‾     ‾‾‾‾‾     ‾‾‾‾‾     ‾‾‾‾‾     ‾‾‾‾‾


   73        82        74        81        64
−  27     −  38     −  47     −  39     −  47
‾‾‾‾‾     ‾‾‾‾‾     ‾‾‾‾‾     ‾‾‾‾‾     ‾‾‾‾‾

‾‾‾‾‾     ‾‾‾‾‾     ‾‾‾‾‾     ‾‾‾‾‾     ‾‾‾‾‾


   61        52        61        53        73
−  14     −  17     −  19     −  23     −  44
‾‾‾‾‾     ‾‾‾‾‾     ‾‾‾‾‾     ‾‾‾‾‾     ‾‾‾‾‾

‾‾‾‾‾     ‾‾‾‾‾     ‾‾‾‾‾     ‾‾‾‾‾     ‾‾‾‾‾


   70        63        83        53        47
−  26     −   7     −  56     −  36     −  43
‾‾‾‾‾     ‾‾‾‾‾     ‾‾‾‾‾     ‾‾‾‾‾     ‾‾‾‾‾

‾‾‾‾‾     ‾‾‾‾‾     ‾‾‾‾‾     ‾‾‾‾‾     ‾‾‾‾‾
```

# 2 times table

Count in 2s, color, and find a pattern.

| | | | | |
|---|---|---|---|---|
| 1 | 2 | 3 | 4 | 5 |
| 6 | 7 | 8 | 9 | 10 |
| 11 | 12 | 13 | 14 | 15 |
| 16 | 17 | 18 | 19 | 20 |
| 21 | 22 | 23 | 24 | 25 |

Write the answers.

$1 \times 2 = \boxed{2}$       $2 \times 2 = \boxed{\phantom{0}}$       $3 \times 2 = \boxed{\phantom{0}}$       $4 \times 2 = \boxed{\phantom{0}}$

$5 \times 2 = \boxed{\phantom{0}}$       $6 \times 2 = \boxed{\phantom{0}}$       $7 \times 2 = \boxed{\phantom{0}}$       $8 \times 2 = \boxed{\phantom{0}}$

$9 \times 2 = \boxed{\phantom{0}}$       $10 \times 2 = \boxed{\phantom{0}}$

How many ears?

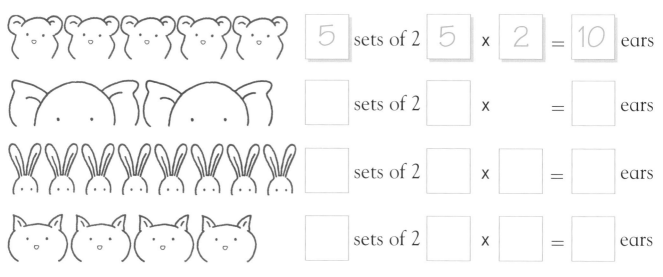

| | sets of 2 | | x | | = | | ears |
|---|---|---|---|---|---|---|---|
| 5 | sets of 2 | 5 | x | 2 | = | 10 | ears |
| | sets of 2 | | x | | = | | ears |
| | sets of 2 | | x | | = | | ears |
| | sets of 2 | | x | | = | | ears |

# Multiplying by 2

Write the problems.

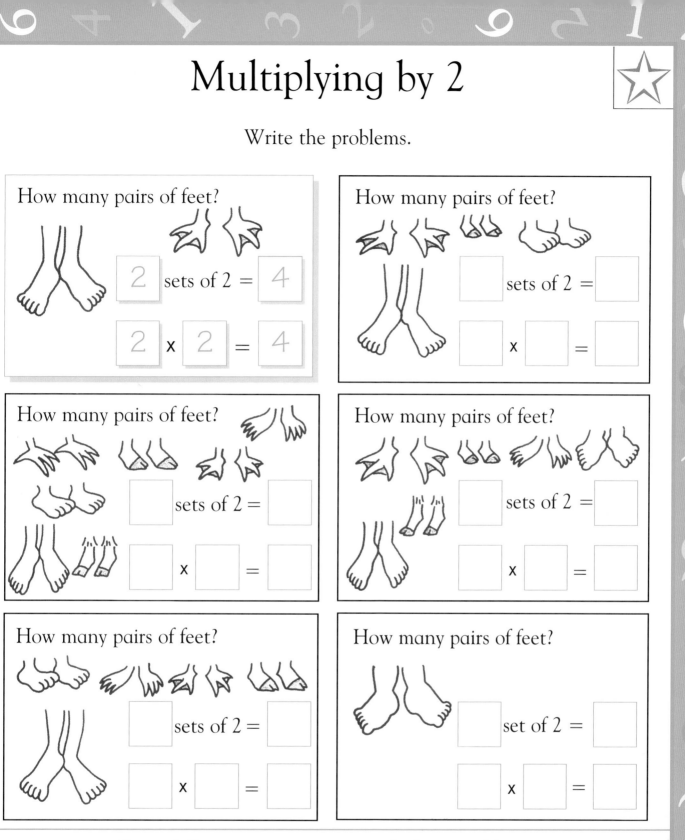

How many pairs of feet?

2 sets of 2 = 4

2 x 2 = 4

How many pairs of feet?

☐ sets of 2 = ☐

☐ x ☐ = ☐

How many pairs of feet?

☐ sets of 2 = ☐

☐ x ☐ = ☐

How many pairs of feet?

☐ sets of 2 = ☐

☐ x ☐ = ☐

How many pairs of feet?

☐ sets of 2 = ☐

☐ x ☐ = ☐

How many pairs of feet?

☐ set of 2 = ☐

☐ x ☐ = ☐

Draw different pictures to go with these problems.

8 x 2 = 16

10 x 2 = 20

# Dividing by 2

Share the eggs equally between the nests.

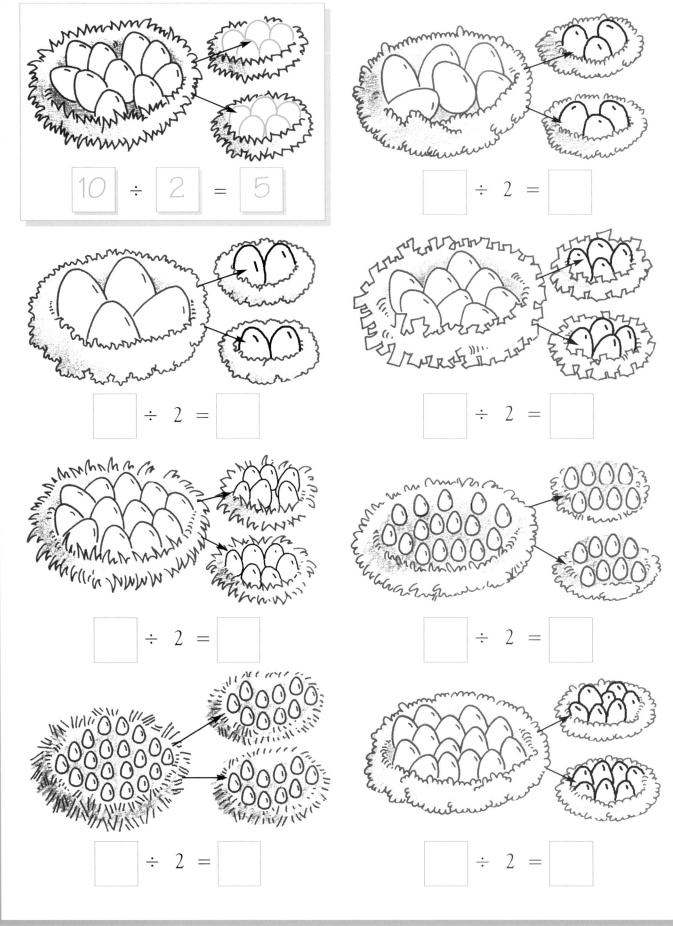

$10 \div 2 = 5$

$\boxed{\phantom{0}} \div 2 = \boxed{\phantom{0}}$

$\boxed{\phantom{0}} \div 2 = \boxed{\phantom{0}}$

$\boxed{\phantom{0}} \div 2 = \boxed{\phantom{0}}$

$\boxed{\phantom{0}} \div 2 = \boxed{\phantom{0}}$

$\boxed{\phantom{0}} \div 2 = \boxed{\phantom{0}}$

$\boxed{\phantom{0}} \div 2 = \boxed{\phantom{0}}$

$\boxed{\phantom{0}} \div 2 = \boxed{\phantom{0}}$

# Using the 2 times table

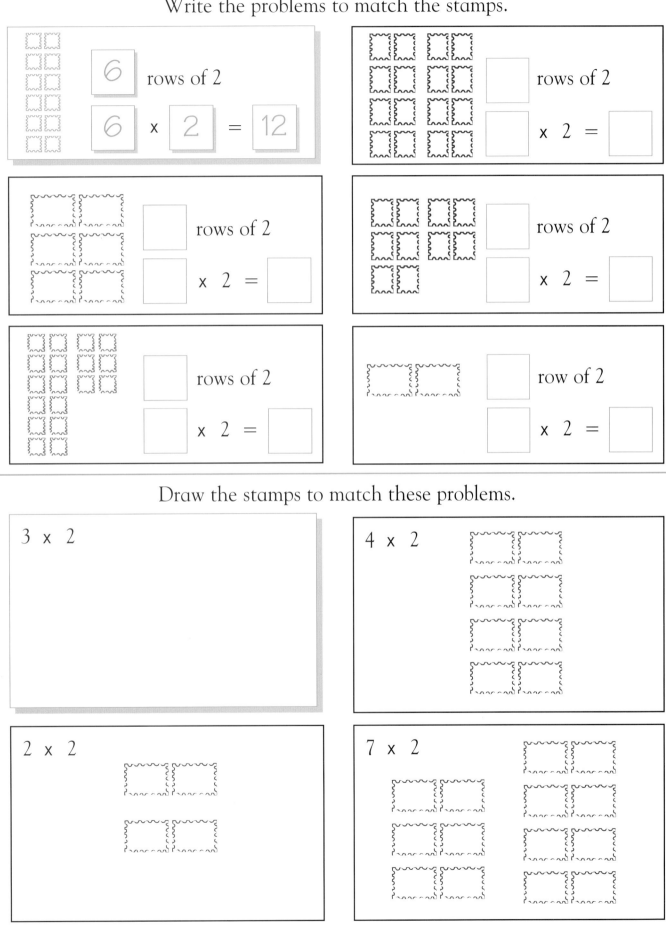

Write the problems to match the stamps.

6 rows of 2

6 x 2 = 12

rows of 2

x 2 =

rows of 2

x 2 =

rows of 2

x 2 =

rows of 2

x 2 =

row of 2

x 2 =

Draw the stamps to match these problems.

3 x 2

4 x 2

2 x 2

7 x 2

# Using the 2 times table

Each face stands for 2. Join each set of faces to the correct number.

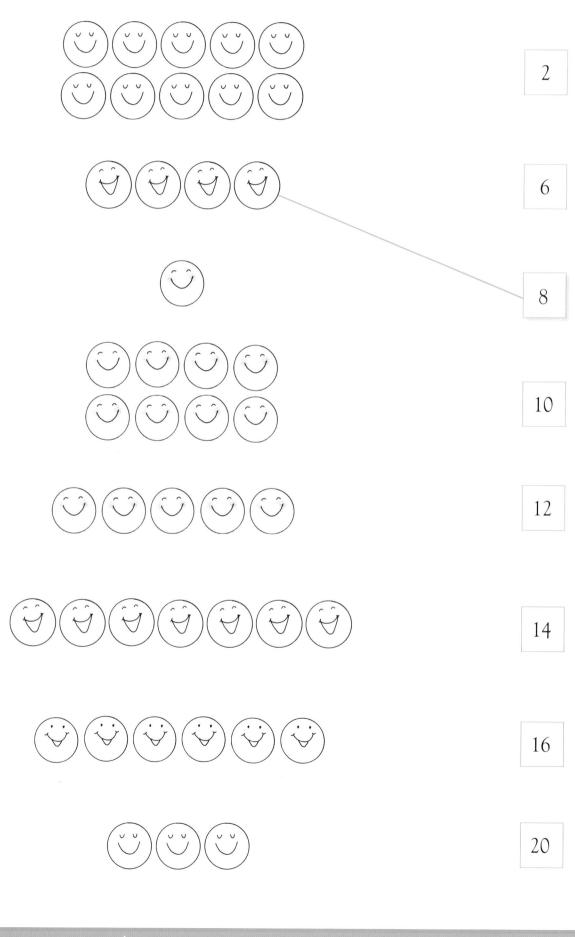

# Using the 2 times table

How many eyes?

| 3 | x | 2 | = | 6 | eyes |

| | x | | = | | eyes |

| | x | | = | | eyes |

| | x | | = | | eyes |

| | x | | = | | eyes |

| | x | | = | | eyes |

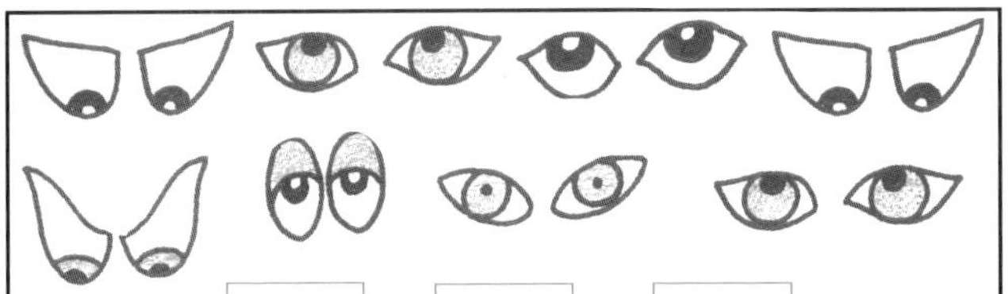

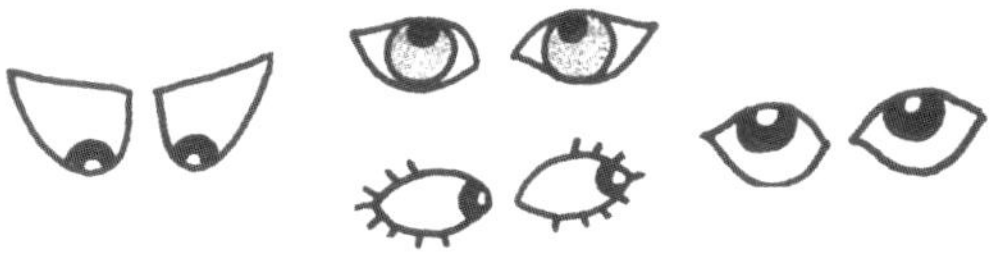

Draw your own pictures to match these number sentences.

2 x 2 = 4

10 x 2 = 20

3 x 2 = 6

7 x 2 = 14

# 5 times table

Count in 5s, color, and find a pattern.

| 1 | 2 | 3 | 4 | 5 | 6 | 7 | 8 | 9 | 10 |
|---|---|---|---|---|---|---|---|---|---|
| 11 | 12 | 13 | 14 | 15 | 16 | 17 | 18 | 19 | 20 |
| 21 | 22 | 23 | 24 | 25 | 26 | 27 | 28 | 29 | 30 |
| 31 | 32 | 33 | 34 | 35 | 36 | 37 | 38 | 39 | 40 |
| 41 | 42 | 43 | 44 | 45 | 46 | 47 | 48 | 49 | 50 |
| 51 | 52 | 53 | 54 | 55 | 56 | 57 | 58 | 59 | 60 |
| 61 | 62 | 63 | 64 | 65 | 66 | 67 | 68 | 69 | 70 |
| 71 | 72 | 73 | 74 | 75 | 76 | 77 | 78 | 79 | 80 |
| 81 | 82 | 83 | 84 | 85 | 86 | 87 | 88 | 89 | 90 |
| 91 | 92 | 93 | 94 | 95 | 96 | 97 | 98 | 99 | 100 |

Write the answers.

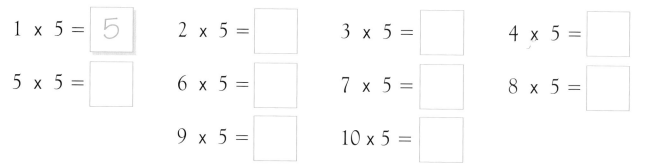

$1 \times 5 = \boxed{5}$     $2 \times 5 = \boxed{\phantom{0}}$     $3 \times 5 = \boxed{\phantom{0}}$     $4 \times 5 = \boxed{\phantom{0}}$

$5 \times 5 = \boxed{\phantom{0}}$     $6 \times 5 = \boxed{\phantom{0}}$     $7 \times 5 = \boxed{\phantom{0}}$     $8 \times 5 = \boxed{\phantom{0}}$

$9 \times 5 = \boxed{\phantom{0}}$     $10 \times 5 = \boxed{\phantom{0}}$

How many candies?

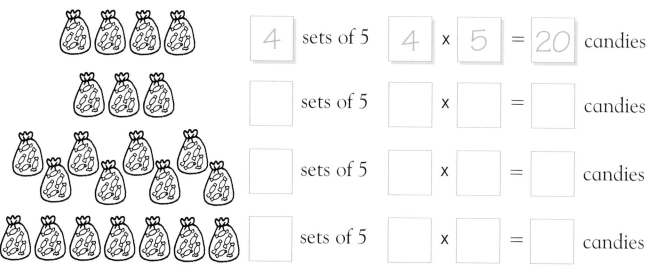

$\boxed{4}$ sets of 5     $\boxed{4} \times \boxed{5} = \boxed{20}$ candies

$\boxed{\phantom{0}}$ sets of 5     $\boxed{\phantom{0}} \times \boxed{\phantom{0}} = \boxed{\phantom{0}}$ candies

$\boxed{\phantom{0}}$ sets of 5     $\boxed{\phantom{0}} \times \boxed{\phantom{0}} = \boxed{\phantom{0}}$ candies

$\boxed{\phantom{0}}$ sets of 5     $\boxed{\phantom{0}} \times \boxed{\phantom{0}} = \boxed{\phantom{0}}$ candies

# Multiplying by 5

Draw a ring around rows of 5. Complete the problem.

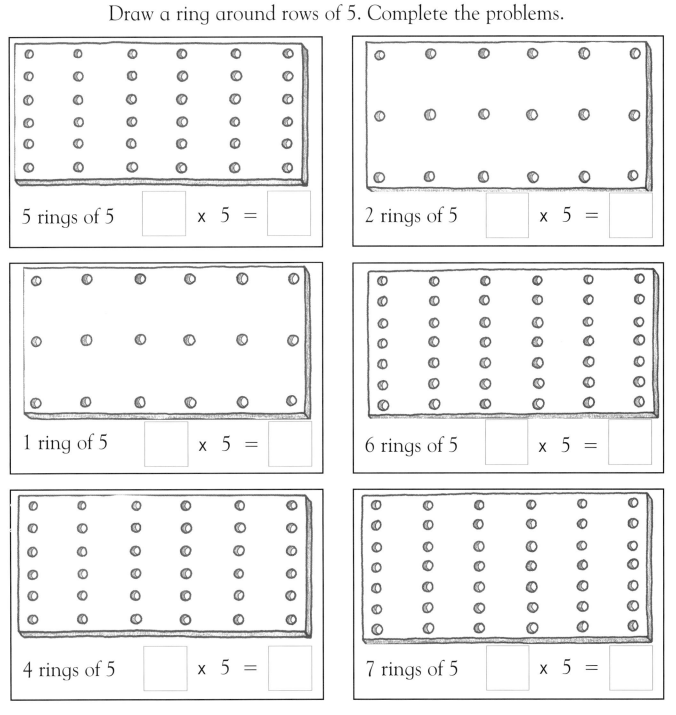

Draw a ring around rows of 5. Complete the problems.

5 rings of 5   ☐ x 5 = ☐

2 rings of 5   ☐ x 5 = ☐

1 ring of 5   ☐ x 5 = ☐

6 rings of 5   ☐ x 5 = ☐

4 rings of 5   ☐ x 5 = ☐

7 rings of 5   ☐ x 5 = ☐

# Dividing by 5

Write a number sentence to show how many cubes are in each stack.

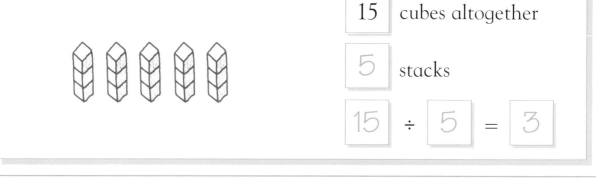

| 15 | cubes altogether |

| 5 | stacks |

15 ÷ 5 = 3

Write a number sentence to show how many cubes are in each stack.

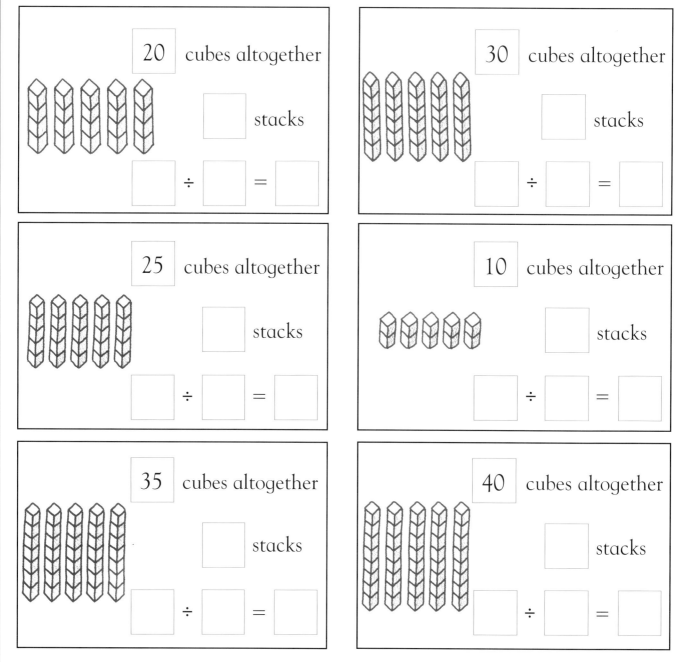

| 20 | cubes altogether |

stacks

____ ÷ ____ = ____

| 30 | cubes altogether |

stacks

____ ÷ ____ = ____

| 25 | cubes altogether |

stacks

____ ÷ ____ = ____

| 10 | cubes altogether |

stacks

____ ÷ ____ = ____

| 35 | cubes altogether |

stacks

____ ÷ ____ = ____

| 40 | cubes altogether |

stacks

____ ÷ ____ = ____

# Using the 5 times table

Write the number that is hiding under the star.

⭐ 4  x 5 = 20

---

Write the number that is hiding under the star.

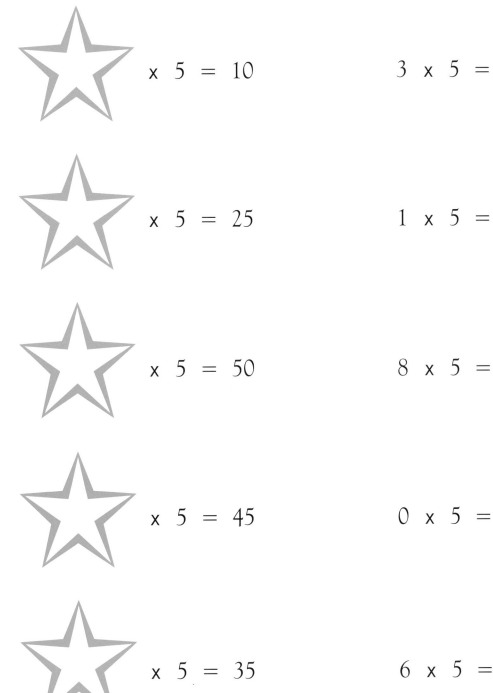

⭐ x 5 = 10            3 x 5 = ⭐

⭐ x 5 = 25            1 x 5 = ⭐

⭐ x 5 = 50            8 x 5 = ⭐

⭐ x 5 = 45            0 x 5 = ⭐

⭐ x 5 = 35            6 x 5 = ⭐

# Using the 5 times table

Each frog stands for 5. Join each set of frogs to the correct number.

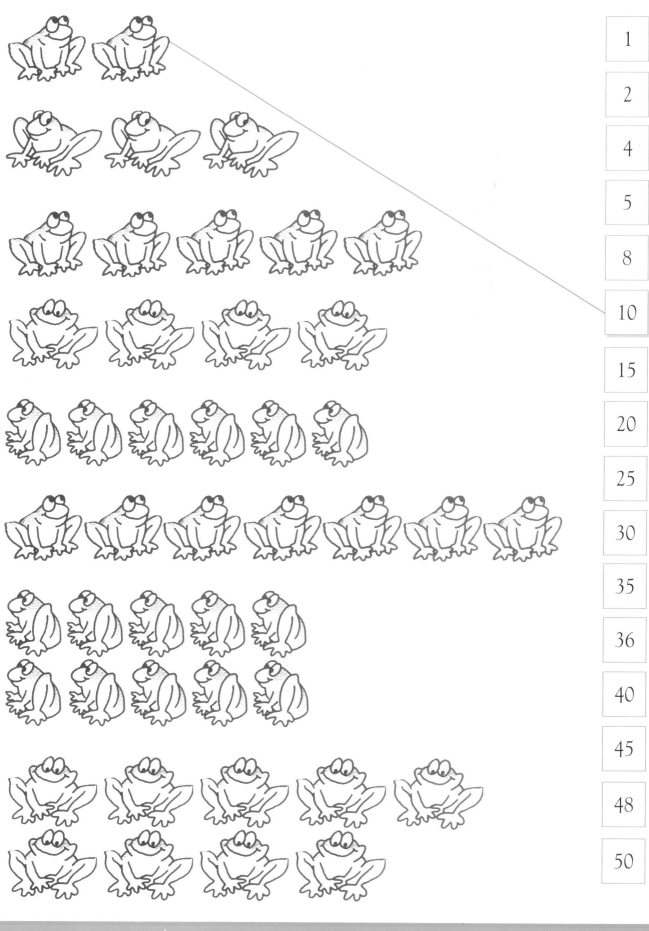

| 1 |
| 2 |
| 4 |
| 5 |
| 8 |
| 10 |
| 15 |
| 20 |
| 25 |
| 30 |
| 35 |
| 36 |
| 40 |
| 45 |
| 48 |
| 50 |

# Using the 5 times table

## How many altogether?

Georgia had 7 cats. Each cat had 5 kittens. How many kittens were there altogether?

$$7 \times 5 = 35 \text{ kittens}$$

## How many altogether?

Charlie had 6 boxes. He had 5 trains in each box. How many trains did he have altogether?

$$\boxed{\phantom{0}} \times \boxed{\phantom{0}} = \boxed{\phantom{0}} \text{ trains}$$

Zoe had 3 jackets. Each jacket had 5 buttons. How many buttons were there altogether?

$$\boxed{\phantom{0}} \times \boxed{\phantom{0}} = \boxed{\phantom{0}} \text{ buttons}$$

Yan had 8 fish tanks. Each tank had 5 fish in it. How many fish were there altogether?

$$\boxed{\phantom{0}} \times \boxed{\phantom{0}} = \boxed{\phantom{0}} \text{ fish}$$

## How many in each?

Joe had 45 pencils and 5 pencil cases. How many pencils were in each case?

$$45 \div 5 = 9 \text{ pencils}$$

## How many in each?

Heather had 10 mice and 5 cages. How many mice were in each cage?

$$\boxed{\phantom{0}} \div \boxed{\phantom{0}} = \boxed{\phantom{0}} \text{ mice}$$

Shannon had 35 candies in 5 bags. How many candies were in each bag?

$$\boxed{\phantom{0}} \div \boxed{\phantom{0}} = \boxed{\phantom{0}} \text{ candies}$$

Mark put 25 seeds into 5 pots. How many seeds were in each pot?

$$\boxed{\phantom{0}} \div \boxed{\phantom{0}} = \boxed{\phantom{0}} \text{ seeds}$$

# 10 times table

Count in 10s, color, and find a pattern.

| 1 | 2 | 3 | 4 | 5 | 6 | 7 | 8 | 9 | 10 |
|---|---|---|---|---|---|---|---|---|---|
| 11 | 12 | 13 | 14 | 15 | 16 | 17 | 18 | 19 | 20 |
| 21 | 22 | 23 | 24 | 25 | 26 | 27 | 28 | 29 | 30 |
| 31 | 32 | 33 | 34 | 35 | 36 | 37 | 38 | 39 | 40 |
| 41 | 42 | 43 | 44 | 45 | 46 | 47 | 48 | 49 | 50 |
| 51 | 52 | 53 | 54 | 55 | 56 | 57 | 58 | 59 | 60 |
| 61 | 62 | 63 | 64 | 65 | 66 | 67 | 68 | 69 | 70 |
| 71 | 72 | 73 | 74 | 75 | 76 | 77 | 78 | 79 | 80 |
| 81 | 82 | 83 | 84 | 85 | 86 | 87 | 88 | 89 | 90 |
| 91 | 92 | 93 | 94 | 95 | 96 | 97 | 98 | 99 | 100 |

Write the answers.

1 x 10 = 10    2 x 10 =    3 x 10 =    4 x 10 =

5 x 10 =    6 x 10 =    7 x 10 =    8 x 10 =

10 x 10 =    9 x 10 =

Each box contains 10 crayons. How many crayons are there altogether?

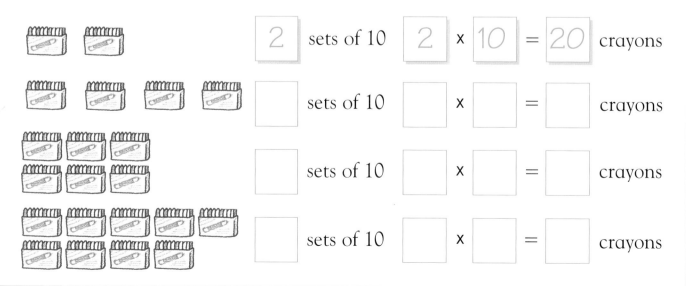

2 sets of 10    2 x 10 = 20 crayons

    sets of 10    x = crayons

    sets of 10    x = crayons

    sets of 10    x = crayons

# Multiplying and dividing

Each pod contains 10 peas. How many peas are there altogether?

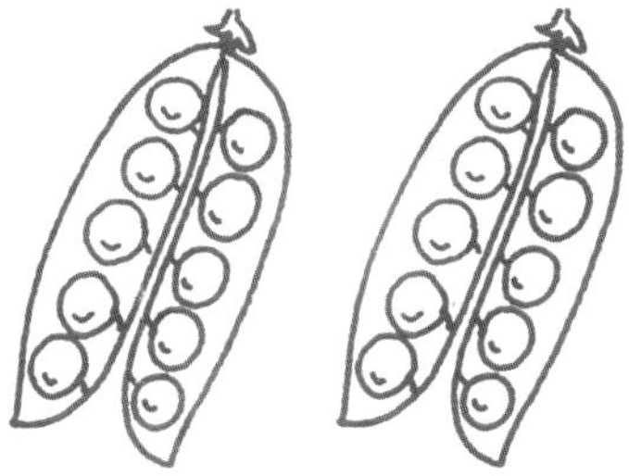

How many pods?  2

2  ×  10  =  20  peas

Write how many peas.

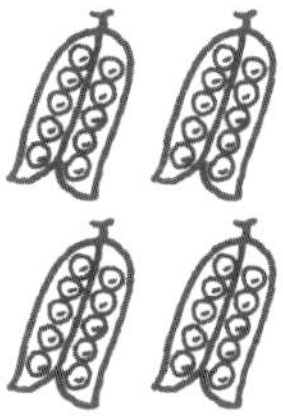

How many pods? ☐

☐ × 10 = ☐ peas

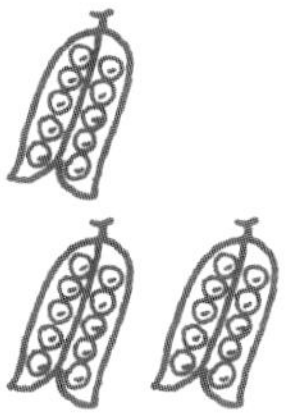

How many pods? ☐

☐ × ☐ = ☐ peas

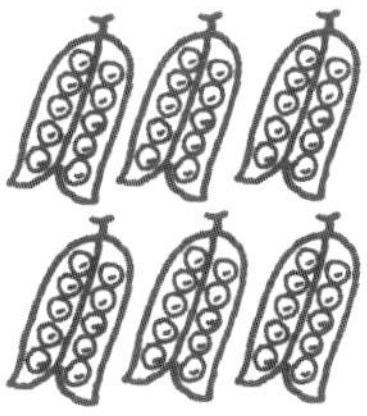

How many pods? ☐

☐ × ☐ = ☐ peas

How many pods? ☐

☐ × ☐ = ☐ peas

How many pods did the peas come from?

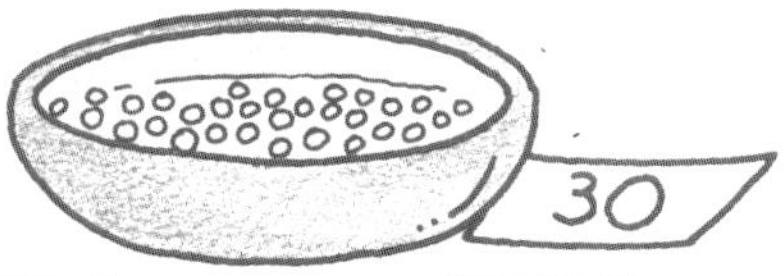

30

30 ÷ 10 = 3 pods

Write how many pods.

10

☐ ÷ 10 = ☐ pod

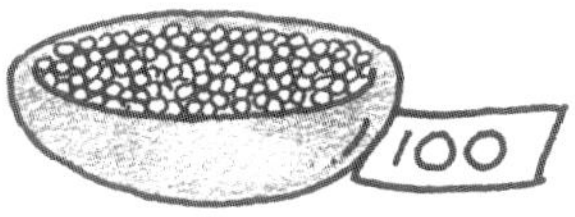

100

☐ ÷ 10 = ☐ pods

20

☐ ÷ 10 = ☐ pods

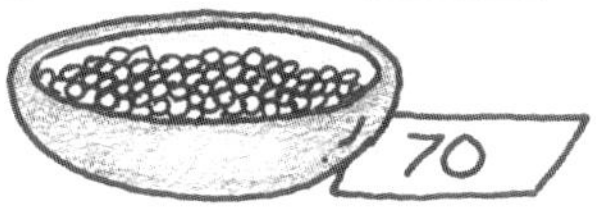

70

☐ ÷ 10 = ☐ pods

# Dividing by 10

One dollar is worth the same as ten dimes.

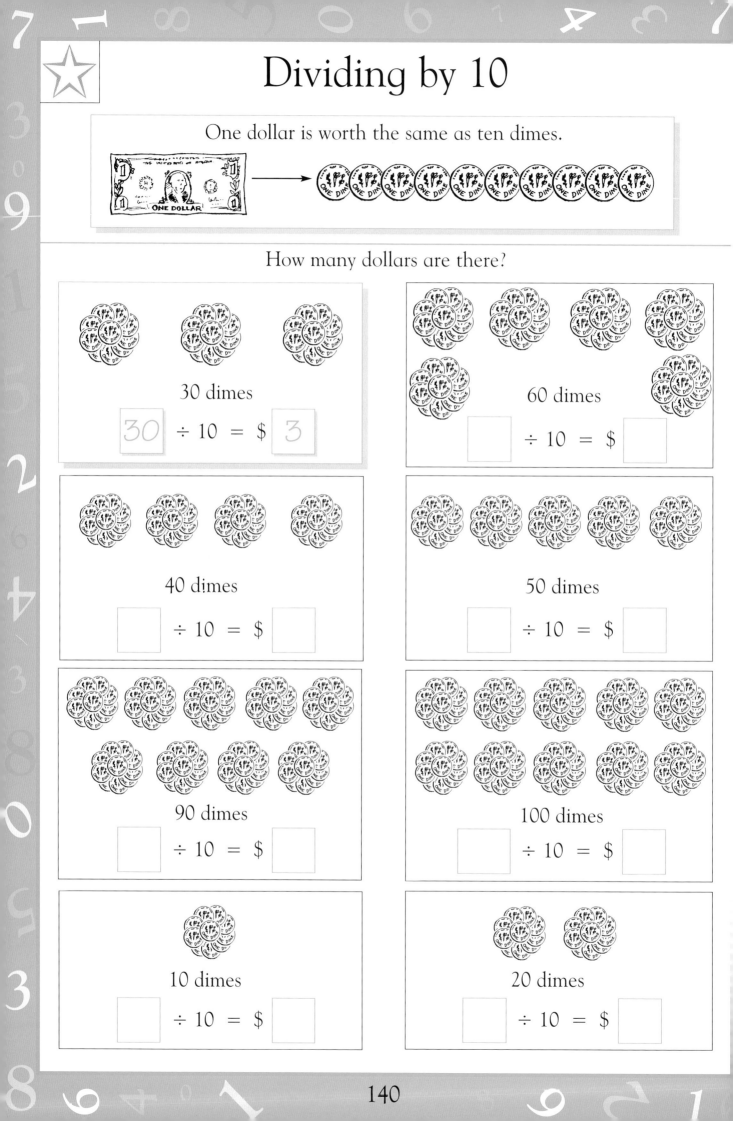

How many dollars are there?

30 dimes

$\boxed{30} \div 10 = \$ \boxed{3}$

60 dimes

$\boxed{\phantom{00}} \div 10 = \$ \boxed{\phantom{0}}$

40 dimes

$\boxed{\phantom{00}} \div 10 = \$ \boxed{\phantom{0}}$

50 dimes

$\boxed{\phantom{00}} \div 10 = \$ \boxed{\phantom{0}}$

90 dimes

$\boxed{\phantom{00}} \div 10 = \$ \boxed{\phantom{0}}$

100 dimes

$\boxed{\phantom{00}} \div 10 = \$ \boxed{\phantom{0}}$

10 dimes

$\boxed{\phantom{00}} \div 10 = \$ \boxed{\phantom{0}}$

20 dimes

$\boxed{\phantom{00}} \div 10 = \$ \boxed{\phantom{0}}$

# Using the 10 times table

## How many altogether?

The squirrels had 4 food dens. Each den had 10 acorns. How many acorns were there altogether?

$$4 \times 10 = 40 \text{ acorns}$$

## How many altogether?

The monkeys had 6 trees. There were 10 bananas in each tree. How many bananas did they have altogether?

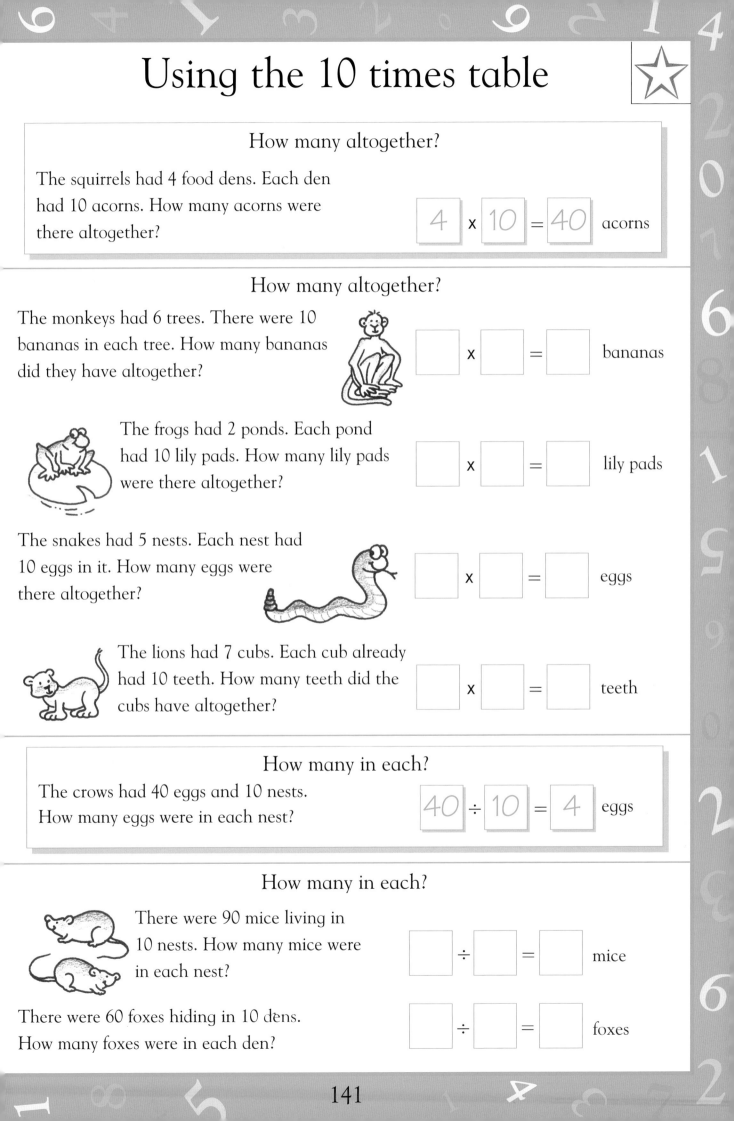

□ x □ = □ bananas

The frogs had 2 ponds. Each pond had 10 lily pads. How many lily pads were there altogether?

□ x □ = □ lily pads

The snakes had 5 nests. Each nest had 10 eggs in it. How many eggs were there altogether?

□ x □ = □ eggs

The lions had 7 cubs. Each cub already had 10 teeth. How many teeth did the cubs have altogether?

□ x □ = □ teeth

## How many in each?

The crows had 40 eggs and 10 nests. How many eggs were in each nest?

$$40 \div 10 = 4 \text{ eggs}$$

## How many in each?

There were 90 mice living in 10 nests. How many mice were in each nest?

□ ÷ □ = □ mice

There were 60 foxes hiding in 10 dens. How many foxes were in each den?

□ ÷ □ = □ foxes

# Using the 10 times table

Match each dog to the right bone.

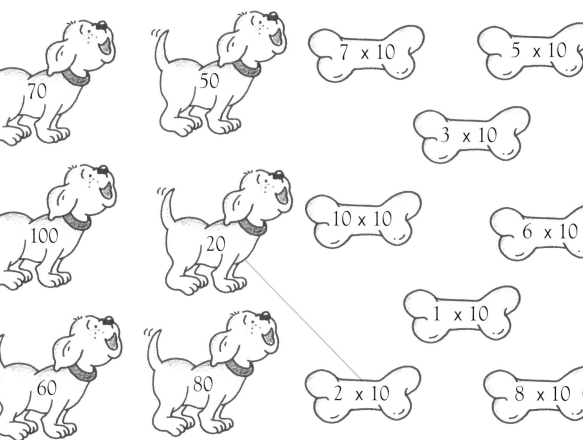

Match each mouse to the right cheese.

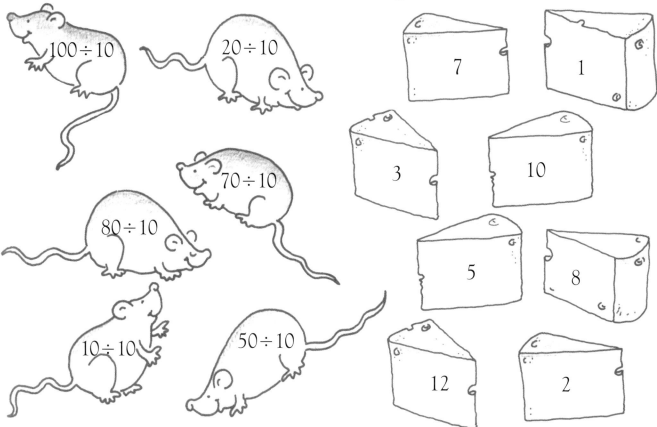

# Using the 10 times table

Write in the missing numbers.

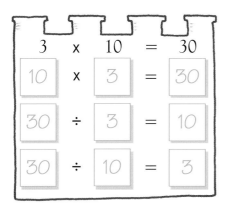

$3 \times 10 = 30$

$10 \times 3 = 30$

$30 \div 3 = 10$

$30 \div 10 = 3$

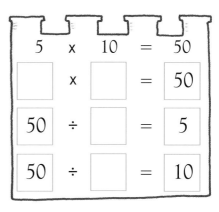

$5 \times 10 = 50$

$\square \times \square = 50$

$50 \div \square = 5$

$50 \div \square = 10$

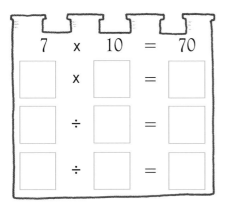

$7 \times 10 = 70$

$\square \times \square = \square$

$\square \div \square = \square$

$\square \div \square = \square$

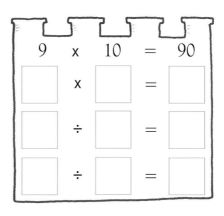

$9 \times 10 = 90$

$\square \times \square = \square$

$\square \div \square = \square$

$\square \div \square = \square$

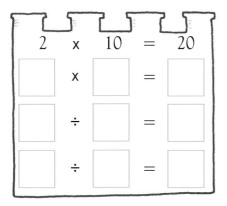

$2 \times 10 = 20$

$\square \times \square = \square$

$\square \div \square = \square$

$\square \div \square = \square$

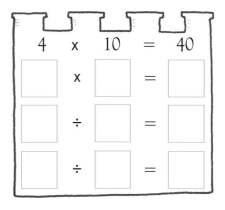

$4 \times 10 = 40$

$\square \times \square = \square$

$\square \div \square = \square$

$\square \div \square = \square$

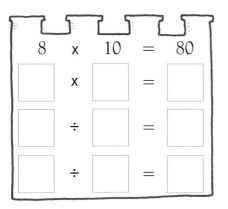

$8 \times 10 = 80$

$\square \times \square = \square$

$\square \div \square = \square$

$\square \div \square = \square$

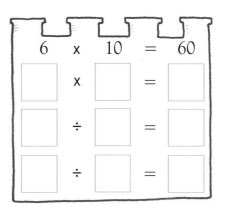

$6 \times 10 = 60$

$\square \times \square = \square$

$\square \div \square = \square$

$\square \div \square = \square$

# 3 times table

Count in 3s, color, and find a pattern.

| | | | | |
|---|---|---|---|---|
| 1 | 2 | 3 | 4 | 5 |
| 6 | 7 | 8 | 9 | 10 |
| 11 | 12 | 13 | 14 | 15 |
| 16 | 17 | 18 | 19 | 20 |
| 21 | 22 | 23 | 24 | 25 |

Write the answers.

$1 \times 3 = \boxed{3}$    $2 \times 3 = \boxed{\phantom{0}}$    $3 \times 3 = \boxed{\phantom{0}}$    $4 \times 3 = \boxed{\phantom{0}}$    $5 \times 3 = \boxed{\phantom{0}}$

How many flowers?

$\boxed{2}$ sets of 3   $\boxed{2} \times \boxed{3} = \boxed{6}$

$\boxed{\phantom{0}}$ sets of 3   $\boxed{\phantom{0}} \times \boxed{\phantom{0}} = \boxed{\phantom{0}}$

$\boxed{\phantom{0}}$ sets of 3   $\boxed{\phantom{0}} \times \boxed{\phantom{0}} = \boxed{\phantom{0}}$

$\boxed{\phantom{0}}$ sets of 3   $\boxed{\phantom{0}} \times \boxed{\phantom{0}} = \boxed{\phantom{0}}$

# Multiplying by 3

Write the number sentences to match the pictures.

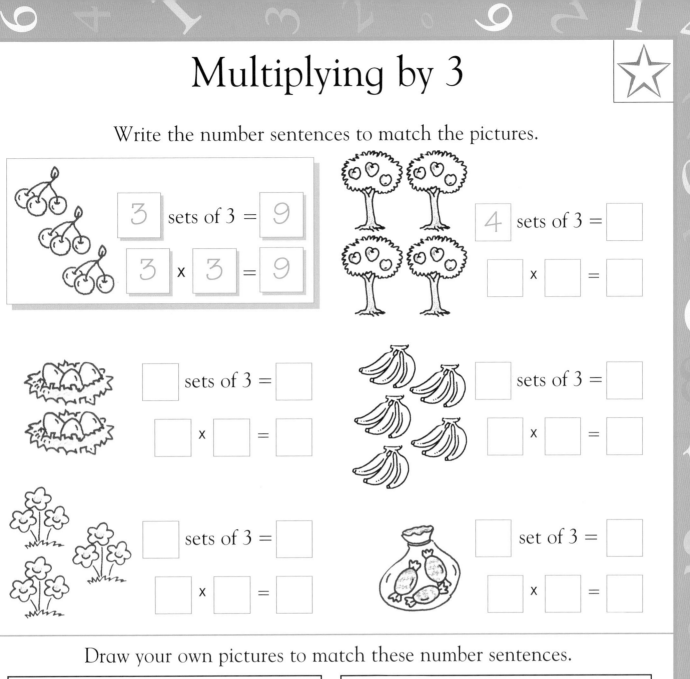

3 sets of 3 = 9

3 x 3 = 9

4 sets of 3 =

☐ x ☐ = ☐

☐ sets of 3 = ☐

☐ x ☐ = ☐

☐ sets of 3 = ☐

☐ x ☐ = ☐

☐ sets of 3 = ☐

☐ x ☐ = ☐

☐ set of 3 = ☐

☐ x ☐ = ☐

Draw your own pictures to match these number sentences.

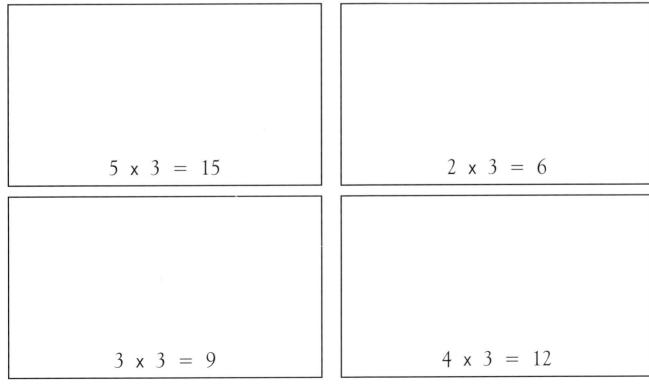

5 x 3 = 15

2 x 3 = 6

3 x 3 = 9

4 x 3 = 12

# Dividing by 3

Divide the money equally among the purses.
Write a problem to show what you have done.
You might find it easier to change all the money into 1¢ coins.

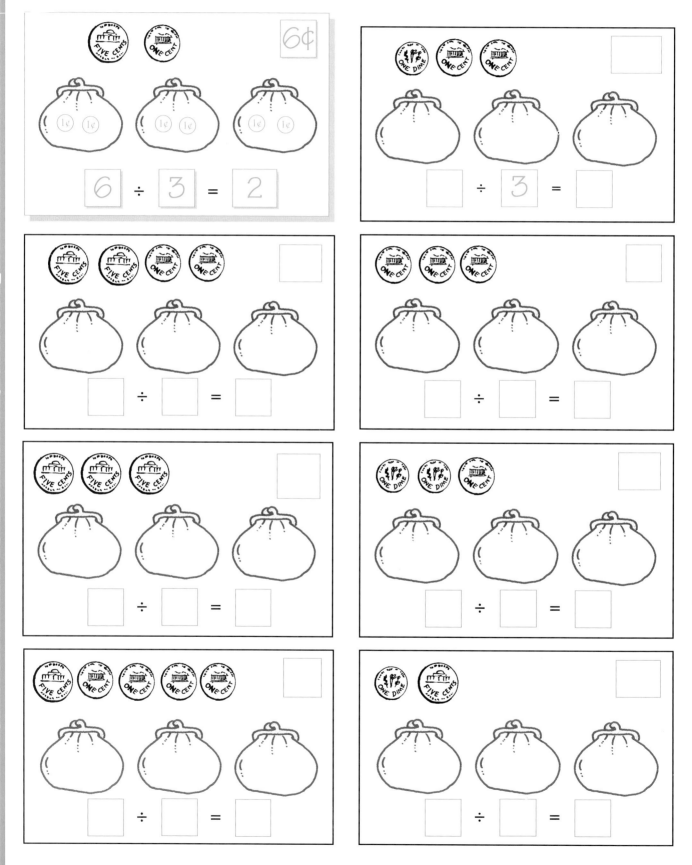

# 4 times table

Count in 4s, color, and find a pattern.

| | | | | |
|---|---|---|---|---|
| 1 | 2 | 3 | 4 | 5 |
| 6 | 7 | 8 | 9 | 10 |
| 11 | 12 | 13 | 14 | 15 |
| 16 | 17 | 18 | 19 | 20 |
| 21 | 22 | 23 | 24 | 25 |

Write the answers.

$1 \times 4 = \boxed{4}$   $2 \times 4 = \boxed{\phantom{0}}$   $3 \times 4 = \boxed{\phantom{0}}$   $4 \times 4 = \boxed{\phantom{0}}$   $5 \times 4 = \boxed{\phantom{0}}$

How many flowers?

$\boxed{4}$ sets of 4   $\boxed{4} \times \boxed{4} = \boxed{16}$

$\boxed{\phantom{0}}$ sets of 4   $\boxed{\phantom{0}} \times \boxed{\phantom{0}} = \boxed{\phantom{0}}$

$\boxed{\phantom{0}}$ sets of 4   $\boxed{\phantom{0}} \times \boxed{\phantom{0}} = \boxed{\phantom{0}}$

$\boxed{\phantom{0}}$ sets of 4   $\boxed{\phantom{0}} \times \boxed{\phantom{0}} = \boxed{\phantom{0}}$

# Multiplying by 4

Write number sentences to match the pictures.

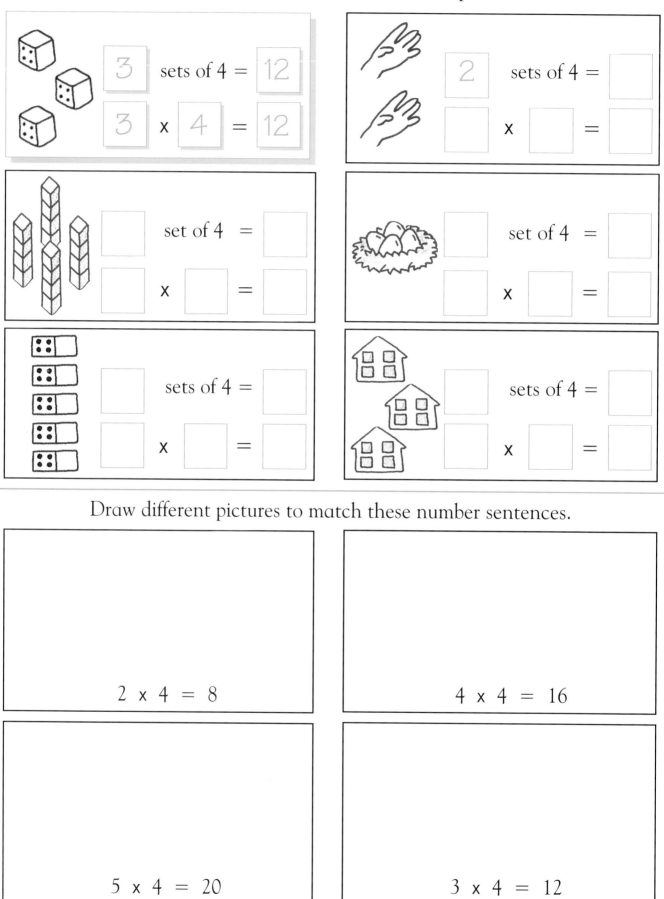

| | |
|---|---|
| 3 sets of 4 = 12 | 2 sets of 4 = ☐ |
| 3 x 4 = 12 | ☐ x ☐ = ☐ |
| ☐ set of 4 = ☐ | ☐ set of 4 = ☐ |
| ☐ x ☐ = ☐ | ☐ x ☐ = ☐ |
| ☐ sets of 4 = ☐ | ☐ sets of 4 = ☐ |
| ☐ x ☐ = ☐ | ☐ x ☐ = ☐ |

Draw different pictures to match these number sentences.

| 2 x 4 = 8 | 4 x 4 = 16 |
|---|---|
| 5 x 4 = 20 | 3 x 4 = 12 |

# Dividing by 4

How many on each plate?

There are 4 children. How many things will each child have?
Draw the objects in the circles.

**8 sandwiches**

$8 \div 4 = 2$ each

**12 cookies**

$\boxed{\phantom{0}} \div 4 = \boxed{\phantom{0}}$ each

**4 drinks**

$\boxed{\phantom{0}} \div \boxed{\phantom{0}} = \boxed{\phantom{0}}$ each

**20 cherries**

$\boxed{\phantom{0}} \div \boxed{\phantom{0}} = \boxed{\phantom{0}}$ each

**16 cupcakes**

$\boxed{\phantom{0}} \div \boxed{\phantom{0}} = \boxed{\phantom{0}}$ each

**8 cheese triangles**

$\boxed{\phantom{0}} \div \boxed{\phantom{0}} = \boxed{\phantom{0}}$ each

# Mixed tables

How many pegs are there in each pegboard?

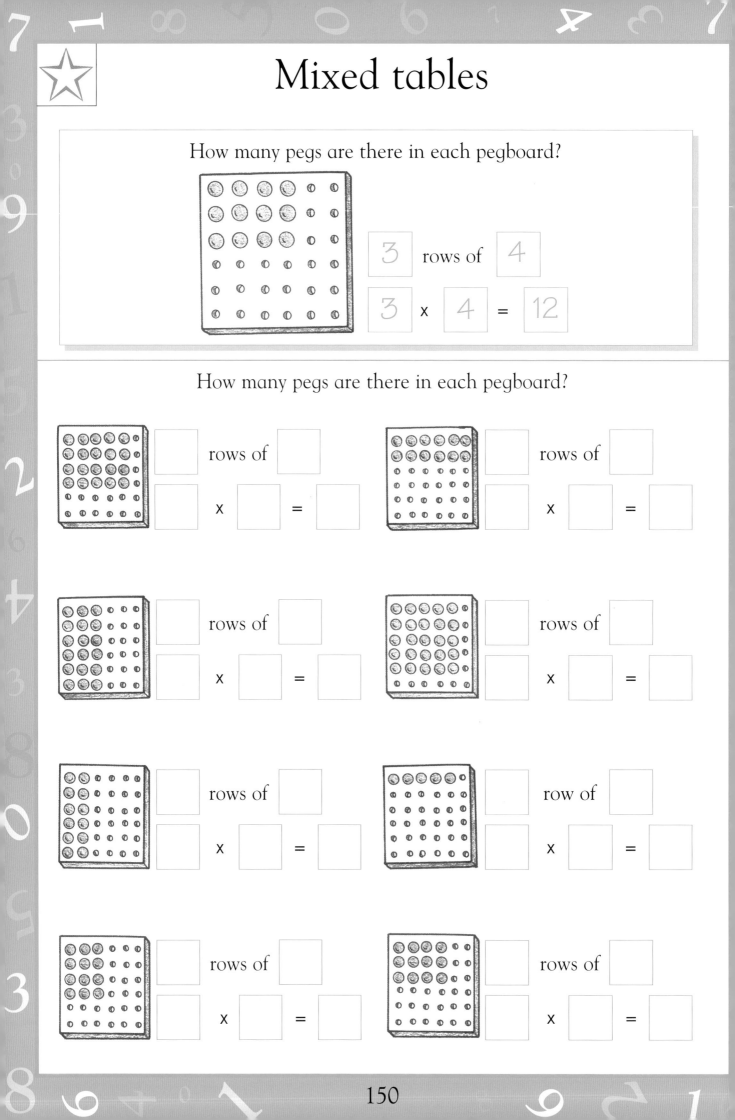

3 rows of 4

3 x 4 = 12

How many pegs are there in each pegboard?

___ rows of ___

___ x ___ = ___

___ rows of ___

___ x ___ = ___

___ rows of ___

___ x ___ = ___

___ rows of ___

___ x ___ = ___

___ rows of ___

___ x ___ = ___

___ row of ___

___ x ___ = ___

___ rows of ___

___ x ___ = ___

___ rows of ___

___ x ___ = ___

# Mixed tables

Divide the 12 pennies equally. Draw the coins
and write the problem to show how many each person gets.

12 ÷ 3 = 4

4 ¢ each

☐ ÷ ☐ = ☐

☐ ¢ each

☐ ÷ ☐ = ☐

☐ ¢ each

☐ ÷ ☐ = ☐

☐ ¢ each

☐ ÷ ☐ = ☐

☐ ¢ each

# Mixed tables

How much will they get paid?

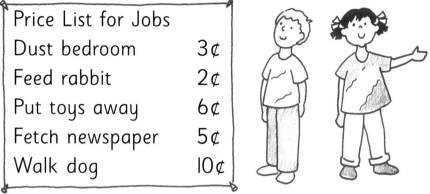

Price List for Jobs
Dust bedroom        3¢
Feed rabbit         2¢
Put toys away       6¢
Fetch newspaper     5¢
Walk dog           10¢

Write a problem to show how much money
Joe and Jasmine will get for these jobs.

Feed 4 rabbits            4  x  2¢  =  8¢

Dust 2 bedrooms           ☐  x  ☐  =  ☐ ¢

Walk the dog 4 times      ☐  x  ☐  =  ☐ ¢

Put the toys away 3 times ☐  x  ☐  =  ☐ ¢

Fetch the newspaper 5 times ☐  x  ☐  =  ☐ ¢

How much will they get for these jobs?
Use the space to work out the problems.

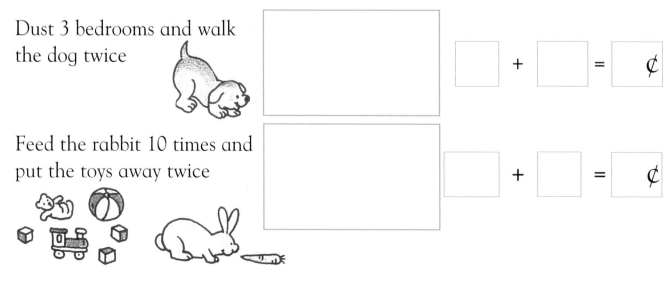

Dust 3 bedrooms and walk
the dog twice

☐ + ☐ = ☐ ¢

Feed the rabbit 10 times and
put the toys away twice

☐ + ☐ = ☐ ¢

# Mixed tables

Write the numbers that the raindrops are hiding.

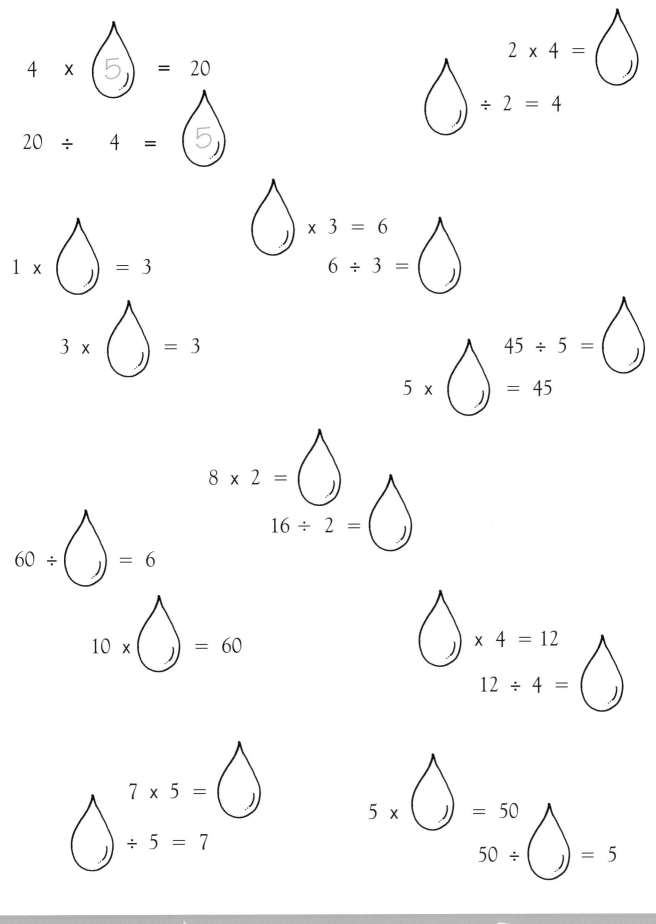

4  x  5  =  20

20  ÷  4  =  5

2 x 4 =

÷ 2 = 4

1 x  = 3

x 3 = 6

6 ÷ 3 =

3 x  = 3

45 ÷ 5 =

5 x  = 45

8 x 2 =

16 ÷ 2 =

60 ÷  = 6

10 x  = 60

x 4 = 12

12 ÷ 4 =

7 x 5 =

÷ 5 = 7

5 x  = 50

50 ÷  = 5

# Mixed tables

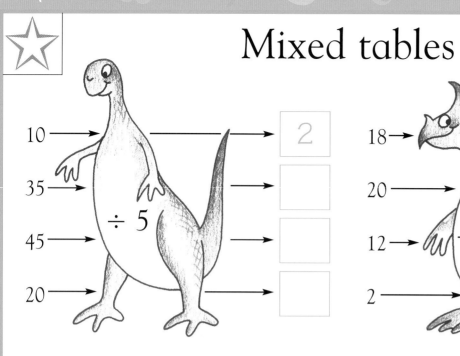

10 →  ÷ 5  → 2

35 →

45 →

20 →

18 →  ÷ 2  → 9

20 →

12 →

2 →

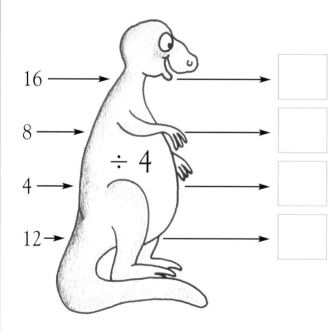

16 →  ÷ 4  →

8 →

4 →

12 →

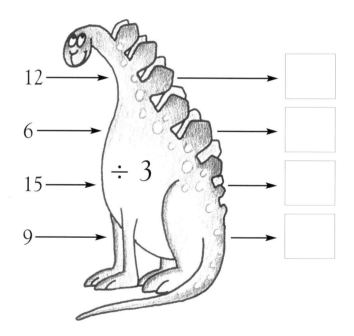

12 →  ÷ 3  →

6 →

15 →

9 →

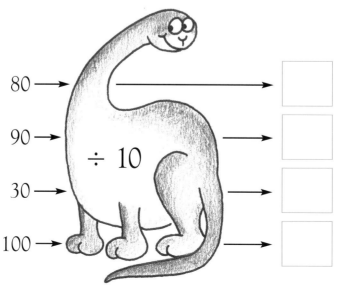

80 →  ÷ 10  →

90 →

30 →

100 →

# Mixed tables

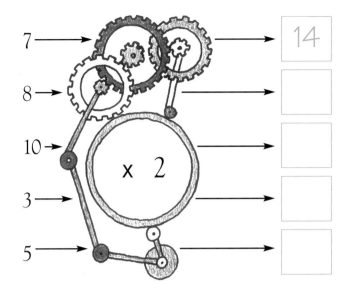

7 →

8 →

10 →  x 2

3 →

5 →

14

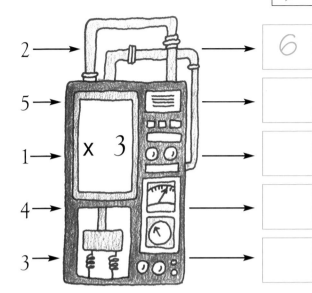

2 →

5 →

1 →  x 3

4 →

3 →

6

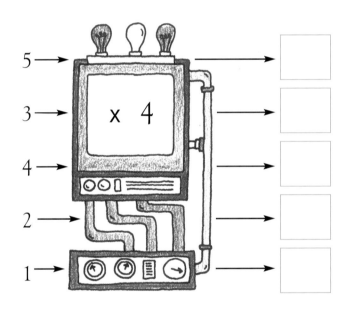

5 →

3 →  x 4

4 →

2 →

1 →

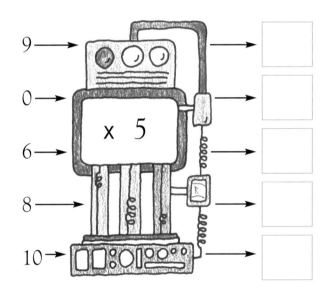

9 →

0 →

6 →  x 5

8 →

10 →

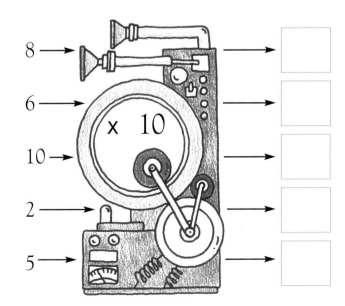

8 →

6 →

10 →  x 10

2 →

5 →

# Mixed tables

Work out how many.

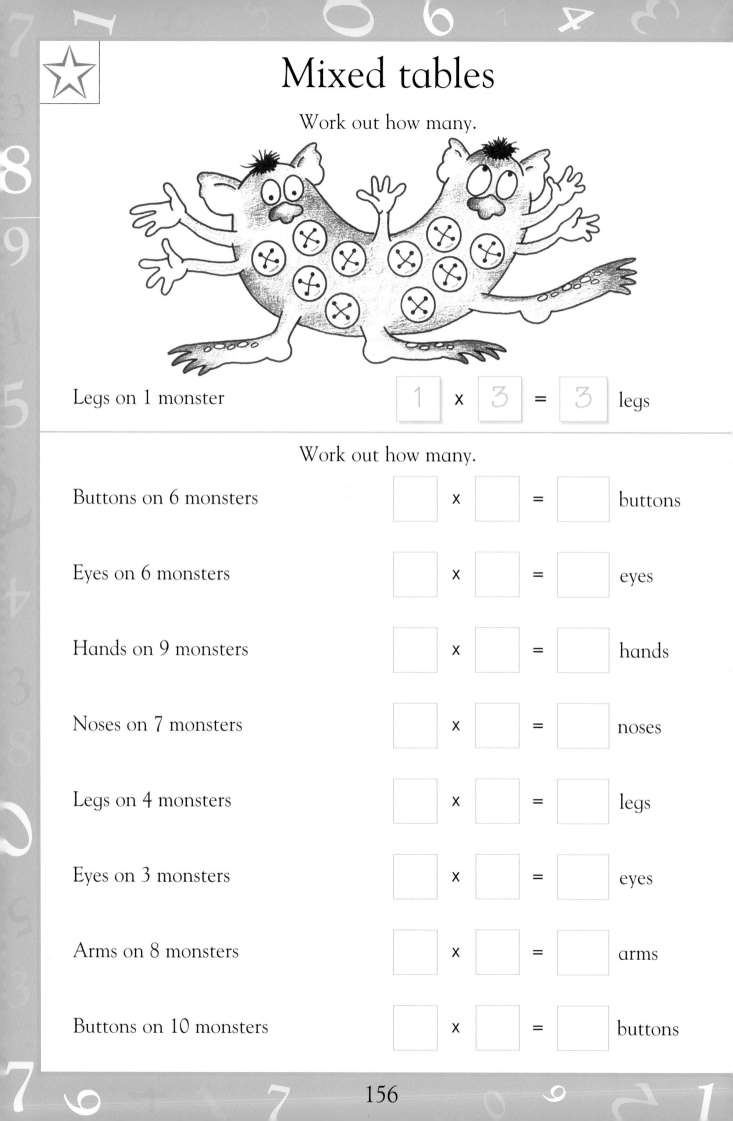

Legs on 1 monster  $\boxed{1}$ x $\boxed{3}$ = $\boxed{3}$ legs

Work out how many.

Buttons on 6 monsters  $\boxed{\phantom{0}}$ x $\boxed{\phantom{0}}$ = $\boxed{\phantom{0}}$ buttons

Eyes on 6 monsters  $\boxed{\phantom{0}}$ x $\boxed{\phantom{0}}$ = $\boxed{\phantom{0}}$ eyes

Hands on 9 monsters  $\boxed{\phantom{0}}$ x $\boxed{\phantom{0}}$ = $\boxed{\phantom{0}}$ hands

Noses on 7 monsters  $\boxed{\phantom{0}}$ x $\boxed{\phantom{0}}$ = $\boxed{\phantom{0}}$ noses

Legs on 4 monsters  $\boxed{\phantom{0}}$ x $\boxed{\phantom{0}}$ = $\boxed{\phantom{0}}$ legs

Eyes on 3 monsters  $\boxed{\phantom{0}}$ x $\boxed{\phantom{0}}$ = $\boxed{\phantom{0}}$ eyes

Arms on 8 monsters  $\boxed{\phantom{0}}$ x $\boxed{\phantom{0}}$ = $\boxed{\phantom{0}}$ arms

Buttons on 10 monsters  $\boxed{\phantom{0}}$ x $\boxed{\phantom{0}}$ = $\boxed{\phantom{0}}$ buttons

# Answer Section with Parents' Notes

## Grade 2
## ages 7–8
## Workbook

This section provides answers to all the activities in the book. These pages will enable you to mark your children's work, or they can be used by your children if they prefer to do their own marking.

The notes for each page help to explain common errors and problems and, where appropriate, indicate the kind of practice needed to ensure that your children understand where and how they have made errors.

---

☆ Counting by 1s, 10s, and 100s

Finish each row.

| | | | | | |
|---|---|---|---|---|---|
| Count by 1s. | 24 | 25 | 26 | 27 | 28 | 29 |
| Count by 10s. | 31 | 41 | 51 | 61 | 71 | 81 |
| Count by 100s. | 134 | 234 | 334 | 434 | 534 | 634 |

Finish each row. Count by 1s.

| | | | | | | | |
|---|---|---|---|---|---|---|---|
| 17 | 18 | 19 | 20 | 21 | 22 | 23 | 24 |
| 36 | 37 | 38 | 39 | 40 | 41 | 42 | 43 |
| 69 | 70 | 71 | 72 | 73 | 74 | 75 | 76 |
| 45 | 46 | 47 | 48 | 49 | 50 | 51 | 52 |
| 85 | 86 | 87 | 88 | 89 | 90 | 91 | 92 |

Finish each row. Count by 10s.

| | | | | | | | |
|---|---|---|---|---|---|---|---|
| 34 | 44 | 54 | 64 | 74 | 84 | 94 | 104 |
| 47 | 57 | 67 | 77 | 87 | 97 | 107 | 117 |
| 78 | 88 | 98 | 108 | 118 | 128 | 138 | 148 |
| 9 | 19 | 29 | 39 | 49 | 59 | 69 | 79 |
| 167 | 177 | 187 | 197 | 207 | 217 | 227 | 237 |
| 305 | 315 | 325 | 335 | 345 | 355 | 365 | 375 |

Finish each row. Count by 100s.

| | | | | | | | |
|---|---|---|---|---|---|---|---|
| 146 | 246 | 346 | 446 | 546 | 646 | 746 | 846 |
| 312 | 412 | 512 | 612 | 712 | 812 | 912 | 1012 |
| 508 | 608 | 708 | 808 | 908 | 1008 | 1108 | 1208 |
| 757 | 857 | 957 | 1057 | 1157 | 1257 | 1357 | 1457 |
| 274 | 374 | 474 | 574 | 674 | 774 | 874 | 974 |

For each row, children should realize that they need only increase the digit in the appropriate place value by 1. Some may have difficulty with a number such as 96 when they have to increase by ten, or a number such as, 957 when they have to increase by 100.

---

## 3

Counting by 2s ☆

| | | | | | | |
|---|---|---|---|---|---|---|
| Count by 2s. | 12 | 14 | 16 | 18 | 20 | 22 |
| Count by 2s. | 31 | 33 | 35 | 37 | 39 | 41 |

Finish each row. Count by 2s.

| | | | | | | | |
|---|---|---|---|---|---|---|---|
| 17 | 19 | 21 | 23 | 25 | 27 | 29 | 31 |
| 36 | 38 | 40 | 42 | 44 | 46 | 48 | 50 |
| 72 | 74 | 76 | 78 | 80 | 82 | 84 | 86 |
| 43 | 45 | 47 | 49 | 51 | 53 | 55 | 57 |
| 14 | 16 | 18 | 20 | 22 | 24 | 26 | 28 |
| 39 | 41 | 43 | 45 | 47 | 49 | 51 | 53 |

Finish each row. Count by 2s.

| | | | | | | | |
|---|---|---|---|---|---|---|---|
| 20 | 22 | 24 | 26 | 28 | 30 | 32 | 34 |
| 75 | 77 | 79 | 81 | 83 | 85 | 87 | 89 |
| 44 | 46 | 48 | 50 | 52 | 54 | 56 | 58 |
| 69 | 71 | 73 | 75 | 77 | 79 | 81 | 83 |
| 31 | 33 | 35 | 37 | 39 | 41 | 43 | 45 |
| 88 | 90 | 92 | 94 | 96 | 98 | 100 | 102 |

Continue each row. Count by 2s.

| | | | | | | | |
|---|---|---|---|---|---|---|---|
| 20 | 22 | 24 | 26 | 28 | 30 | 32 | 34 |
| 47 | 49 | 51 | 53 | 55 | 57 | 59 | 61 |
| 77 | 79 | 81 | 83 | 85 | 87 | 89 | 91 |
| 46 | 48 | 50 | 52 | 54 | 56 | 58 | 60 |
| 87 | 89 | 91 | 93 | 95 | 97 | 99 | 101 |
| 46 | 48 | 50 | 52 | 54 | 56 | 58 | 60 |

As on the previous page, some children will need help crossing a tens or hundreds "border." Show them counting by 2s by counting by 1 two times.

---

☆ Odd and even

| Numbers ending in | 0 | 2 | 4 | 6 | 8 | are called even numbers. |
| Numbers ending in | 1 | 3 | 5 | 7 | 9 | are called odd numbers. |

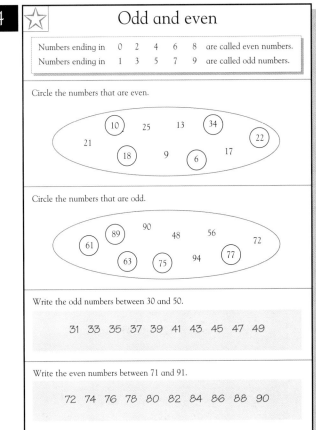

Circle the numbers that are even.

10 25 13 34 21 22 18 9 6 17

Circle the numbers that are odd.

90 89 48 56 61 72 63 75 94 77

Write the odd numbers between 30 and 50.

31 33 35 37 39 41 43 45 47 49

Write the even numbers between 71 and 91.

72 74 76 78 80 82 84 86 88 90

Children should realize that all even numbers are multiples of 2 and that they can all be divided by 2 to give a whole-number quotient. Odd numbers cannot be divided by two. If unsure, a child can use counters and try to share them equally.

# Reading and writing numbers ☆

Write this number in words.  278  *two hundred seventy-eight*

Write this number in digits.  four hundred twelve  *412*

**Write each of these numbers in words.**

624  six hundred twenty-four
175  one hundred seventy-five
392  three hundred ninety-two
926  nine hundred twenty-six
852  eight hundred fifty-two

**Write each of these numbers in digits.**

three hundred eighty-four  384
four hundred sixty-one  461
nine hundred forty-five  945
seven hundred twenty-six  726

**Write each of these numbers in words.**

340  three hundred forty
407  four hundred seven
870  eight hundred seventy

**Write each of these numbers in digits.**

two hundred eight  208
six hundred nine  609
eight hundred seventy  870
five hundred one  501

Children may miss the significance of a 0 in the tens position, and write 407 as four hundred and seventy, and six hundred and nine may be written as 690. Have them read the numbers they have written and then write those numbers as words, or vice versa.

---

## 6

# ☆ Place value

Write the correct number in the box.  426 = 400 + 20 + *6*
Write the number that is the same as ...
4 hundreds 2 tens 6 ones.  *4  2  6*

**Write the correct number in the box.**

634 = 600 + 30 + *4*        285 = 200 + *80* + 5
539 = 500 + *30* + 9        497 = *400* + 90 + 7
825 = 800 + 20 + *5*        738 = 700 + 30 + *8*
698 = *600* + 90 + 8        715 = *700* + 10 + 5
579 = 500 + *70* + 9        953 = 900 + *50* + 3

**Write the correct number in the box.**

307 = 300 + *0* + 7         850 = 800 + 50 + *0*
601 = 600 + *0* + 1         503 = 500 + *0* + 3

**Write the number that is the same as the word:**

two hundreds, seven tens, three ones.  *2  7  3*
four hundreds, six tens, nine ones.  *4  6  9*
eight hundreds, five tens, three ones.  *8  5  3*
seven hundreds, six tens, eight ones.  *7  6  8*
nine hundreds, four tens, six ones.  *9  4  6*

**Look at the cards.**

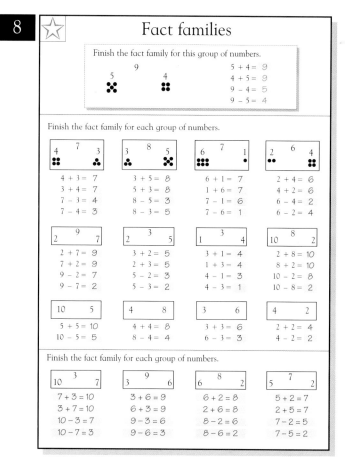

Make the greatest number you can from the digits.  *8  5  2*

Make the smallest number you can from the digits.  *2  5  8*

Children may use zeros incorrectly in numbers. In word form, zeros are omitted, but children should take care to include them when writing numbers in standard form.

---

## 7

# More and less ☆

Which number is 1 more than 49?  *50*
Which number is 10 less than 764?  *754*
Which number is 100 less than 187?  *87*

**Write the number that is 1 more than each of these.**

35 *36*    78 *79*    69 *70*    53 *54*    9 *10*    654 *655*
41 *42*    124 *125*    167 *168*    40 *41*    236 *237*    473 *474*

**Write the number that is 1 less than each of these.**

52 *51*    18 *17*    20 *19*    76 *75*    37 *36*    150 *149*
50 *49*    154 *153*    423 *422*    100 *99*    531 *530*    483 *482*

**Write the number that is 10 more than each of these.**

46 *56*    21 *31*    86 *96*    153 *163*    216 *226*
185 *195*    298 *308*    399 *409*    538 *548*    490 *500*
601 *611*    990 *1000*    590 *600*    323 *333*    480 *490*

**Write the number that is 10 less than each of these.**

56 *46*    75 *65*    86 *76*    185 *175*    230 *220*
680 *670*    451 *441*    503 *493*    407 *397*    805 *795*
600 *590*    902 *892*    605 *595*    702 *692*    908 *898*

**Write the number that is 100 more than each of these.**

365 *465*    76 *176*
960 *1060*    601 *701*

**Write the number that is 100 less than each of these.**

502 *402*    100 *0*
809 *709*    750 *650*

Children may be uncertain when addition or subtraction takes them over a tens or hundreds "border," for example, where the child is asked to write 10 more than 298.

---

# ☆ Fact families

Finish the fact family for this group of numbers.

9    5    4

5 + 4 = 9
4 + 5 = 9
9 – 4 = 5
9 – 5 = 4

**Finish the fact family for each group of numbers.**

| 4  7  3 | 3  8  5 | 6  7  1 | 2  6  4 |
|---|---|---|---|
| 4 + 3 = 7 | 3 + 5 = 8 | 6 + 1 = 7 | 2 + 4 = 6 |
| 3 + 4 = 7 | 5 + 3 = 8 | 1 + 6 = 7 | 4 + 2 = 6 |
| 7 – 3 = 4 | 8 – 5 = 3 | 7 – 1 = 6 | 6 – 4 = 2 |
| 7 – 4 = 3 | 8 – 3 = 5 | 7 – 6 = 1 | 6 – 2 = 4 |

| 9  2  7 | 3  2  5 | 3  1  4 | 8  10  2 |
|---|---|---|---|
| 2 + 7 = 9 | 3 + 2 = 5 | 3 + 1 = 4 | 2 + 8 = 10 |
| 7 + 2 = 9 | 2 + 3 = 5 | 1 + 3 = 4 | 8 + 2 = 10 |
| 9 – 2 = 7 | 5 – 2 = 3 | 4 – 1 = 3 | 10 – 2 = 8 |
| 9 – 7 = 2 | 5 – 3 = 2 | 4 – 3 = 1 | 10 – 8 = 2 |

| 10  5 | 4  8 | 3  6 | 4  2 |
|---|---|---|---|
| 5 + 5 = 10 | 4 + 4 = 8 | 3 + 3 = 6 | 2 + 2 = 4 |
| 10 – 5 = 5 | 8 – 4 = 4 | 6 – 3 = 3 | 4 – 2 = 2 |

**Finish the fact family for each group of numbers.**

| 10  3  7 | 9  3  6 | 8  6  2 | 7  5  2 |
|---|---|---|---|
| 7 + 3 = 10 | 3 + 6 = 9 | 6 + 2 = 8 | 5 + 2 = 7 |
| 3 + 7 = 10 | 6 + 3 = 9 | 2 + 6 = 8 | 2 + 5 = 7 |
| 10 – 3 = 7 | 9 – 3 = 6 | 8 – 2 = 6 | 7 – 2 = 5 |
| 10 – 7 = 3 | 9 – 6 = 3 | 8 – 6 = 2 | 7 – 5 = 2 |

Children should understand that subtraction "undoes" addition. You may want to use counters to demonstrate addition fact families.

# Fractions

Color one-third ($\frac{1}{3}$) of each shape.

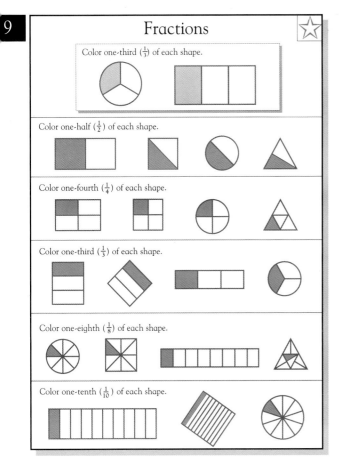

Color one-half ($\frac{1}{2}$) of each shape.

Color one-fourth ($\frac{1}{4}$) of each shape.

Color one-third ($\frac{1}{3}$) of each shape.

Color one-eighth ($\frac{1}{8}$) of each shape.

Color one-tenth ($\frac{1}{10}$) of each shape.

It does not matter if children color alternative sections than those shown above, as long as only one section in each shape is colored. Children should realize that the bottom number represents how many parts the whole has been divided into.

---

## 10

# Money

Change the amount into dollars and cents.   235¢   $2.35

Change each amount into dollars and cents.

| | | | | | |
|---|---|---|---|---|---|
| 153¢ | $1.53 | 428¢ | $4.28 | 392¢ | $3.92 |
| 372¢ | $3.72 | 563¢ | $5.63 | 290¢ | $2.90 |
| 827¢ | $8.27 | 526¢ | $5.26 | 483¢ | $4.83 |
| 460¢ | $4.60 | 729¢ | $7.29 | 926¢ | $9.26 |

Change each amount into cents.

| | | | | | |
|---|---|---|---|---|---|
| $3.27 | 327¢ | $7.28 | 728¢ | $5.17 | 517¢ |
| $6.72 | 672¢ | $4.15 | 415¢ | $8.35 | 835¢ |
| $9.38 | 938¢ | $6.20 | 620¢ | $4.63 | 463¢ |
| $7.20 | 720¢ | $6.50 | 650¢ | $4.31 | 431¢ |

Change each amount into dollars and cents.

| | | | | | |
|---|---|---|---|---|---|
| 150¢ | $1.50 | 208¢ | $2.08 | 480¢ | $4.80 |
| 410¢ | $4.10 | 706¢ | $7.06 | 302¢ | $3.02 |
| 205¢ | $2.05 | 620¢ | $6.20 | 950¢ | $9.50 |
| 609¢ | $6.09 | 204¢ | $2.04 | 606¢ | $6.06 |

Change each amount into cents.

| | | | | | |
|---|---|---|---|---|---|
| $3.50 | 350¢ | $2.07 | 207¢ | $7.50 | 750¢ |
| $6.01 | 601¢ | $3.06 | 306¢ | $10.00 | 1000¢ |
| $4.90 | 490¢ | $5.00 | 500¢ | $4.06 | 406¢ |
| $1.01 | 101¢ | $0.40 | 40¢ | $5.05 | 505¢ |

Make sure that children understand that when they change cents into dollars and cents, they should include the dollar sign but not the cent sign: for example, $3.46.

---

## 11

# Adding

Write the answer in the box.   25 + 30 =   55

Write the answer in the box.

| | | |
|---|---|---|
| 39 + 40 = 79 | 28 + 60 = 88 | 53 + 70 = 123 |
| 27 + 30 = 57 | 73 + 30 = 103 | 46 + 50 = 96 |
| 42 + 60 = 102 | 74 + 50 = 124 | 84 + 40 = 124 |
| 30 + 45 = 75 | 60 + 38 = 98 | 90 + 17 = 107 |

Write the answer in the box.

| | |
|---|---|
| 20 + 30 + 12 = 62 | 50 + 20 + 18 = 88 |
| 45 + 10 + 20 = 75 | 60 + 20 + 7 = 87 |
| 30 + 40 + 18 = 88 | 30 + 50 + 12 = 92 |
| 60 + 20 + 30 = 110 | 46 + 30 + 20 = 96 |
| 52 + 40 + 20 = 112 | 30 + 45 + 20 = 95 |
| 17 + 30 + 3 = 50 | 28 + 50 + 2 = 80 |

Write the answer in the box.

| | | |
|---|---|---|
| 63¢ + 20¢ = 83¢ | 48¢ + 30¢ = 78¢ | 65¢ + 20¢ = 85¢ |
| 50¢ + 37¢ = 87¢ | 39¢ + 60¢ = 99¢ | 40¢ + 56¢ = 96¢ |
| 12¢ + 15¢ = 27¢ | 18¢ + 32¢ = 50¢ | 34¢ + 16¢ = 50¢ |
| 44¢ + 14¢ = 58¢ | 63¢ + 24¢ = 87¢ | 38¢ + 22¢ = 60¢ |

Write the answer in the box.

| | |
|---|---|
| 12 ft + 20 ft + 60 ft = 92 ft | 17 ft + 40 ft + 40 ft = 97 ft |
| 10 ft + 15 ft + 20 ft = 45 ft | 30 ft + 15 ft + 40 ft = 85 ft |

Children should be able to add quickly if they know that adding a 10s number requires adding only to the tens digit. Make sure that children include units (such as cents and feet) for problems in which units are given.

---

# Adding

Write the answers between the lines.

$$35 + 16 = 51 \qquad 17 + 9 = 26 \qquad 24 + 8 = 32$$

Write the answers between the lines.

| 24 + 9 = 33 | 43 + 6 = 49 | 21 + 7 = 28 | 46 + 5 = 51 |
|---|---|---|---|
| 43 + 7 = 50 | 72 + 5 = 77 | 64 + 7 = 71 | 38 + 8 = 46 |
| 46 + 10 = 56 | 37 + 11 = 48 | 53 + 12 = 65 | 49 + 9 = 58 |

Write the answers between the lines.

| 9 + 7 + 9 = 25 | 8 + 9 + 7 = 24 | 7 + 9 + 6 = 22 | 8 + 8 + 9 = 25 |
|---|---|---|---|
| 12¢ + 6¢ + 10¢ = 28¢ | 18¢ + 7¢ + 10¢ = 35¢ | 8¢ + 11¢ + 6¢ = 25¢ | 13¢ + 9¢ + 6¢ = 28¢ |
| 20¢ + 7¢ + 10¢ = 37¢ | 15¢ + 10¢ + 2¢ = 27¢ | 8¢ + 10¢ + 4¢ = 22¢ | 10¢ + 8¢ + 10¢ = 28¢ |

Many of the problems require children to regroup. For the final two rows of the second section, children should make sure to add up the ones column first.

## Subtracting

Write the answers in the boxes.
16 – 9 = 7        23 – 12 = 11

Write the answers in the boxes.

| | | | |
|---|---|---|---|
| 15 – 8 = 7 | 13 – 8 = 5 | 26 – 5 = 21 | 18 – 4 = 14 |
| 22 – 11 = 11 | 28 – 13 = 15 | 14 – 12 = 2 | 15 – 6 = 9 |
| 24 – 10 = 14 | 30 – 20 = 10 | 18 – 12 = 6 | 8 – 0 = 8 |
| 14 – 6 = 8 | 17 – 9 = 8 | 25 – 13 = 12 | 12 – 9 = 3 |
| 29 – 13 = 16 | 28 – 14 = 14 | 19 – 11 = 8 | 36 – 14 = 22 |

Write the answers in the boxes.

| | | | |
|---|---|---|---|
| 45¢ – 20¢ = 25¢ | 35¢ – 12¢ = 23¢ | 25¢ – 10¢ = 15¢ | 40¢ – 25¢ = 15¢ |
| 38¢ – 16¢ = 22¢ | 25¢ – 15¢ = 10¢ | 39¢ – 18¢ = 21¢ | 50¢ – 35¢ = 15¢ |
| 34¢ – 14¢ = 20¢ | 28¢ – 16¢ = 12¢ | 42¢ – 12¢ = 30¢ | 24¢ – 12¢ = 12¢ |
| 45¢ – 25¢ = 20¢ | 50¢ – 15¢ = 35¢ | 27¢ – 16¢ = 11¢ | 45¢ – 35¢ = 10¢ |
| 55¢ – 22¢ = 33¢ | 33¢ – 21¢ = 12¢ | 49¢ – 8¢ = 41¢ | 35¢ – 14¢ = 21¢ |

Write the answers in the boxes.

| | |
|---|---|
| How much less than 24¢ is 17¢? **7¢** | How much less than 40 in. is 16 in.? **24 in.** |
| Take 14¢ away from 30¢. **16¢** | Mandy has 50¢. She spends 26¢ on ice cream. How much does she have left? **24¢** |
| How much is 50¢ minus 14¢? **36¢** | |
| Take away 18¢ from 34¢. **16¢** | What is the difference between 90 in. and 35 in.? **55 in.** |
| What is the difference between 60¢ and 25¢? **35¢** | |

If children need to, they may rewrite each subtraction in vertical form.

---

## Subtracting

Write the answers between the lines.

| 28 | 31 | 40 |
|---|---|---|
| – 16 | – 14 | – 17 |
| 12 | 17 | 23 |

Write the answers between the lines.

| 27 | 41 | 60 | 53 |
|---|---|---|---|
| – 14 | – 25 | – 37 | – 38 |
| 13 | 16 | 23 | 15 |

| 32 | 45 | 33 | 50 |
|---|---|---|---|
| – 14 | – 26 | – 20 | – 27 |
| 18 | 19 | 13 | 23 |

| 47 | 25 | 63 | 36 |
|---|---|---|---|
| – 28 | – 6 | – 44 | – 28 |
| 19 | 19 | 19 | 8 |

| 28¢ | 43¢ | 50¢ | 48¢ |
|---|---|---|---|
| – 16¢ | – 35¢ | – 26¢ | – 37¢ |
| 12¢ | 8¢ | 24¢ | 11¢ |

| 53¢ | 37¢ | 70¢ | 45¢ |
|---|---|---|---|
| – 35¢ | – 28¢ | – 47¢ | – 38¢ |
| 18¢ | 9¢ | 23¢ | 7¢ |

| 40¢ | 60¢ | 41¢ | 54¢ |
|---|---|---|---|
| – 8¢ | – 26¢ | – 14¢ | – 36¢ |
| 32¢ | 34¢ | 27¢ | 18¢ |

In some of these exercises, children may incorrectly subtract the smaller digit from the larger one, when they should be subtracting the larger digit from the smaller one. In such cases, point out that they should regroup.

---

## 15

## Estimating length

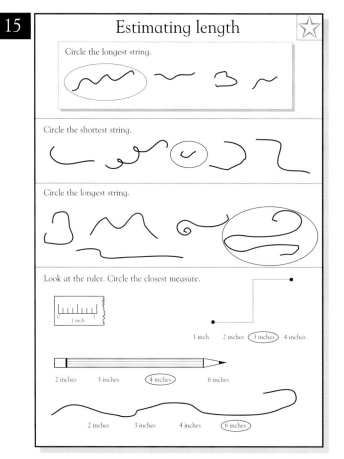

Circle the longest string.

Circle the shortest string.

Circle the longest string.

Look at the ruler. Circle the closest measure.

1 inch   2 inches   (3 inches)   4 inches

2 inches   3 inches   (4 inches)   6 inches

2 inches   3 inches   4 inches   (6 inches)

Children should be able to compare the lengths by sight. For the last section of the page, allow them to use a benchmark (such as, the length of one joint of a finger) to estimate length.

---

## Addition properties

Circle the number that makes the sentence true.

___ + 7 = 7          43 + 21 = 21 + ___

1   (0)   14          22   64   (43)

Circle the number that makes the sentence true.

___ + 3 = 3          15 + ___ = 15

(0)   3   6          30   (0)   5

___ + 23 = 23 + 16          25 + 41 = 41 + ___

(16)   23   46          16   66   (25)

___ + 45 = 45          70 + 0 = 0 + ___

45   (0)   1          (70)   0   700

Complete the number sentences.

| | | |
|---|---|---|
| 0 + 27 = 27 | 90 + 0 = 90 | 13 + 28 = 28 + 13 |
| 52 + 3 = 3 + 52 | 67 + 0 = 67 | 56 + 43 = 43 + 56 |
| 2 + 83 = 83 + 2 | 0 + 12 = 12 | 28 + 64 = 64 + 28 |
| 55 + 0 = 55 | 10 + 0 = 10 | 200 + 800 = 800 + 200 |
| 647 + 0 = 647 | 8 + 0 = 8 | 345 + 871 = 871 + 345 |

This page tests children's understanding of the zero property and the commutative property of addition. Make sure that children understand that the order of addends does not affect the answer.

## Add or subtract?

Write + or – in the box.
12 + 7 = 19     20 – 8 = 12     15 + 7 = 22

Write + or – in the box.

| | | | |
|---|---|---|---|
| 6 + 7 = 13 | 9 + 3 = 12 | 8 + 6 = 14 | 5 + 9 = 14 |
| 13 – 6 = 7 | 10 – 6 = 4 | 3 + 8 = 11 | 15 – 7 = 8 |
| 8 – 6 = 2 | 12 + 6 = 18 | 9 + 6 = 15 | 12 – 3 = 9 |
| 17 – 10 = 7 | 14 – 5 = 9 | 15 – 8 = 7 | 18 – 10 = 8 |

Write the answer in the box.

I add 4 to a number and the answer is 7. What number did I start with? — 3

7 added to a number gives a total of 12. What is the number? — 5

I take 5 from a number and have 6 left. What number did I start with? — 11

9 added to a number makes 16. What is the number? — 7

I subtract 7 from a number and the answer is 12. What number did I start with? — 19

Two numbers add up to 17. One of the numbers is 8. What is the other number? — 9

Write + or – in the box.

| | | | |
|---|---|---|---|
| 15 + 10 = 25 | 20 – 5 = 15 | 28 – 15 = 13 | 40 – 22 = 18 |
| 35 – 15 = 20 | 34 + 14 = 48 | 18 + 12 = 30 | 45 – 17 = 28 |
| 37 + 6 = 43 | 65 – 4 = 61 | 50 – 26 = 24 | 84 – 34 = 50 |
| 43 + 17 = 60 | 62 – 17 = 45 | 31 – 14 = 17 | 17 – 6 = 11 |

Children must choose between addition and subtraction to solve each problem. If they make an error, have them substitute their answer in the problem to show them that the answer is not correct.

## Subtracting

Write the answer between the lines.

| 976 | 574 | $3.84 |
|---|---|---|
| – 553 | – 262 | – $2.51 |
| 423 | 312 | $1.33 |

Write the answer between the lines.

| 487 | 648 | 768 | 556 | 845 |
|---|---|---|---|---|
| – 345 | – 136 | – 427 | – 333 | – 714 |
| 142 | 512 | 341 | 223 | 131 |

| 956 | 298 | 379 | 456 | 885 |
|---|---|---|---|---|
| – 331 | – 157 | – 226 | – 314 | – 363 |
| 625 | 141 | 153 | 142 | 522 |

| 277 | 497 | 575 | 692 | 957 |
|---|---|---|---|---|
| – 113 | – 255 | – 321 | – 531 | – 425 |
| 164 | 242 | 254 | 161 | 532 |

| 853 | 589 | 673 | 367 | 725 |
|---|---|---|---|---|
| – 642 | – 435 | – 542 | – 232 | – 313 |
| 211 | 154 | 131 | 135 | 412 |

Write the answer between the lines.

| $9.64 | $8.97 | $4.57 | $6.71 | $5.99 |
|---|---|---|---|---|
| – $4.32 | – $5.71 | – $1.25 | – $5.50 | – $3.76 |
| $5.32 | $3.26 | $3.32 | $1.21 | $2.23 |

Regrouping is not needed to subtract the numbers on this page. Discuss any mistakes with children to determine whether they are due to lapses of concentration or a basic misunderstanding of the concept.

## 19

## Working with coins

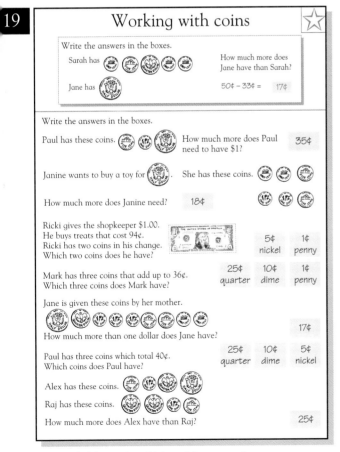

Write the answers in the boxes.

Sarah has [coins]     How much more does Jane have than Sarah?

Jane has [coin]     50¢ – 33¢ = 17¢

Write the answers in the boxes.

Paul has these coins. [coins]     How much more does Paul need to have $1? — 35¢

Janine wants to buy a toy for [coin].     She has these coins. [coins]

How much more does Janine need? — 18¢     [coins]

Ricki gives the shopkeeper $1.00. He buys treats that cost 94¢. Ricki has two coins in his change. Which two coins does he have? — 5¢ nickel, 1¢ penny

Mark has three coins that add up to 36¢. Which three coins does Mark have? — 25¢ quarter, 10¢ dime, 1¢ penny

Jane is given these coins by her mother. [coins]

How much more than one dollar does Jane have? — 17¢

Paul has three coins which total 40¢. Which coins does Paul have? — 25¢ quarter, 10¢ dime, 5¢ nickel

Alex has these coins. [coins]

Raj has these coins. [coins]

How much more does Alex have than Raj? — 25¢

Most children should be able to work out correct answers by counting by 5s and 10s.

## Money problems

Look at these coins. [coins]     How much is 15¢ and 19¢? — 34¢
How much more is needed to make 75¢? — 35¢

Write the answers in the boxes.

What is the total of 20¢ and 70¢? — 90¢

What is 35¢ less 20¢? — 15¢

Jasmine collects nickels and has 45¢ worth. How many nickels does Jasmine have? — 9 nickels

Don has these coins. [coins] Which coin does he need to make $1.00? — 10¢ dime

Jim starts out with 80¢ but loses 35¢. How much does he have left? — 45¢

Mary has four coins that add up to 17¢. Which coins does Mary have? — 10¢ dime, 5¢ nickel, 1¢ penny, 1¢ penny

Which four of the these [coins] coins add up to $0.86? — 50¢ half dollar, 25¢ quarter, 10¢ dime, 1¢ penny

60¢ is shared equally by 4 children. How much do they each get? — 15¢

How much is four groups of coins with 1 dime and 1 nickel in each group? — 60¢ [coins]

These coins are shared equally by two children. How much does each child get? — 55¢ [coins]

Write the answers in the boxes.

| | | |
|---|---|---|
| 5¢ + 40¢ = 45¢ | 10¢ + 46¢ = 56¢ | 21¢ + 8¢ = 29¢ |
| 20¢ – 10¢ = 10¢ | 49¢ – 5¢ = 44¢ | 18¢ – 12¢ = 6¢ |
| 35¢ + 45¢ = 80¢ | 62¢ + 17¢ = 79¢ | 80¢ + 18¢ = 98¢ |

If children have difficulty with these exercises, you may want to use actual coins to work with.

## Measurement problems

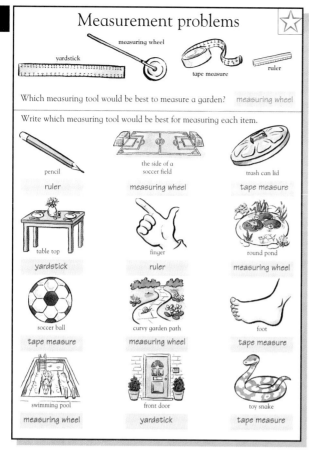

Which measuring tool would be best to measure a garden?  measuring wheel

Write which measuring tool would be best for measuring each item.

| pencil | the side of a soccer field | trash can lid |
|---|---|---|
| ruler | measuring wheel | tape measure |

| table top | finger | round pond |
|---|---|---|
| yardstick | ruler | measuring wheel |

| soccer ball | curvy garden path | foot |
|---|---|---|
| tape measure | measuring wheel | tape measure |

| swimming pool | front door | toy snake |
|---|---|---|
| measuring wheel | yardstick | tape measure |

Although it is possible to measure most of these items with any of the instruments the question is "which is best?". Help children understand why a tape measure is more useful than a ruler for measuring curved lengths.

## 22

## Telling time

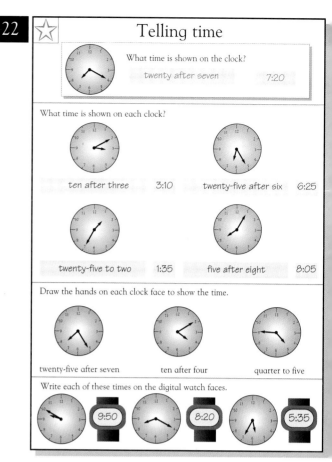

What time is shown on the clock?  twenty after seven  7:20

What time is shown on each clock?

ten after three  3:10    twenty-five after six  6:25

twenty-five to two  1:35    five after eight  8:05

Draw the hands on each clock face to show the time.

twenty-five after seven    ten after four    quarter to five

Write each of these times on the digital watch faces.

9:50    8:20    5:35

Children may need help with some of these exercises. Show them that they can count by 5s (in minutes) for each division on the clock face.

## 23

## Simple tally charts and bar graphs

Look at the tally chart and then answer the question.

| blue | ЦЦ ЦЦ ЦЦ ׀׀׀ |
|---|---|
| red | ЦЦ ׀ |

How many votes did blue receive?  18

Look at the tally chart and then answer the questions.

Favorite ice cream flavors

| vanilla | ЦЦ ЦЦ ׀ |
|---|---|
| chocolate | ЦЦ ЦЦ ЦЦ ЦЦ ЦЦ |
| strawberry | ЦЦ ЦЦ ЦЦ ׀׀׀ |

Which flavor had the most votes?  chocolate

Which flavor had 11 votes?  vanilla

What was the difference in votes between the most popular flavor and strawberry?  6

Look at the bar graph and then answer the questions.

Favorite sports

Which sport did four children vote for?  football

How many votes did volleyball receive?  5

Which was the least popular sport?  running

How many children voted altogether?  13

How many more voted for football than for hockey?  1

Children usually accept the concept of tally marks quickly. They can count by 5s for completed tallies.

## Naming 2-dimensional shapes

Write the name of each shape inside it.    circle    square

Write the name of each shape inside it. Use the words in the Word Box.

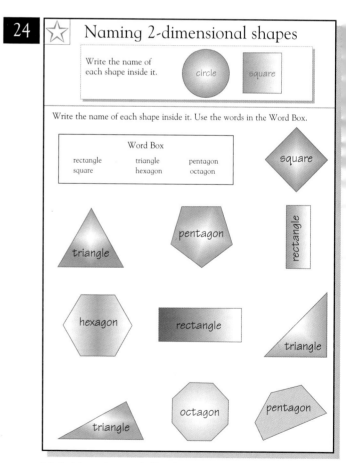

Word Box

| rectangle | triangle | pentagon |
|---|---|---|
| square | hexagon | octagon |

square

pentagon

rectangle

triangle

hexagon    rectangle    triangle

triangle    octagon    pentagon

If children have difficulty identifying any of the shapes, have them count the number of sides of the shape first.

## Sorting 2-dimensional shapes

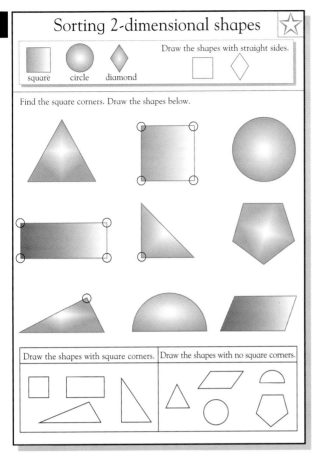

square  circle  diamond

Draw the shapes with straight sides.

Find the square corners. Draw the shapes below.

Draw the shapes with square corners. | Draw the shapes with no square corners.

Children should find the right angles for most of the shapes without much difficulty. The orientation of some of the shapes may confuse children, for example, the pentagon. Explain that the shape remains the same regardless of orientation.

## 26

## Picture graphs

Look at this picture graph. Then answer the questions.

**Mina's marbles**

| | |
|---|---|
| Clear | |
| Blue | |
| Green | |
| Red | |
| Yellow | |

How many blue marbles does Mina have? 3

Does Mina have more green marbles or yellow marbles? green

How many marbles does Mina have in all? 16

Look at this picture graph. Then answer the questions.

**Books on Pablo's shelf**

| | |
|---|---|
| Cats | |
| Sports | |
| Mysteries | |
| Cartoons | |
| Science | |

How many science books does Pablo have? 3

Does he have more books about cats than mysteries? no

How many more cartoon books does he have than mysteries? 2

How many books about cats and science does he have? 6

Look at this picture graph. Then answer the questions.

**Pets on Redmond Road**

| | |
|---|---|
| Cats | |
| Dogs | |
| Fish | |
| Birds | |

On Redmond Road, are there more cats or dogs? dogs

How many more fish are there than dogs? 2 more

How many cats and dogs are there? 9

How many pets are there in all? 19

Children need to count the items for each category, and then add, subtract, and compare data.

## 27

## Equations

Circle the correct number sentence.

7 + 3 = 10   (4 + 3 = 7)   4 – 3 = 1   2 + 4 = 6   2 + 3 = 5   (5 – 3 = 2)

Circle the correct addition sentence.

5 + 2 = 7   (3 + 2 = 5)   3 – 2 = 1   4 + 2 = 6   5 – 1 = 4   (5 + 1 = 6)

Circle the correct subtraction sentence.

3 + 3 = 6   3 – 3 = 0   (6 – 3 = 3)   (6 – 2 = 4)   6 + 2 = 8   4 – 2 = 2

Circle the correct number sentence.

(9 – 3 = 6)   5 – 3 = 2   6 – 3 = 3   5 – 2 = 3   (2 + 5 = 7)   7 – 5 = 2

6 – 4 = 2   (4 + 2 = 6)   6 + 2 = 8   5 – 1 = 4   4 + 5 = 9   (9 – 4 = 5)

For the final section, make sure that children understand that animals approaching each other represent addition and animals moving away from each other represent subtraction.

## 3-dimensional shapes

Write the name of each shape.

sphere   cube

Write the name of each shape. Use the words in the word box.

**Word Box**
sphere   prism   cone   cube   cylinder   pyramid

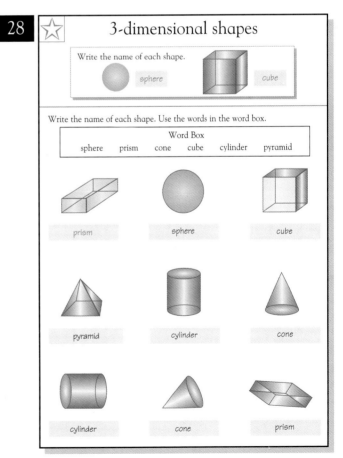

prism   sphere   cube

pyramid   cylinder   cone

cylinder   cone   prism

If children have difficulty, help them identify each shape and learn its name.

## Sorting 3-dimensional shapes

Look at the shape. Then answer the questions.

How many curved surfaces ? 1

How many flat surfaces ? 0

Look at each shape. Then answer the questions below.

sphere    cylinder    cone

cube    prism    pyramid

| Shape | How many curved surfaces? | How many flat surfaces? |
|---|---|---|
| sphere | 1 | 0 |
| cylinder | 1 | 2 |
| cone | 1 | 1 |
| cube | 0 | 6 |
| prism | 0 | 6 |
| pyramid | 0 | 5 |

Children may find it easier to use a physical model of the shapes, but point out that each of the diagrams does show the hidden surfaces.

## 30

## Location on a grid

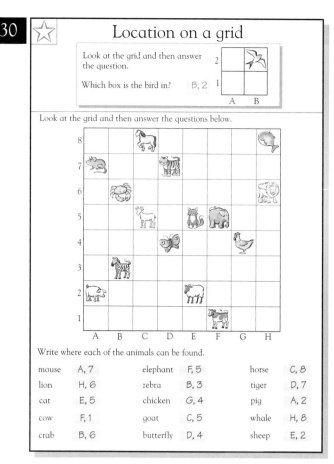

Look at the grid and then answer the question.

Which box is the bird in? B, 2

Look at the grid and then answer the questions below.

Write where each of the animals can be found.

| | | | | | |
|---|---|---|---|---|---|
| mouse | A, 7 | elephant | F, 5 | horse | C, 8 |
| lion | H, 6 | zebra | B, 3 | tiger | D, 7 |
| cat | E, 5 | chicken | G, 4 | pig | A, 2 |
| cow | F, 1 | goat | C, 5 | whale | H, 8 |
| crab | B, 6 | butterfly | D, 4 | sheep | E, 2 |

To label the squares on the grid, children should understand that the letter should precede the number. This will prepare them to learn about coordinates on graphs where the value from the x-axis is written before the value from the y-axis.

## 31

## Placing on a grid

Draw each picture in the correct box.

✳ in B, 2

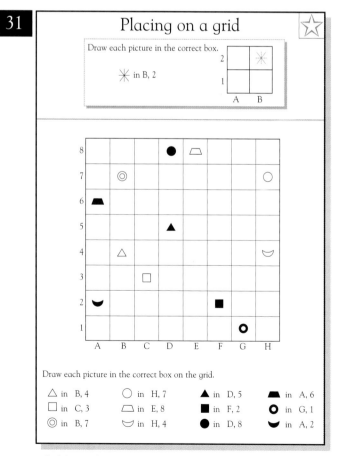

Draw each picture in the correct box on the grid.

△ in B, 4          ◯ in H, 7          ▲ in D, 5          ◣ in A, 6
▢ in C, 3          ▱ in E, 8          ■ in F, 2          ◉ in G, 1
◎ in B, 7          ⌣ in H, 4          ● in D, 8          ◠ in A, 2

Children should be careful to draw the pictures within the boxes, not on the lines.

## Counting by 3s, 4s, and 5s

Find the pattern. Continue each row.

| Count by 3s. | 9 | 12 | 15 | 18 | 21 | 24 | 27 |
|---|---|---|---|---|---|---|---|
| Count by 4s. | 8 | 12 | 16 | 20 | 24 | 28 | 32 |
| Count by 5s. | 55 | 50 | 45 | 40 | 35 | 30 | 25 |

Find the pattern. Continue each row.

| | | | | | | | |
|---|---|---|---|---|---|---|---|
| 0 | 3 | 6 | 9 | 12 | 15 | 18 | 21 |
| 8 | 12 | 16 | 20 | 24 | 28 | 32 | 36 |
| 38 | 41 | 44 | 47 | 50 | 53 | 56 | 59 |
| 40 | 45 | 50 | 55 | 60 | 65 | 70 | 75 |
| 63 | 67 | 71 | 75 | 79 | 83 | 87 | 91 |
| 85 | 90 | 95 | 100 | 105 | 110 | 115 | 120 |
| 6 | 10 | 14 | 18 | 22 | 26 | 30 | 34 |
| 21 | 18 | 15 | 12 | 9 | 6 | 3 | 0 |
| 68 | 65 | 62 | 59 | 56 | 53 | 50 | 47 |
| 85 | 80 | 75 | 70 | 65 | 60 | 55 | 50 |
| 43 | 40 | 37 | 34 | 31 | 28 | 25 | 22 |
| 49 | 45 | 41 | 37 | 33 | 29 | 25 | 21 |
| 71 | 67 | 63 | 59 | 55 | 51 | 47 | 43 |
| 83 | 78 | 73 | 68 | 63 | 58 | 53 | 48 |
| 39 | 34 | 29 | 24 | 19 | 14 | 9 | 4 |

Some of the patterns show an increase, while others show a decrease. Children should be able to complete these questions using mental math.

## Adding

Write the answer between the lines.

| 300 | 520 | 205 |
|---|---|---|
| + 100 | + 136 | + 324 |
| 400 | 656 | 529 |

Write the answer between the lines.

| 500 | 200 | 300 | 100 | 600 |
|---|---|---|---|---|
| + 300 | + 400 | + 400 | + 700 | + 300 |
| 800 | 600 | 700 | 800 | 900 |

| 240 | 110 | 540 | 320 | 860 |
|---|---|---|---|---|
| + 430 | + 830 | + 220 | + 510 | + 130 |
| 670 | 940 | 760 | 830 | 990 |

| 204 | 402 | 554 | 701 | 324 |
|---|---|---|---|---|
| + 163 | + 283 | + 304 | + 108 | + 601 |
| 367 | 685 | 858 | 809 | 925 |

| 284 | 621 | 507 | 417 | 105 |
|---|---|---|---|---|
| + 100 | + 261 | + 170 | + 280 | + 802 |
| 384 | 882 | 677 | 697 | 907 |

Write the answer between the lines.

| $5.72 | $9.07 | $5.50 | $3.09 | $5.80 |
|---|---|---|---|---|
| +$0.22 | +$1.21 | +$3.45 | +$4.80 | +$1.07 |
| $5.94 | $10.28 | $8.95 | $7.89 | $6.87 |

None of these addition problems require regrouping. Make sure that children understand that adding zero to a digit does not change the value of the digit.

## 34

## Comparing and ordering

Write these numbers in order, starting with the smallest.

431  678  273  586    273  431  586  678

Write these numbers in order, starting with the smallest.

| 267 | 931 | 374 | 740 | 267 | 374 | 740 | 931 |
|---|---|---|---|---|---|---|---|
| 734 | 218 | 625 | 389 | 218 | 389 | 625 | 734 |
| 836 | 590 | 374 | 669 | 374 | 590 | 669 | 836 |
| 572 | 197 | 469 | 533 | 197 | 469 | 533 | 572 |
| 948 | 385 | 846 | 289 | 289 | 385 | 846 | 948 |
| 406 | 560 | 460 | 650 | 406 | 460 | 560 | 650 |
| 738 | 837 | 378 | 783 | 378 | 738 | 783 | 837 |
| 582 | 285 | 528 | 852 | 285 | 528 | 582 | 852 |
| 206 | 620 | 602 | 260 | 206 | 260 | 602 | 620 |
| 634 | 436 | 364 | 463 | 364 | 436 | 463 | 634 |
| 47 | 740 | 74 | 704 | 47 | 74 | 704 | 740 |
| 501 | 150 | 51 | 105 | 51 | 105 | 150 | 501 |
| 290 | 92 | 209 | 29 | 29 | 92 | 209 | 290 |
| 803 | 380 | 83 | 38 | 38 | 83 | 380 | 803 |
| 504 | 450 | 54 | 45 | 45 | 54 | 450 | 504 |

Make sure that children do not simply order the numbers according to the first digits.

## 35

## Comparing and ordering

Circle the numbers that are greater than 207.
72    158    (210)    (230)    208

Circle the numbers that are greater than 705.
698    (834)    590    (711)    (812)

Circle the numbers that are less than 512.
(268)    (507)    600    (378)    564

Circle the numbers that are between 494 and 508.
492    512    406    (504)    (499)

Circle the amounts that are greater than $1.00.
76¢    $0.35    ($1.28)    (104¢)    ($1.79)

Circle the amounts that are less than $2.50.
309¢    ($1.76)    ($2.38)    (245¢)    $3.05

Circle the amounts that are between $1.80 and $2.00.
167¢    (190¢)    $2.94    (183¢)    $1.79

Children should make sure to circle all the numbers or amounts that satisfy each question. For the final question, children may want to rename $1.80 and $2.00 as cents.

## Missing addends

Write the missing addend.

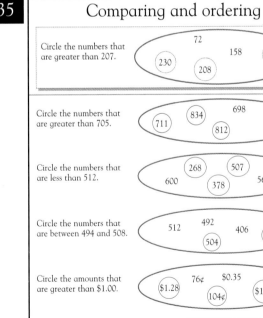

6 + 7 = 13

Write the missing addend.

3 + 6 = 9          5 + 7 = 12

9 + 2 = 11          8 + 8 = 16

Write the missing addend.

| 3 + 4 = 7 | 5 + 9 = 14 | 9 + 3 = 12 | 8 + 2 = 10 |
|---|---|---|---|
| 7 + 5 = 12 | 7 + 8 = 15 | 7 + 5 = 12 | 9 + 8 = 17 |
| 7 + 6 = 13 | 8 + 6 = 14 | 10 + 3 = 13 | 4 + 9 = 13 |
| 4 + 3 = 7 | 3 + 6 = 9 | 2 + 9 = 11 | 8 + 5 = 13 |
| 6 + 2 = 8 | 5 + 4 = 9 | 7 + 1 = 8 | 8 + 4 = 12 |
| 8 + 1 = 9 | 6 + 7 = 13 | 8 + 8 = 16 | 5 + 6 = 11 |
| 4 + 7 = 11 | 10 + 5 = 15 | 8 + 3 = 11 | 4 + 6 = 10 |
| 7 + 7 = 14 | 8 + 7 = 15 | 9 + 5 = 14 | 6 + 9 = 15 |
| 9 + 7 = 16 | 9 + 9 = 18 | 3 + 7 = 10 | 5 + 4 = 9 |

Children can use any method they wish to answer these problems—using related subtraction facts, counting, or number sense. They should be able to complete the page using mental math.

## Reading tables

Read the table. Then answer the questions.

**Ages of cousins**

| NAME | AGE |
|------|-----|
| Kinta | 8 |
| Paul | 7 |
| Clara | 9 |
| Meg | 7 |
| Lee | 6 |

How old is Paul?  7

Who is older than Kinta?  Clara

Who is the same age as Meg?  Paul

Who is the youngest?  Lee

Read the table. Then answer the questions.

**Favorite juice**

| Apple | 6 |
|-------|---|
| Cranberry | 2 |
| Grape | 3 |
| Cherry | 1 |
| Orange | 9 |

How many people chose orange juice?  9

Which juice did 2 people choose?  cranberry

How many more people like orange juice than apple juice?  3 more

Did more people choose grape juice or cranberry juice?  grape juice

Read the table. Then answer the questions.

**Weight of dogs**

| NAME | Bear | Mike | Perry | Spike | Marca |
|------|------|------|-------|-------|-------|
| POUNDS | 64 | 13 | 20 | 11 | 6 |

Which dog weighs more than 50 pounds?  Bear

Which dog weighs less than 10 pounds?  Marca

How much more does Perry weigh than Mike?  7 pounds

How much less does Spike weigh than Mike?  2 pounds

If children have difficulty reading the information in the last table, help them with one question, reading across the appropriate row and down the appropriate column, showing them the intersection of the two.

## 38

## Extending geometric patterns

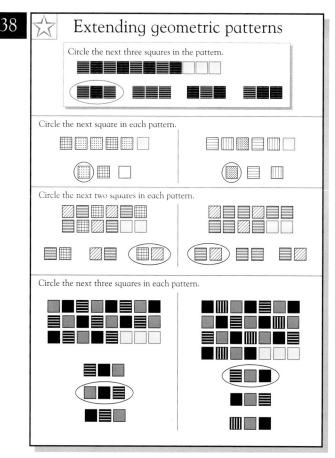

Circle the next three squares in the pattern.

Circle the next square in each pattern.

Circle the next two squares in each pattern.

Circle the next three squares in each pattern.

Children may have difficulty with the final two patterns. Point out that the patterns run horizontally and diagonally.

## 39

## Adding

Write the answer in each box.

21 + 13 + 15 = 49     16 + 12 + 20 = 48

Write the answer in each box.

| | | |
|---|---|---|
| 25 + 30 + 20 = 75 | 60 + 25 + 15 = 100 | 14 + 14 + 30 = 58 |
| 72 + 12 + 10 = 94 | 35 + 15 + 30 = 80 | 30 + 13 + 14 = 57 |
| 23 + 24 + 30 = 77 | 42 + 16 + 20 = 78 | 21 + 40 + 34 = 95 |
| 32 + 10 + 45 = 87 | 30 + 34 + 21 = 85 | 15 + 15 + 60 = 90 |
| 12 + 13 + 14 = 39 | 10 + 11 + 12 = 33 | 12 + 14 + 13 = 39 |
| 15 + 21 + 32 = 68 | 25 + 35 + 7 = 67 | 20 + 14 + 5 = 39 |
| 41 + 22 + 6 = 69 | 42 + 13 + 4 = 59 | 32 + 40 + 7 = 79 |
| 62 + 8 + 11 = 81 | 45 + 21 + 12 = 78 | 31 + 51 + 6 = 88 |
| 40 + 30 + 20 = 90 | 50 + 40 + 20 = 110 | 30 + 40 + 50 = 120 |
| 8 + 11 + 80 = 99 | 25 + 41 + 13 = 79 | 43 + 30 + 6 = 79 |
| 22 + 33 + 44 = 99 | 13 + 70 + 11 = 94 | 11 + 14 + 60 = 85 |
| 17 + 12 + 60 = 89 | 24 + 26 + 50 = 100 | 31 + 8 + 20 = 59 |

Write the answer in each box.

6 + 7 + 8 + 9 = 30     4 + 6 + 8 + 10 = 28

3 + 5 + 7 + 9 = 24     8 + 9 + 10 + 11 = 38

1 + 4 + 7 + 11 = 23     8 + 6 + 4 + 2 = 20

10 + 7 + 5 + 2 = 24     9 + 7 + 5 + 3 = 24

For these questions, some children may want to find partial sums first.

## 40

## Adding

Write the answer in the box.

| 34 | 26 | 73 |
|----|----|----|
| + 13 | + 15 | + 27 |
| 47 | 41 | 100 |

Write the answer in the box.

| | | | |
|---|---|---|---|
| 45 + 24 = 69 | 31 + 18 = 49 | 53 + 26 = 79 | 62 + 16 = 78 |
| 37 + 10 = 47 | 26 + 13 = 39 | 72 + 15 = 87 | 45 + 24 = 69 |
| 39 + 10 = 49 | 24 + 15 = 39 | 52 + 17 = 69 | 36 + 13 = 49 |
| 56 + 14 = 70 | 12 + 16 = 28 | 67 + 11 = 78 | 54 + 16 = 70 |
| 48 + 12 = 60 | 64 + 14 = 78 | 36 + 13 = 49 | 55 + 15 = 70 |
| 26 + 17 = 43 | 37 + 14 = 51 | 48 + 19 = 67 | 56 + 17 = 73 |
| 28 + 16 = 44 | 64 + 26 = 90 | 56 + 27 = 83 | 38 + 23 = 61 |
| 29 + 24 = 53 | 37 + 27 = 64 | 28 + 17 = 45 | 19 + 26 = 45 |
| 26 + 38 = 64 | 36 + 76 = 112 | 46 + 44 = 90 | 34 + 66 = 100 |

Most of the problems require regrouping. Make sure that children do not neglect to add 10 to the tens column when they regroup.

## 41 — Subtracting

Write the answer in the box.

54 − 12 = 42    51 − 21 = 30

Write the answer in the box.

39 − 17 = 22    48 − 16 = 32    53 − 21 = 32    57 − 33 = 24

78 − 26 = 52    47 − 24 = 23    67 − 25 = 42    79 − 27 = 52

64 − 33 = 31    73 − 23 = 50    48 − 26 = 22    77 − 34 = 43

47 − 26 = 21    66 − 26 = 40    35 − 13 = 22    98 − 36 = 62

69 − 48 = 21    57 − 34 = 23    63 − 41 = 22    76 − 53 = 23

Write the answer in the box.

77¢ − 36¢ = 41¢    47¢ − 23¢ = 24¢    58¢ − 46¢ = 12¢    69¢ − 46¢ = 23¢

79¢ − 39¢ = 40¢    76¢ − 34¢ = 42¢    89¢ − 36¢ = 53¢    91¢ − 41¢ = 50¢

75¢ − 35¢ = 40¢    68¢ − 26¢ = 42¢    78¢ − 43¢ = 35¢    45¢ − 35¢ = 10¢

87¢ − 63¢ = 24¢    49¢ − 34¢ = 15¢    58¢ − 38¢ = 20¢    47¢ − 34¢ = 13¢

98¢ − 26¢ = 72¢    79¢ − 29¢ = 50¢    59¢ − 26¢ = 33¢    67¢ − 35¢ = 32¢

Write the answer in the box.

How much is 70¢ minus 23¢?    47¢

Take 46¢ away from $1.00.    54¢

How much is 85¢ minus 46¢?    39¢

Take away 47¢ from 94¢.    47¢

What is the difference between 56¢ and $1.00?    44¢

How much less than 72 in. is 36 in.?    36 in.

Mia has 60¢. She spends 32¢ on candy. How much does she have left?    28¢

Take away 48 in. from 94 in.    46 in.

None of the subtraction problems on this page require regrouping, so children should be able to calculate their answers mentally. For the money problems, make sure that children include units in their answers.

## 42 — Subtracting

Write the answer in the box.

⁶¹³ 7̷3̷    ³¹⁵ 4̷5̷    ⁶¹² 7̷2̷
− 48    − 26    − 36
25    19    36

Write the answer in the box.

| 67 | 43 | 63 | 72 |
| − 48 | − 26 | − 46 | − 45 |
| 19 | 17 | 17 | 27 |

| 71 | 82 | 63 | 90 |
| − 47 | − 36 | − 44 | − 47 |
| 24 | 46 | 19 | 43 |

| 80 | 90 | 65 | 81 |
| − 46 | − 63 | − 37 | − 47 |
| 34 | 27 | 28 | 34 |

Write the answer in the box.

| 46 in. | 59 in. | 74 in. | 60 in. |
| − 18 in. | − 36 in. | − 27 in. | − 44 in. |
| 28 in. | 23 in. | 47 in. | 16 in. |

| 70 in. | 54 in. | 39 in. | 91 in. |
| − 47 in. | − 26 in. | − 4 in. | − 47 in. |
| 23 in. | 28 in. | 35 in. | 44 in. |

Write the answer in the box.

| 43¢ | 61¢ | 73¢ | 71¢ |
| − 17¢ | − 24¢ | − 36¢ | − 46¢ |
| 26¢ | 37¢ | 37¢ | 25¢ |

| 70¢ | 81¢ | 63¢ | 74¢ |
| − 44¢ | − 37¢ | − 46¢ | − 44¢ |
| 26¢ | 44¢ | 17¢ | 30¢ |

| 90 in. | 94 in. | 96 in. | 98¢ |
| − 34 in. | − 47 in. | − 78 in. | − 45¢ |
| 56 in. | 47 in. | 18 in. | 53¢ |

Most of the subtraction problems require regrouping. Make sure children remember to regroup correctly.

## 43 — Reading a calendar

Look at this calendar. Then answer the questions.

**September**

| S | M | T | W | T | F | S |
|---|---|---|---|---|---|---|
| | 1 | 2 | 3 | 4 | 5 | 6 |
| 7 | 8 | 9 | 10 | 11 | 12 | 13 |
| 14 | 15 | 16 | 17 | 18 | 19 | 20 |
| 21 | 22 | 23 | 24 | 25 | 26 | 27 |
| 28 | 29 | 30 | | | | |

What day of the week is the first day of September on this calendar?    Monday

What date is the last Tuesday in September?    September 30

Look at this calendar. Then answer the questions.

**July**

| S | M | T | W | T | F | S |
|---|---|---|---|---|---|---|
| | | | | 1 | 2 | 3 |
| 4 | 5 | 6 | 7 | 8 | 9 | 10 |
| 11 | 12 | 13 | 14 | 15 | 16 | 17 |
| 18 | 19 | 20 | 21 | 22 | 23 | 24 |
| 25 | 26 | 27 | 28 | 29 | 30 | 31 |

How many days are in the month of July?    31 days

What day of the week is the last day of July on this calendar?    Saturday

A camp starts on July 5 and ends on July 9. How many camp days are there?    5 days

The campers go swimming on Tuesday and Thursday. On which dates will they swim?    July 6 and July 8

Look at this calendar. Then answer the questions.

**November**

| S | M | T | W | T | F | S |
|---|---|---|---|---|---|---|
| | | | | | | 1 |
| 2 | 3 | 4 | 5 | 6 | 7 | 8 |
| 9 | 10 | 11 | 12 | 13 | 14 | 15 |
| 16 | 17 | 18 | 19 | 20 | 21 | 22 |
| 23 | 24 | 25 | 26 | 27 | 28 | 29 |
| 30 | | | | | | |

What date is the first Sunday of November?    November 2

What day of the week is November 14?    Friday

How many Saturdays are shown in November?    5

Jenna's birthday is November 23. What day of the week is it?    Sunday

If children have difficulty with these exercises, make sure they understand the abbreviations used in the calendars, and are able to read the calendars accurately.

## 44 — Multiplication as repeated addition

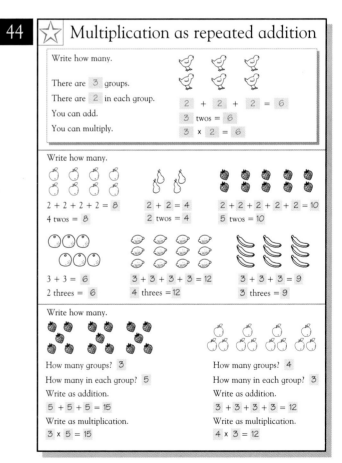

Write how many.

There are 3 groups.

There are 2 in each group.

You can add.

You can multiply.

2 + 2 + 2 = 6

3 twos = 6

3 x 2 = 6

Write how many.

2 + 2 + 2 + 2 = 8    2 + 2 = 4    2 + 2 + 2 + 2 + 2 = 10
4 twos = 8    2 twos = 4    5 twos = 10

3 + 3 = 6    3 + 3 + 3 + 3 = 12    3 + 3 + 3 = 9
2 threes = 6    4 threes = 12    3 threes = 9

Write how many.

How many groups? 3    How many groups? 4

How many in each group? 5    How many in each group? 3

Write as addition.    Write as addition.

5 + 5 + 5 = 15    3 + 3 + 3 + 3 = 12

Write as multiplication.    Write as multiplication.

3 x 5 = 15    4 x 3 = 12

This page reinforces the 2 and 3 times tables. Children can count the items shown to verify their addition.

## 45

## Choose the operation

Put either + or – in the box to make each answer correct.

20 + 13 = 33     24 – 18 = 6     17 + 14 = 31

Put either + or – in the box to make each answer correct.

15 + 19 = 34     21 – 9 = 12     16 – 11 = 5     29 + 23 = 52

60 – 25 = 35     45 + 18 = 63     65 – 30 = 35     42 + 18 = 60

71 + 36 = 107     60 – 37 = 23     57 – 12 = 45     66 + 16 = 82

59 – 20 = 39     72 – 40 = 32     84 – 32 = 52     38 + 38 = 76

29 – 29 = 0     45 + 45 = 90     29 + 45 = 74     73 – 16 = 57

Write the answer in the box.

I add 26 to a number and the answer is 50. What number did I start with? **24**

67 added to a number makes 80. What is the number? **13**

36 added to a number gives a total of 64. What is the number? **28**

I subtract 18 from a number and the result is 24. What number did I start with? **42**

I take 22 away from a number and have 15 left. What number did I start with? **37**

Two numbers add up to 55. One of the numbers is 25. What is the other number? **30**

Two numbers are added together and the total is 84. One of the numbers is 66. What is the other number? **18**

After spending 34¢, I have 65¢ left. How much did I start with? **99¢**

Write + or – in the box.

17¢ + 35¢ = 52¢     46¢ – 37¢ = 9¢     72¢ – 31¢ = 41¢

68¢ – 68¢ = 0¢     25¢ – 3¢ = 22¢     80¢ – 46¢ = 34¢

74¢ + 20¢ = 94¢     28¢ + 14¢ = 42¢     52¢ – 17¢ = 35¢

53¢ + 24¢ = 77¢     63¢ – 27¢ = 36¢     56¢ + 23¢ = 79¢

Children should realize that if the answer is larger than the first number then they must add, and if the answer is smaller than the first number then they must subtract. They should check some of their answers to make sure that they are correct.

---

## 46

## Venn diagrams

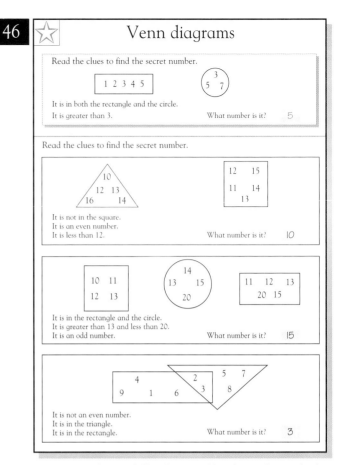

Read the clues to find the secret number.

1 2 3 4 5     3 5 7

It is in both the rectangle and the circle.
It is greater than 3.     What number is it?  **5**

Read the clues to find the secret number.

It is not in the square.
It is an even number.
It is less than 12.     What number is it?  **10**

It is in the rectangle and the circle.
It is greater than 13 and less than 20.
It is an odd number.     What number is it?  **15**

It is not an even number.
It is in the triangle.
It is in the rectangle.     What number is it?  **3**

If children have difficulty, "walk" them through the example. The final question is a Venn diagram showing which numbers are in both figures. You may want to ask children which numbers are in both the triangle and the rectangle.

---

## 47

## Working with coins

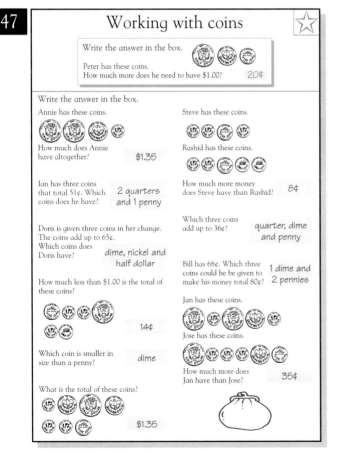

Write the answer in the box.

Peter has these coins.
How much more does he need to have $1.00?  **20¢**

Write the answer in the box.

Annie has these coins.
How much does Annie have altogether?  **$1.35**

Steve has these coins.

Rashid has these coins.

Ian has three coins that total 51¢. Which coins does he have?  **2 quarters and 1 penny**

How much more money does Steve have than Rashid?  **8¢**

Doris is given three coins in her change. The coins add up to 65¢. Which coins does Doris have?  **dime, nickel and half dollar**

Which three coins add up to 36¢?  **quarter, dime and penny**

Bill has 68¢. Which three coins could he be given to make his money total 80¢?  **1 dime and 2 pennies**

How much less than $1.00 is the total of these coins?  **14¢**

Jan has these coins.

Jose has these coins.

Which coin is smaller in size than a penny?  **dime**

How much more does Jan have than Jose?  **35¢**

What is the total of these coins?  **$1.35**

For some of these questions, children may have to use guess-and-check.

---

## Money problems

Write the answer in the box.

How much needs to be added to 65¢ to make $1.00?  **35¢**

What is the total of  **0**

Write the answer in the box.

How many 5¢ coins are needed to make a total of 50¢?  **10**

Julie has $2.60 and is given $2.40. How much does Julie have now?  **$5.00**

One dollar is shared equally by four children. How much will they each get?  **25¢**

How much do three dimes make?  **30¢**

How many groups of $2.50 are needed to make $10.00?  **4**

Andrea spends $1.63 and gives the storekeeper $2.00. How much change does she get?  **37¢**

Wendy needs $5.00 for a T-shirt but only has $1.60. How much more does Wendy need?  **$3.40**

After spending $1.50, Andrew has 90¢ left. How much did Andrew start with?  **$2.40**

How many 25¢ coins are equal to $1.00?  **4**

Sean has $2.05 but needs $4.00 to buy a toy. How much more does Sean need?  **$1.95**

Write the answer in the box.

$1.10 – $0.60 = **$0.50**     $2.50 + $2.50 = **$5.00**     $1.50 + $0.65 = **$2.15**

$1.20 – $0.90 = **$0.30**     $5.00 + $2.35 = **$7.35**     75¢ – 35¢ = **40¢**

65¢ – 45¢ = **20¢**     $2.27 + $3.33 = **$5.60**     56¢ – 45¢ = **11¢**

50¢ + 60¢ = **110¢**     80¢ – 30¢ = **50¢**     $1.60 + $4.50 = **$6.10**

$1.80 – $0.50 = **$1.30**     $2.00 – $0.50 = **$1.50**     $2.60 + $2.35 = **$4.95**

Children should be able to find the answers to most of these questions using mental math. In some cases, they may want to write the information as a subtraction problem.

# Measurement problems

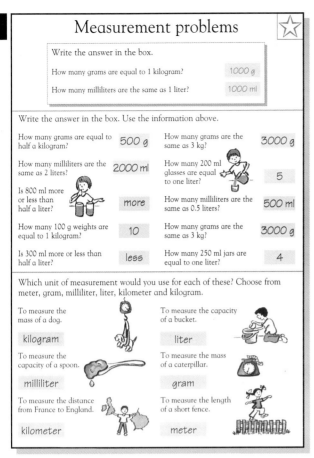

Write the answer in the box.

How many grams are equal to 1 kilogram? **1000 g**

How many milliliters are the same as 1 liter? **1000 ml**

Write the answer in the box. Use the information above.

How many grams are equal to half a kilogram? **500 g**

How many grams are the same as 3 kg? **3000 g**

How many milliliters are the same as 2 liters? **2000 ml**

How many 200 ml glasses are equal to one liter? **5**

Is 800 ml more or less than half a liter? **more**

How many milliliters are the same as 0.5 liters? **500 ml**

How many 100 g weights are equal to 1 kilogram? **10**

How many grams are the same as 3 kg? **3000 g**

Is 300 ml more or less than half a liter? **less**

How many 250 ml jars are equal to one liter? **4**

Which unit of measurement would you use for each of these? Choose from meter, gram, milliliter, liter, kilometer and kilogram.

To measure the mass of a dog. **kilogram**

To measure the capacity of a bucket. **liter**

To measure the capacity of a spoon. **milliliter**

To measure the mass of a caterpillar. **gram**

To measure the distance from France to England. **kilometer**

To measure the length of a short fence. **meter**

For most of these problems, children will have to count, rather than using multiplication or division. You may want to provide counters that children can use to represent the amounts.

## 50

# Telling time

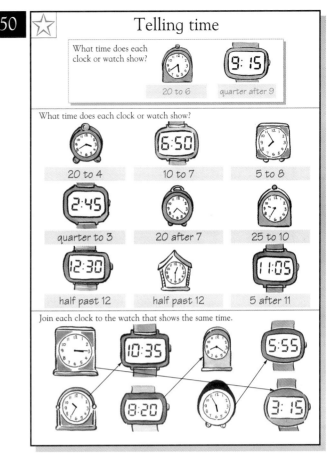

What time does each clock or watch show?

**20 to 6**     **quarter after 9**

What time does each clock or watch show?

**20 to 4**     **10 to 7**     **5 to 8**

**quarter to 3**     **20 after 7**     **25 to 10**

**half past 12**     **half past 12**     **5 after 11**

Join each clock to the watch that shows the same time.

Children may need help with answers that are a certain number of minutes to the hour. On the analog clocks, show them how to count back by 5s from the 12 o'clock mark.

## 51

# Telling time

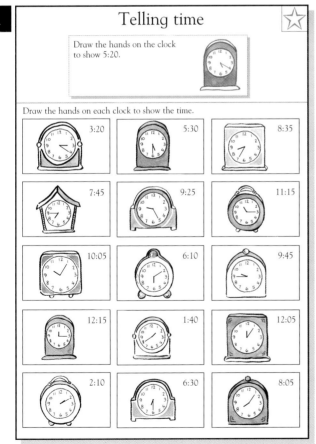

Draw the hands on the clock to show 5:20.

Draw the hands on each clock to show the time.

3:20     5:30     8:35

7:45     9:25     11:15

10:05     6:10     9:45

12:15     1:40     12:05

2:10     6:30     8:05

If children are not familiar with the minutes on the clock face, have them count by 5s from the 12 o'clock mark . Children need only draw the hour hands in an approximate position between the correct numbers.

# Telling time

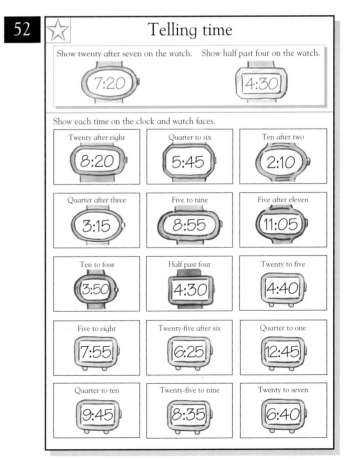

Show twenty after seven on the watch.     Show half past four on the watch.

**7:20**     **4:30**

Show each time on the clock and watch faces.

Twenty after eight **8:20**     Quarter to six **5:45**     Ten after two **2:10**

Quarter after three **3:15**     Five to nine **8:55**     Five after eleven **11:05**

Ten to four **3:50**     Half past four **4:30**     Twenty to five **4:40**

Five to eight **7:55**     Twenty-five after six **6:25**     Quarter to one **12:45**

Quarter to ten **9:45**     Twenty-five to nine **8:35**     Twenty to seven **6:40**

For questions asking to show minutes before an hour, children may need to subtract from 60. Make sure they do not write the hour incorrectly in such cases.

# Bar graphs

Look at the bar graph. Then answer the question.

Robbie
Maggie

0  2  4  6
Number of cherries

How many cherries does Robbie have?   6

Look at the bar graph. Then answer the questions.

Favorite seasons

This graph shows the favorite seasons of a group of children. How many children were asked which season they liked best?   20

How many children liked autumn best?   6

Which season did 4 children like?   spring

Which was the favorite season?   summer

How many more children liked autumn than liked winter?   4

Look at the bar graph. Then answer the questions.

Favorite pets

This graph shows the favorite pets of a group of children. How many children were asked about which pets they liked?   14

Which pet did 8 children like?   guinea pigs

How many children liked rabbits?   3

How many children liked hamsters?   1

How many more children liked rabbits than liked hamsters?   2

If children need help reading bar graphs, show them how to read across and up from the axis labels. To answer some of the questions, children will need to add and compare data.

## 54

# 2-dimensional shapes

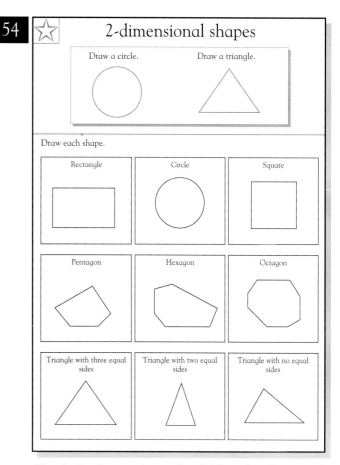

Draw a circle.          Draw a triangle.

Draw each shape.

| Rectangle | Circle | Square |
| Pentagon | Hexagon | Octagon |
| Triangle with three equal sides | Triangle with two equal sides | Triangle with no equal sides |

Check the figures drawn by children for shape and appropriate lengths of sides.

## 55

# Properties of polygons

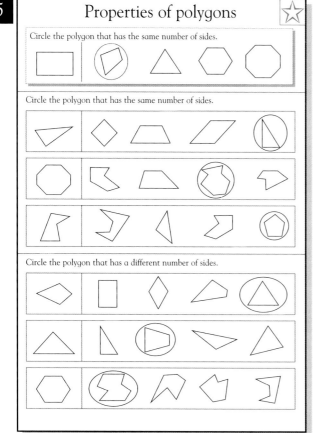

Circle the polygon that has the same number of sides.

Circle the polygon that has the same number of sides.

Circle the polygon that has a different number of sides.

Make sure that children understand that they are not looking for identical shapes, but figures with the given number of sides.

# Pictographs

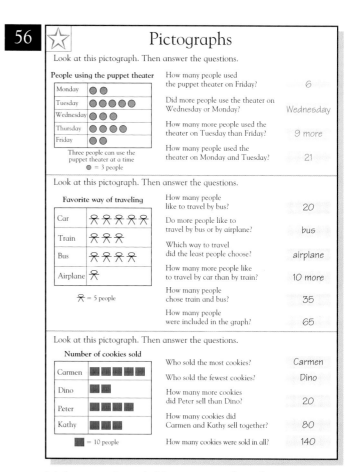

Look at this pictograph. Then answer the questions.

People using the puppet theater

| Monday |
| Tuesday |
| Wednesday |
| Thursday |
| Friday |

Three people can use the puppet theater at a time
● = 3 people

How many people used the puppet theater on Friday?   6

Did more people use the theater on Wednesday or Monday?   Wednesday

How many more people used the theater on Tuesday than Friday?   9 more

How many people used the theater on Monday and Tuesday?   21

Look at this pictograph. Then answer the questions.

Favorite way of traveling

| Car |
| Train |
| Bus |
| Airplane |

= 5 people

How many people like to travel by bus?   20

Do more people like to travel by bus or by airplane?   bus

Which way to travel did the least people choose?   airplane

How many more people like to travel by car than by train?   10 more

How many people chose train and bus?   35

How many people were included in the graph?   65

Look at this pictograph. Then answer the questions.

Number of cookies sold

| Carmen |
| Dino |
| Peter |
| Kathy |

= 10 people

Who sold the most cookies?   Carmen

Who sold the fewest cookies?   Dino

How many more cookies did Peter sell than Dino?   20

How many cookies did Carmen and Kathy sell together?   80

How many cookies were sold in all?   140

Make sure that children notice that the units on the scale are not in ones. To answer some of the questions, children will need to add, subtract, and compare data.

## Most likely/least likely

Look at the marbles. Then answer the questions.

Which kind of marble would you be least likely to pick without looking?

Which kind of marble would you be most likely to pick without looking?

Look at the spinner. Then answer the questions.

Is the spinner more likely to land on 1 or 2?   1

Is the spinner more likely to land on 2 or 3?   2

Which number is the spinner most likely to land on?   1

Which number is the spinner least likely to land on?   3

Look at the tally chart. Then answer the questions.

Imagine that each time you shake the bag, one coin falls out.

Tally of coins in the bag

| COLOR | TALLIES |
|---|---|
| Pennies | IIII |
| Dimes | II |
| Nickels | ЖIII |
| Quarters | Ж |

Is a penny or a dime more likely to fall out?   penny

Is a quarter or a nickel more likely to fall out?   nickel

Which coin is most likely to fall out?   nickel

Which coin is least likely to fall out?   dime

Children should realize that the more of a particular item there is in a set, the more likely it is to be picked.

## 58

## 3-dimensional shapes

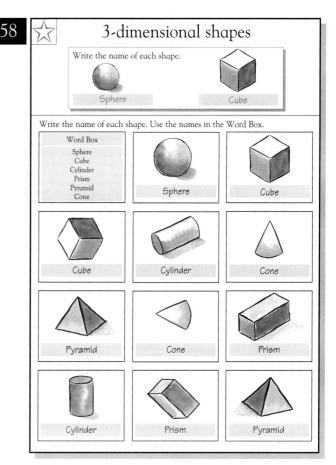

Write the name of each shape.

Sphere      Cube

Write the name of each shape. Use the names in the Word Box.

Word Box
Sphere
Cube
Cylinder
Prism
Pyramid
Cone

Sphere | Cube
Cube | Cylinder | Cone
Pyramid | Cone | Prism
Cylinder | Prism | Pyramid

Children may find figures with unusual orientations a little confusing.

## 59

## Sorting 3-dimensional shapes

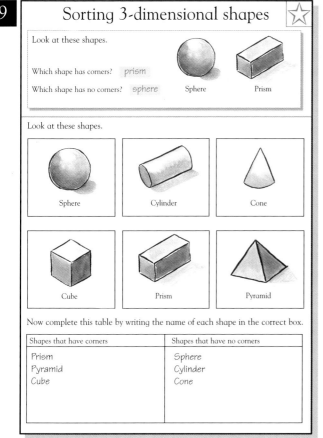

Look at these shapes.

Which shape has corners?   prism

Which shape has no corners?   sphere

Sphere      Prism

Look at these shapes.

Sphere | Cylinder | Cone
Cube | Prism | Pyramid

Now complete this table by writing the name of each shape in the correct box.

| Shapes that have corners | Shapes that have no corners |
|---|---|
| Prism | Sphere |
| Pyramid | Cylinder |
| Cube | Cone |

If necessary, point out that a shape must have flat surfaces to have corners.

## Location on a grid

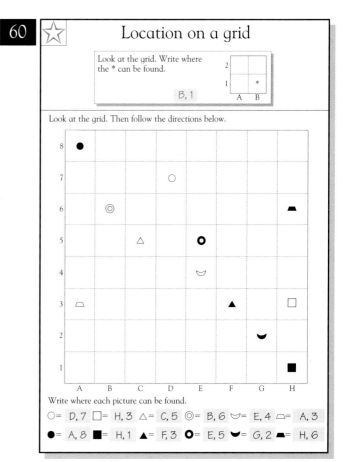

Look at the grid. Write where the * can be found.

B, 1

Look at the grid. Then follow the directions below.

Write where each picture can be found.

○= D, 7   □= H, 3   △= C, 5   ◎= B, 6   ⌣= E, 4   ▱= A, 3

●= A, 8   ■= H, 1   ▲= F, 3   ○= E, 5   ⌣= G, 2   ◗= H, 6

To write the location of the shapes on the grid, children should understand that the letter should precede the number. This will prepare them to learn about coordinates on graphs where the value from the x-axis is written before the value from the y-axis.

# Location on a grid

Color B, 2 on the grid.

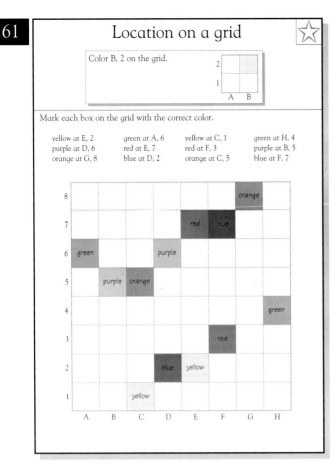

Mark each box on the grid with the correct color.

| | | | |
|---|---|---|---|
| yellow at E, 2 | green at A, 6 | yellow at C, 1 | green at H, 4 |
| purple at D, 6 | red at E, 7 | red at F, 3 | purple at B, 5 |
| orange at G, 8 | blue at D, 2 | orange at C, 5 | blue at F, 7 |

See the comments for the previous page.

---

## 62

# Square corners

Circle the square corners on each shape.

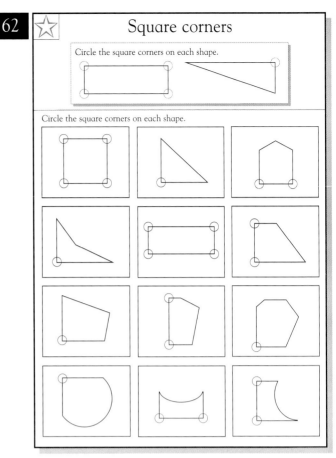

Circle the square corners on each shape.

Most of the right angles should be quite clear, but make sure that the children spot all of them, especially on the later figures.

---

# Square corners

Circle the square corners on these shapes.

Circle the square corners on these shapes.

See the comments for the previous page.

---

# Adding

Write the answer between the lines.

```
  721        646        502
+  35      +  98      +  25
-----      -----      -----
  756        744        527
```

Write the answer between the lines.

```
  220     491     560     709     312
+  36   +  50   +  64   +  53   +  30
-----   -----   -----   -----   -----
  256     541     624     762     342

  203     970     348     470     662
+  41   +  12   +  25   +  10   +  49
-----   -----   -----   -----   -----
  244     982     373     480     711

  241     371     437     421     752
+  12   +  83   +  45   + 168   +  67
-----   -----   -----   -----   -----
  253     454     482     589     819

  792     534     615     185     658
+  38   +  99   +  25   +  87   +  17
-----   -----   -----   -----   -----
  830     633     640     272     675
```

Write the answer between the lines.

```
 $9.45      $5.60      $8.35      $6.50      $1.65
+$0.68     +$0.43     +$0.89     +$0.70     +$0.95
-------    -------    -------    -------    -------
$10.13      $6.03      $9.24      $7.20      $2.60

 $7.29      $4.82     $10.19      $3.78      $9.12
+$0.12     +$0.18     +$ 0.94    +$0.47     +$0.74
-------    -------    -------    -------    -------
 $7.41      $5.00     $11.13      $4.25      $9.86
```

Most of these addition problems require regrouping. In some problems, children need to regroup more than once.

## Ordering

Write these numbers in order starting with the smallest.
670    760    607    706
*607    670    706    760*

Write these numbers in order starting with the smallest.

| 270 | 720 | 207 | 702 | | 870 | 780 | 807 | 708 |
|---|---|---|---|---|---|---|---|---|
| *207* | *270* | *702* | *720* | | *708* | *780* | *807* | *870* |

| 906 | 690 | 960 | 609 | | 106 | 610 | 601 | 160 |
|---|---|---|---|---|---|---|---|---|
| *609* | *690* | *906* | *960* | | *106* | *160* | *601* | *610* |

| 560 | 506 | 650 | 605 | | 849 | 489 | 948 | 984 |
|---|---|---|---|---|---|---|---|---|
| *506* | *560* | *605* | *650* | | *489* | *849* | *948* | *984* |

| 890 | 980 | 809 | 908 | | 486 | 684 | 864 | 648 |
|---|---|---|---|---|---|---|---|---|
| *809* | *890* | *908* | *980* | | *486* | *648* | *684* | *864* |

| 405 | 450 | 540 | 504 | | 746 | 647 | 764 | 674 |
|---|---|---|---|---|---|---|---|---|
| *405* | *450* | *504* | *540* | | *647* | *674* | *746* | *764* |

| 570 | 586 | 490 | 92 | | 76 | 104 | 200 | 92 |
|---|---|---|---|---|---|---|---|---|
| *92* | *490* | *570* | *586* | | *76* | *92* | *104* | *200* |

| 440 | 66 | 781 | 177 | | 632 | 236 | 77 | 407 |
|---|---|---|---|---|---|---|---|---|
| *66* | *177* | *440* | *781* | | *77* | *236* | *407* | *632* |

| 842 | 587 | 99 | 88 | | 74 | 101 | 12 | 800 |
|---|---|---|---|---|---|---|---|---|
| *88* | *99* | *587* | *842* | | *12* | *74* | *101* | *800* |

| 500 | 468 | 395 | 288 | | 600 | 304 | 403 | 89 |
|---|---|---|---|---|---|---|---|---|
| *288* | *395* | *468* | *500* | | *89* | *304* | *403* | *600* |

| 78 | 9 | 302 | 470 | | 345 | 543 | 53 | 34 |
|---|---|---|---|---|---|---|---|---|
| *9* | *78* | *302* | *470* | | *34* | *53* | *345* | *543* |

Make sure that children do not simply order the numbers according to the first digits.

---

## 66

## Adding

Write the answer between the lines.

```
  3 2 4        5 3 7        6 0 8
+ 1 5 2      + 1 6 4      + 5 4 9
-------      -------      -------
  4 7 6        7 0 1       1 1 5 7
```

Write the answer between the lines.

```
  5 6 0      3 4 2      3 2 9      2 5 3      6 0 7
+ 3 6 1    + 4 5 0    + 6 2 4    + 5 5 3    + 3 4 9
-------    -------    -------    -------    -------
  9 2 1      7 9 2      9 5 3      8 0 6      9 5 6
```

```
  2 7 3      1 1 7      7 2 1      3 0 8      8 2 2
+ 2 6 5    + 4 8 3    + 1 9 5    + 5 0 0    + 1 0 3
-------    -------    -------    -------    -------
  5 3 8      6 0 0      9 1 6      8 0 8      9 2 5
```

```
  2 2 0      4 9 1      5 6 0      7 0 9      3 1 2
+ 1 6 3    + 2 9 9    + 3 4 0    + 1 6 8    + 3 1 2
-------    -------    -------    -------    -------
  3 8 3      7 9 0      9 0 0      8 7 7      6 2 4
```

```
  8 0 5      3 8 0      1 6 0      6 2 6      7 2 5
+ 1 9 1    + 4 6 1    + 1 7 5    + 3 0 2    + 1 2 5
-------    -------    -------    -------    -------
  9 9 6      8 4 1      3 3 5      9 2 8      8 5 0
```

Write the answer between the lines.

```
  7 3 8      6 0 7      8 2 6      5 9 1      4 5 0
+ 4 8 0    + 5 2 3    + 3 7 2    + 5 3 7    + 9 3 5
-------    -------    -------    -------    -------
 1 2 1 8    1 1 3 0    1 1 9 8    1 1 2 8    1 3 8 5
```

This page is similar to page 64, but all of the addends are three-digit numbers. In the final section, children must regroup to make thousands.

---

## Counting

Write the missing numbers above each ↑.

←23 24 25 26 ○ ○ ○ ○ *30* ○ ○ ○ *33* *34* ○ ○ ○→

Write the missing numbers above each ↑.

←12 ○ 14 ○ ○ 17 ○ ○ ○ 21 ○ ○ 23 24 ○→

| 5 | 6 | | | 9 | 10 | | | | 14 | 15 | 16 | | 18 |

←47 48 49 ○ ○ ○ 53 54 ○ ○ ○ 57 ○ ○ ○ 60→

| 31 | | 33 | 34 | 35 | | | 38 | | 40 | 41 | | | 44 |

←67 ○ ○ ○ 70 ○ 72 73 74 ○ ○ ○ 78 79 80→

| 71 | 72 | | | | 76 | 77 | | 79 | | | | 83 | |

←101 102 103 ○ ○ ○ ○ *108* ○ 110 ○ 112 113 ○ ○→

Each of the sequences involves counting by 1s. Children should fill in only the shapes marked with an arrow.

---

## Place value

The value of 5 in 5<u>2</u>3 is    *500*    or    *five hundred*

The value of 2 in 5<u>2</u>3 is    *20*    or    *twenty*

The value of 3 in 52<u>3</u> is    *3*    or    *three*

Change the 2 in 24 to 3.    *34*    The number is greater by    *10*

What is the value of 5 in these numbers?
Write each value with a number and with a word.

| 35 | 152 | 905 | 512 |
|---|---|---|---|
| *5* | *50* | *5* | *500* |
| *five* | *fifty* | *five* | *five hundred* |
| 65 | 547 | 57 | 950 |
| *5* | *500* | *50* | *50* |
| *five* | *five hundred* | *fifty* | *fifty* |

Circle each number that has a 3 with the value of thirty.
(632)    953    13    (534)    (38)    355

Circle each number that has a 4 with the value of four hundred.
(482)    954    (434)    544    (444)    104

Circle each number that has an 8 with the value of eight.
(38)    83    813    85    (638)    (888)

Write the new number. Then write the value.

Change the 6 in 86 to 9.    *89*    The number is greater by    *3*
Change the 1 in 17 to 4.    *47*    The number is greater by    *30*
Change the 3 in 305 to 5.    *505*    The number is greater by    *200*
Change the 6 in 86 to 5.    *85*    The number is less by    *1*
Change the 4 in 42 to 2.    *22*    The number is less by    *20*
Change the 7 in 704 to 2.    *204*    The number is less by    *500*

If children make errors, have them read each number aloud before answering the question.

# Fractions of shapes

Shade half of each shape.

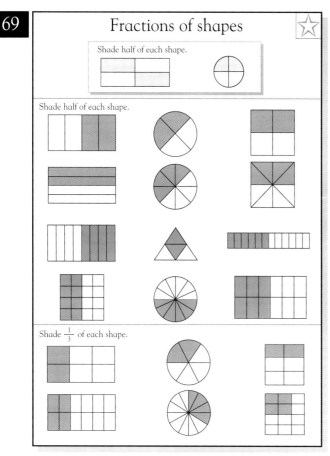

Shade half of each shape.

Shade $\frac{1}{3}$ of each shape.

Children may shade in any combination of the sections as long as the shaded area represents the fraction.

## 70

# Finding patterns

Find the counting pattern. Write the missing numbers.

| 12 | 14 | 16 | 18 | 20 | 22 | 24 | 26 | 28 | 30 |

Find the counting pattern. Write the missing numbers.

5 10 15 20 25 30 35 40 45 50

3 6 9 12 15 18 21 24 27 30

| 31 | 35 | 39 | 43 | 47 | 51 | 55 | 59 | 63 | 67 |

81 83 85 87 89 91 93 95 97 99

19 20 21 22 23 24 25 26 27 28

| 6 | 12 | 18 | 24 | 30 | 36 | 42 | 48 | 54 | 60 |

19 17 15 13 11 9 7 5 3 1

100 90 80 70 60 50 40 30 20 10

| 100 | 200 | 300 | 400 | 500 | 600 | 700 | 800 | 900 | 1000 |

58 55 52 49 46 43 40 37 34 31

| 75 | 70 | 65 | 60 | 55 | 50 | 45 | 40 | 35 | 30 |

42 38 34 30 26 22 18 14 10 6

It may be necessary to point out that some of the patterns show an increase and some a decrease. Children should see what operation turns a number into the next number in a pattern, and then repeat the operation to continue the pattern.

## 71

# Adding

Write the answer in the box.
One child has 46 jacks. Another child has 35 jacks. How many jacks do the children have altogether? **81**

Write the answer in the box.

Scott has 47¢ and Mira has 36¢. How much do they have in all? **83¢**

David has 29¢ and Katie has 62¢. How much do they have altogether? **91¢**

Penny skips for 24 seconds and then Bob skips for 54 seconds. For how many seconds did they skip in total? **78**

Dan finds 44¢ in one pocket and 38¢ in his other pocket. How much does he have altogether? **82¢**

A line is 45 inches long. Peta continues it for another 25 inches. How long is the line now? **70 in.**

What is the sum when 17 is added to 38? **55**

Three girls add their money together. They have $26, $24, and $20. How much do they have altogether? **$70**

A pencil 11 cm long is put end to end with another pencil 12 cm long. What is the total length of the two pencils? **23 cm**

What is the total when 34 is added to 46? **80**

One child has 47 football cards. Another has 48 football cards. How many cards do they have altogether? **95**

One bag of candy has 26 toffee bars. A second bag has 19 bars. How many toffee bars are there altogether? **45**

Abel spends 48¢ on candy and then 38¢ on an ice cream. How much has Abel spent altogether? **86¢**

Martha has 45 marbles in one hand and 56 in the other hand. How many marbles does Martha have altogether? **101**

A bag of cherries has 43 ripe ones and 17 rotten ones. How many cherries are in the bag? **60**

There are 34 children in one class and 36 in another. How many children are there in total? **70**

Ideally, children should work out these problems in their heads, but you should allow them to write the addition problems out in vertical form if they find it easier.

# Adding

Write the answer in the box.
Josh has three piles of blocks. There are 20 blocks in one pile, 18 blocks in the second pile, and 10 blocks in the third pile. How many blocks does Josh have altogether? **48**

Write the answer in the box.

What is the total of 13, 17, and 20? **50**

Joanne is given some money at Christmas. She is given $5.00 by Uncle Eddie, $2.50 by Aunt Jo, and $3.50 by her sister. How much is she given in all? **$11**

A child collects 32 birthday cards and 77 Christmas cards. How many cards does she have? **109**

How much do these coins add up to: 25¢, 50¢, 10¢, and 5¢? **90¢**

Add together 50¢, 20¢, and 50¢. **120¢**

What is the sum of 23, 24, and 25? **72**

Jane has three piggy banks. One has $1.20, the second has $0.80, and the third has $3.00. How much does Jane have altogether? **$5.00**

How much is 50¢ plus 70¢ plus 80¢? **200¢ or $2.00**

One bag holds 24 grapes, another bag holds 34 grapes, and the third bag holds 30 grapes. What is the total number of grapes? **88**

Bill collects comics. He has 120 and is given 60 more by a friend. How many comics does Bill have now? **180**

Jill buys three bars of chocolate. One costs 30¢, another costs 28¢, and the third costs 32¢. What is the total cost of the chocolate? **90¢**

What is the total of 60, 70, and 80? **210**

Three loads of sand are delivered to a building site. They weigh 70 lb, 90 lb, and 100 lb. How much do they weigh altogether? **260 lb**

Add together 12, 24, and 36. **72**

A teacher gives out 33 stars on Monday, 25 on Tuesday, and 35 on Wednesday. How many stars has she given out altogether? **93**

Encourage children to work out these problems mentally. Some of the questions with three addends include two that add up to a multiple of ten. This makes the mental math easier. Children should try to spot these addends.

## Subtracting

Write the answer in the box.
Doris had 40 marbles but then lost 17 in a game.
How many marbles does Doris have left? | 23

Write the answer in the box.

I have 35 jelly beans. Then I eat 12. How many are left? | 23

Two numbers add up to 30. One of the numbers is 18. What is the other number? | 12

A piece of wood is 60 inches long. A section 28 inches long is cut off. How long is the remaining piece of wood? | 32 in.

Two numbers add up to 80. One of the numbers is 45. What is the other number? | 35

A class has 33 children. 15 of the class are boys. How many of the class are girls? | 18

Out of 46 squirrels, 38 are gray and the rest are red. How many squirrels are red? | 8

What is 56 less than 100? | 44

A bag contains 60 cherries. 12 of the cherries are rotten. How many cherries are not rotten? | 48

Two numbers total 65. One of the numbers is 32. What is the other number? | 33

A number added to 15 makes a total of 40. What number has been added? | 25

Mary goes shopping with $5.00. She spends $1.80. How much does Mary have left? | $3.20

Dick goes shopping with $5.00. He returns home with $1.30. How much has Dick spent? | $3.70

The sum of two numbers is 80. One of the numbers is 43. What is the other number? | 37

A child has 50¢ to spend. She gives 24¢ to a friend. How much does she have left? | 26¢

Ideally, children should work out these subtraction problems mentally, but you should allow them to write the problems in a vertical form if they find it easier.

## 74

## Subtracting

Write the answer in the box.
A road is 35 miles long. A section 13 miles long has to be repaired. What length of road does not need repair? | 22 miles

Write the answer in the box.

Shane has to run 100 meters. After running 74 meters he trips. How far did he have left to run? | 26 m

Samantha has to swim for one hour at a swim meet. How much longer must she swim if she has already swum for 38 minutes? | 22 min

Two numbers add up to 80. One of the numbers is 44. What is the other number? | 36

I add 37 to a number and have a total of 66. What is the number? | 29

A school dentist sees 84 children in a day. If she sees 37 in the morning, how many will she see in the afternoon? | 47

What is the difference when I take away 33 from 70? | 37

A box has 60 chocolates. 29 have nuts. The rest are plain. How many chocolates are plain? | 31

A number has been taken away from 90 and the difference is 26. What number has been taken away? | 64

How much money is left if I start with 95¢ and then spend 67¢? | 28¢

A lady grows 100 roses in her garden. 58 of the roses are red and the rest are white. How many of the roses are white? | 42

There are 520 spectators at a football game. 320 are adults and the rest are children. How many are children? | 200

How much money is left if I start with $1.00 and then spend 65¢? | 35¢

Out of 70 sailors, 34 are women. How many are men? | 36

A bag contains 80 marbles. 45 marbles are clear. The rest are colored. How many are colored? | 35

A piece of wood is 30 inches long. It is cut into two sections. One section is 12 inches long. How long is the other section? | 18 in.

See the comments for the previous page.

## 75

## Reading tally charts

Look at the tally chart. Then answer the questions.

**Winners at Tag**

| Kelly | Mark | Sandy | Rita | Brad |
|---|---|---|---|---|
| 卌 II | III | 卌 I | 卌 | 卌 IIII |

Who won the most games? | Brad

Who won more games, Sandy or Kelly? | Kelly

How many more games did Rita win than Mark? | 2 more

Look at the tally chart. Then answer the questions.

**Colors of T-Shirts sold**

| Blue | 卌 卌 I |
|---|---|
| White | 卌 III |
| Green | 卌 IIII |
| Black | 卌 卌 II |

Which color shirt was sold most? | black

How many green shirts were sold? | 9

Which color sold more, blue or green? | blue

How many black shirts were sold? | 12

How many more green shirts were sold than white shirts? | 1 more

How many more black shirts were sold than green shirts? | 3 more

How many T-shirts were sold in all? | 40

Look at the tally chart. Then answer the questions.

**Snack choices**

| Chips | Cherries | Cheese | Cookie | Apple |
|---|---|---|---|---|
| 卌 IIII | 卌 | 卌 卌 I | 卌 III | 卌 II |

How many people chose chips? | 9

Which snack did 7 people choose? | apple

Did more people choose chips or cookies? | chips

Which snack did the fewest people choose? | cherries

How many more people chose cheese than chips? | 2 more

How many people chose apples and cherries? | 12

Children usually accept the concept of tally marks quickly. They can count by 5s for completed tallies.

## 76

## Same shape and size

Which figure has same shape and size?

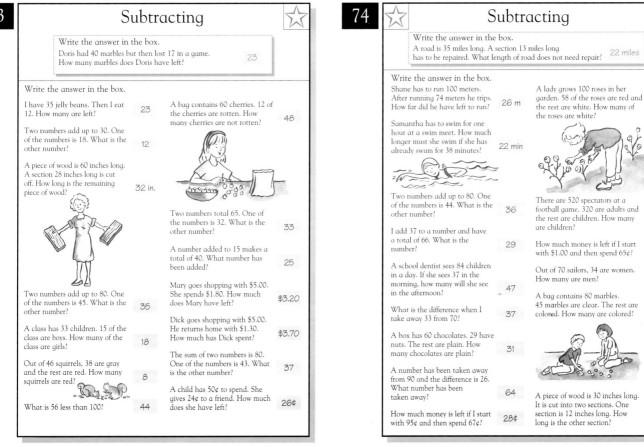

Circle the figure that has same shape and size.

Make sure children compare both size and shape. They may have difficulty if the figures are drawn with different orientations.

## Subtracting

Write the answer between the lines.

```
  4 13            4 11            4 11 13
  3 5 3           5 1 7           5 2 3
- 1 1 7         - 2 8 6         - 1 7 5
  2 3 6           2 3 1           3 4 8
```

Write the answer between the lines.

```
  4 8 2      2 5 4      9 8 6      3 7 1      8 4 2
- 3 5 8    - 1 1 9    - 4 5 8    - 1 3 6    - 7 2 5
  1 2 4      1 3 5      5 2 8      2 3 5      1 1 7

  5 5 5      8 4 2      9 8 4      9 7 8      7 5 6
- 3 7 2    - 4 8 1    - 5 9 2    - 2 9 3    - 3 2 8
  1 8 3      3 6 1      3 9 2      6 8 5      4 2 8

  3 2 5      5 1 9      7 3 2      6 7 1      9 1 2
- 1 5 8    - 3 4 9    - 5 8 7    - 2 9 8    - 2 5 6
  1 6 7      1 7 0      1 4 5      3 7 3      6 5 6

  5 5 1      6 7 3      8 2 4      7 1 1      9 1 5
- 3 7 5    - 1 8 5    - 3 6 7    - 4 8 5    - 5 3 6
  1 7 6      4 8 8      4 5 7      2 2 6      3 7 9
```

Write the answer between the lines.

```
 $6.15      $8.45      $5.55      $8.13      $9.12
-$5.00     -$3.28     -$2.95     -$2.46     -$1.65
 $1.15      $5.17      $2.60      $5.67      $7.47
```

These subtraction problems require multiple regrouping. Some children may neglect to do so. If children make an error, have them check their answers by adding the answer to the number being subtracted.

## Subtracting

Write the answer between the lines.

```
  3 5 9           6 12            4 11 13
  3 5 9           4 7 2           5 2 0
-   3 5         -   3 4         -   2 5
  3 2 4           4 3 8           4 9 5
```

Write the answer between the lines.

```
  9 5 7      5 6 9      4 6 8      2 9 5      7 2 9
-   3 2    -   5 0    -   2 4    -   8 3    -   1 6
  9 2 5      5 1 9      4 4 4      2 1 2      7 1 3

  6 9 2      8 5 0      2 7 4      3 8 7      1 6 3
-   4 3    -   3 6    -   1 7    -   5 7    -   4 9
  6 4 9      8 1 4      2 5 7      3 3 0      1 1 4

  6 4 1      5 2 3      3 1 8      4 2 4      2 5 7
-   5 2    -   7 6    -   7 9    -   6 8    -   8 9
  5 8 9      4 4 7      2 3 9      3 5 6      1 6 8

  9 1 2      4 5 0      9 9 0      3 8 0      7 3 9
-   2 8    -   7 5    -   6 5    -   5 4    -   4 1
  8 8 4      3 7 5      9 2 5      3 2 6      6 9 8
```

Write the answer between the lines.

```
 $5.52      $8.09      $4.82      $3.93      $5.70
-$0.38     -$0.51     -$0.60     -$0.17     -$0.95
 $5.14      $7.58      $4.22      $3.76      $4.75
```

See the comments for the previous page.

## Choosing the operation

Write the answer in the box.

I add 25 to a number and the sum is 40. What number did I start with? | 15

I subtract 13 and have 24 left. What number did I start with? | 37

Write the answer in the box.

22 is added to a number and the sum is 30. What number did I begin with? | 8

I subtract 14 from a number and end up with 17. What number did I start with? | 31

I add 16 to a number and the total of the two numbers is 30. What number did I begin with? | 14

When 26 is subtracted from a number, the difference is 14. What is the number? | 40

After adding 22 to a number the total is 45. What is the number? | 23

What number must you subtract from 19 to find a difference of 7? | 12

I start with 29 and take away a number. The difference is 14. What number did I subtract? | 15

35 is added to a number and the total is 60. What is the number? | 25

I increase a number by 14 and the total is 30. What number did I start with? | 16

After taking 17 away from a number I am left with 3. What number did I start with? | 20

Paul starts with 50¢ but spends some money in a shop. He goes home with 18¢. How much did Paul spend? | 32¢

Sue starts out with 23¢ but is given some money by her aunt. Sue then has 50¢. How much was she given? | 27¢

Alice gives 20¢ to charity. If she started with 95¢, how much has she have left? | 75¢

Jane has a 32-ounce bottle of orange soda. She drinks 12 ounces. How many ounces does she have left? | 20 oz

A box contains 60 pins and then some are added so that the new total is 85. How many pins have been added? | 25

A tower is made up of 30 blocks. 45 more are put on the top. How many blocks are in the tower now? | 75

Children must choose between addition and subtraction to solve each problem. If they make an error, have them substitute their answer in the problem to show them that the answer is not correct.

## Subtracting

Write the answer between the lines.

```
  3 10            3 10            6 9 10
  8 4 0           4 0 5           7 0 0
- 5 0 6         - 1 6 2         - 1 7 5
  3 3 4           2 4 3           5 2 5
```

Write the answer between the lines.

```
  3 5 0      5 6 0      8 6 0      7 7 0      4 8 0
- 1 2 7    - 1 4 5    - 4 3 2    - 3 3 6    - 1 2 3
  2 2 3      4 1 5      4 2 8      4 3 4      3 5 7

  5 0 6      4 0 2      6 0 8      7 0 5      9 0 3
- 3 7 3    - 2 8 1    - 3 7 1    - 4 5 2    - 6 9 2
  1 3 3      1 2 1      2 3 7      2 5 3      2 1 1

  3 0 0      5 1 0      4 0 7      6 3 0      7 0 2
- 1 8 3    - 2 6 7    - 1 6 8    - 3 9 8    - 4 6 3
  1 1 7      2 4 3      2 3 9      2 3 2      2 3 9

  9 0 1      8 0 0      2 0 7      7 0 9      9 0 4
- 2 7 5    - 3 5 0    - 1 0 7    - 3 2 9    - 5 3 6
  6 2 6      4 5 0      1 0 0      3 8 0      3 6 8
```

Write the answer between the lines.

```
 $6.00      $6.05      $9.00      $8.30      $7.00
-$5.00     -$2.82     -$8.56     -$2.06     -$5.62
 $1.00      $3.23      $0.44      $6.24      $1.38
```

See the comments for page 77.

## 81

## Working with money

Write the total in the box.

$5 □  $1 □  ◯ HALF DOLLAR          $6.50

Write the total in the box.

| | |
|---|---|
| $5 $10 $1 ◯◯◯ | $16.80 | $10 $5 $5 ◯◯ | $20.35 |
| $20 $10 $5 $5 $1 | $41 | $20 $10 $10 $10 $5 $5 $5 | $55 |
| $20 $10 $5 ◯◯◯ | $35.75 | $20 $50 $10 $5 | $85 |
| $50 $10 ◯◯◯ | $60.65 | $20 $1 ◯ $5 $1 | $27.05 |
| $20 $10 $20 $10 $50 $5 | $115 | $20 $50 $50 $20 ◯ | $140.10 |
| $10 $20 $50 ◯◯◯ | $80.85 | $1 ◯◯ ◯◯◯ | $1.96 |

Children can add either the dollars or the cents first, since there is no regrouping involved in the problems on this page.

## 82

## Money problems

Write the answer in the box.
Rick goes shopping with a five dollar bill. He spends $2.30. How much does Rick have left?          $2.70

Write the answer in the box.

John has three bills. The total value of the bills is $35. Which three bills does he have?          $20, $10, $5

Patrick has a $5 bill and a 50¢ coin. How much more does he need to have $8.00?          $2.50

After spending $5.50, Ann still has $2.40 left. How much did Ann start with?          $7.90

A package of pens costs $3.45. If Mac pays for them with a $5 bill, how much change will he get?          $1.55

A man buys a Chinese meal that costs $7.80. He pays for the food with a $10 bill. How much change will he get?          $2.20

Three pineapples cost a total of $5.10. A lady pays for the pineapples with a $5 bill and a $1 bill. How much change will she get?          90¢

Apples cost 60¢ a pound. How much will 4 pounds cost?          $2.40

How much change will you get if you buy food for $8.35 and pay for it with a $10 bill?          $1.65

Jan saves 50¢ a week for 10 weeks. How much does she have after the ten weeks?          $5.00

Rob buys a new coat for $34.50 and pays for it with a $50 bill. How much change will he get?          $15.50

The change given to a woman is $1.50. She bought a bag for $8.50. How much had she given the clerk?          $10.00

What is the change from $20.00 when a hat is bought for $14.50?          $5.50

The change from $5.00 is $0.80. How much was spent?          $4.20

After spending $3.20 on food, a man is given $6.80 in change. How much had he given to the storekeeper?          $10.00

A box of chocolates costs $6.28. It is paid for with a $5 bill and two $1 bills. How much extra has been paid?          72¢

These questions involve money in realistic situations. Children must choose between addition and subtraction to solve each problem.

## 83

## Measurement problems

Write the measurement shown by the arrow.          3 cm

Write the measurement shown by the arrow.

7 cm

4 cm

90 cm

73 cm

45 cm

31 cm

28 cm

67 cm

Children should be able to read off scales of this type relatively easily. Make sure that children include the units in their answers.

## Parts of a set

Write the fraction that shows the shaded part of the set.
How many of the fish are shaded?

How many 🐟 ?  3
How many fish in all?  4

Write the fraction.  $\frac{3}{4}$  part of the set
whole set

Circle the fraction that shows the shaded part of the set.

$\frac{1}{3}$   $\frac{2}{3}$   $\frac{3}{2}$          $\frac{2}{3}$   $\frac{3}{5}$   $\frac{2}{5}$

$\frac{1}{4}$   $\frac{3}{4}$   $\frac{2}{4}$          $\frac{4}{5}$   $\frac{1}{5}$   $\frac{1}{4}$

Write the fraction that shows the shaded part of the set.

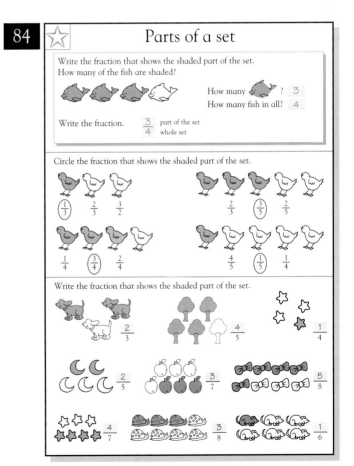

$\frac{2}{3}$          $\frac{4}{5}$          $\frac{1}{4}$

$\frac{2}{5}$          $\frac{3}{7}$          $\frac{5}{8}$

$\frac{4}{7}$          $\frac{3}{8}$          $\frac{1}{6}$

If children have difficulty, point out that the denominator—or bottom number of the fraction—is the total number of parts. The numerator—or top part of the fraction—is the number of shaded parts.

# Bar graphs and pictographs

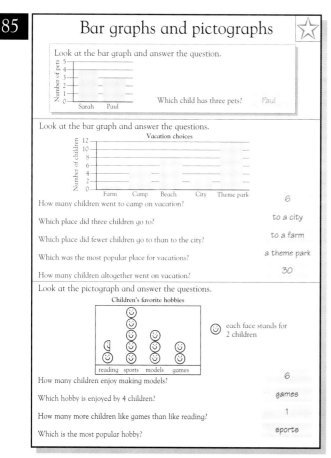

Look at the bar graph and answer the question.

Which child has three pets?   Paul

Look at the bar graph and answer the questions.

Vacation choices

How many children went to camp on vacation?   6

Which place did three children go to?   to a city

Which place did fewer children go to than to the city?   to a farm

Which was the most popular place for vacations?   a theme park

How many children altogether went on vacation?   30

Look at the pictograph and answer the questions.

Children's favorite hobbies

each face stands for 2 children

How many children enjoy making models?   6

Which hobby is enjoyed by 4 children?   games

How many more children like games than like reading?   1

Which is the most popular hobby?   sports

Children should notice that the units on the bar graph scale are in twos rather than ones, as are the icons on the pictograph. To answer some of the questions, children will have to add and compare data.

## 86

# 2-dimensional shapes

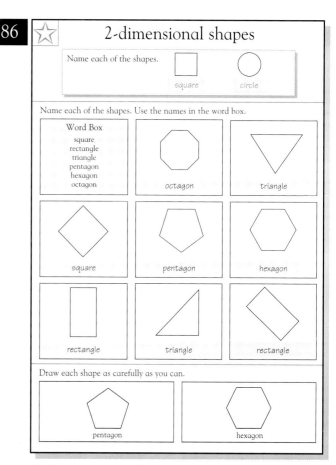

Name each of the shapes.

square   circle

Name each of the shapes. Use the names in the word box.

Word Box
square
rectangle
triangle
pentagon
hexagon
octagon

octagon   triangle

square   pentagon   hexagon

rectangle   triangle   rectangle

Draw each shape as carefully as you can.

pentagon   hexagon

If children have difficulty, help them learn the names of the figures. Allow them to use a ruler for the final section.

## 87

# Sorting 2-dimensional shapes

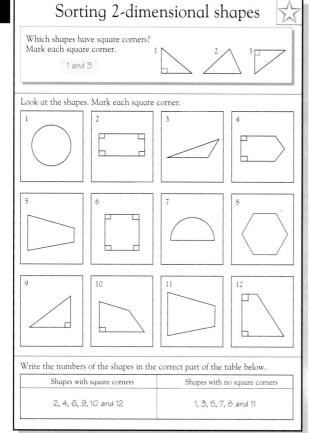

Which shapes have square corners?
Mark each square corner.

1 and 3

Look at the shapes. Mark each square corner.

Write the numbers of the shapes in the correct part of the table below.

| Shapes with square corners | Shapes with no square corners |
| --- | --- |
| 2, 4, 6, 9, 10 and 12 | 1, 3, 5, 7, 8 and 11 |

Most of the right angles should be quite clear, but make sure that the children spot all of them for each figure.

# Symmetry

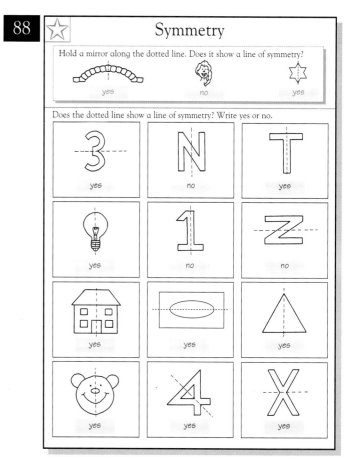

Hold a mirror along the dotted line. Does it show a line of symmetry?

yes   no   yes

Does the dotted line show a line of symmetry? Write yes or no.

yes   no   yes

yes   no   no

yes   yes   yes

yes   yes   yes

Some of these shapes have lines of symmetry in unusual positions. Let children use mirrors on the shapes if they are unsure of their answers.

## Symmetry

Complete each drawing. The dotted line is the line of symmetry.

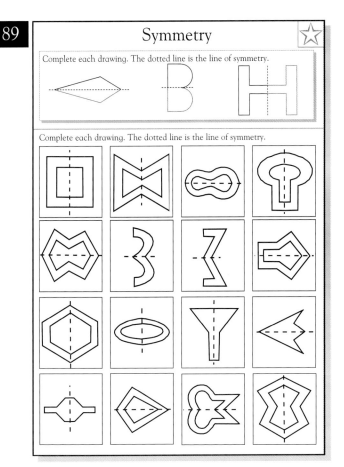

Complete each drawing. The dotted line is the line of symmetry.

Let children use mirrors if they are unsure about any of their drawings.

## Symmetry

Complete each drawing. The dotted line is the line of symmetry.

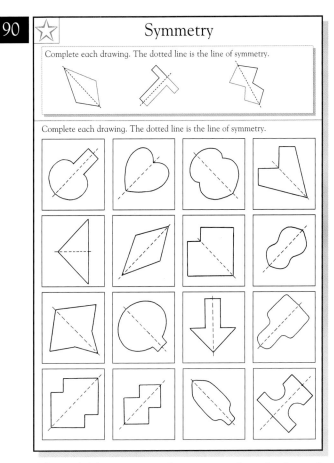

Complete each drawing. The dotted line is the line of symmetry.

Allow children to turn the page so that the line of symmetry is either horizontal or vertical.

## Square corners

Are these corners greater than or less than a square corner? Write greater, less or square corner.

less     greater     square corner

Are these corners greater than or less than a square corner? Write greater, less, or square corner in the box.

| | | | |
|---|---|---|---|
| less | less | greater | square corner |
| greater | less | less | greater |
| square corner | less | square corner | less |
| square corner | greater | greater | square corner |

Allow children to move the book around if they need to. You may want to point out the symbol used to show a right angle.

## 3-dimensional shapes

Write the name of each shape in the box.

prism     sphere

Write the name of each shape in the box.

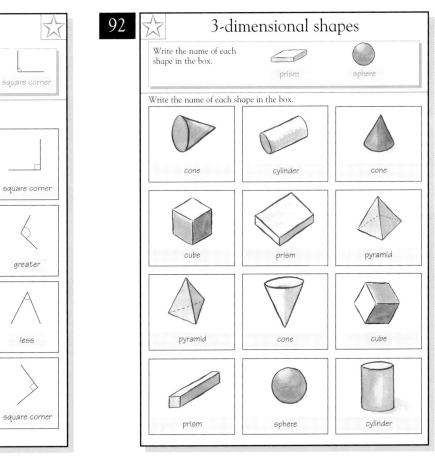

| | | |
|---|---|---|
| cone | cylinder | cone |
| cube | prism | pyramid |
| pyramid | cone | cube |
| prism | sphere | cylinder |

Children may be uncertain of the terms *prism* and *pyramid*. Use real objects to help them visualize.

**93** Sorting 3-dimensional shapes

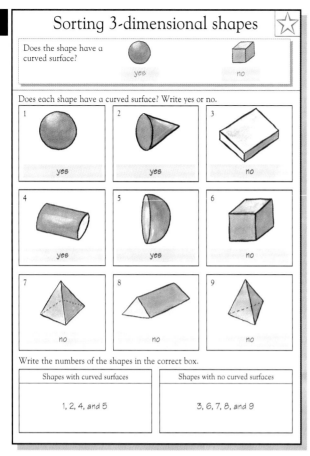

Does the shape have a curved surface?

yes          no

Does each shape have a curved surface? Write yes or no.

| 1 | 2 | 3 |
|---|---|---|
| yes | yes | no |

| 4 | 5 | 6 |
|---|---|---|
| yes | yes | no |

| 7 | 8 | 9 |
|---|---|---|
| no | no | no |

Write the numbers of the shapes in the correct box.

| Shapes with curved surfaces | Shapes with no curved surfaces |
|---|---|
| 1, 2, 4, and 5 | 3, 6, 7, 8, and 9 |

Children should find this simple sorting straightforward. If problems are encountered, you may want to find some household objects that are the same shapes.

**94** Location on a grid

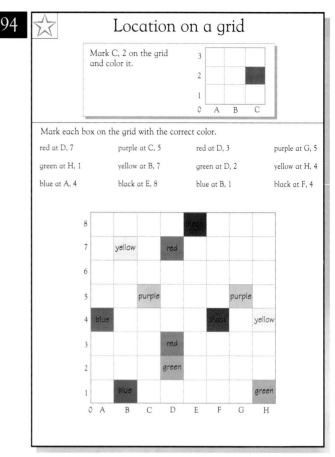

Mark C, 2 on the grid and color it.

Mark each box on the grid with the correct color.

| red at D, 7 | purple at C, 5 | red at D, 3 | purple at G, 5 |
| green at H, 1 | yellow at B, 7 | green at D, 2 | yellow at H, 4 |
| blue at A, 4 | black at E, 8 | blue at B, 1 | black at F, 4 |

Make sure that children understand that the order of the number pairs is important. The first number is from the horizontal or *x*-axis, and the second number is from the vertical or *y*-axis.

**95** Counting by 2s

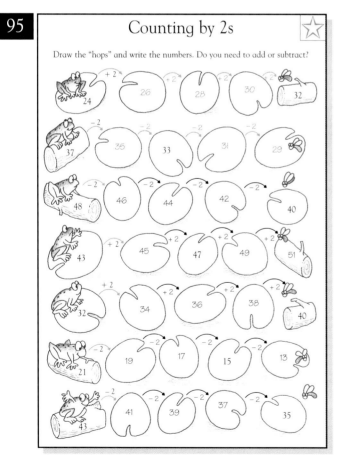

Draw the "hops" and write the numbers. Do you need to add or subtract?

It may be necessary to point out that some of the patterns show an increase and some a decrease. If children have difficulty, they can count by 1s two times for each set.

**96** Counting by 3s, 4s, and 5s

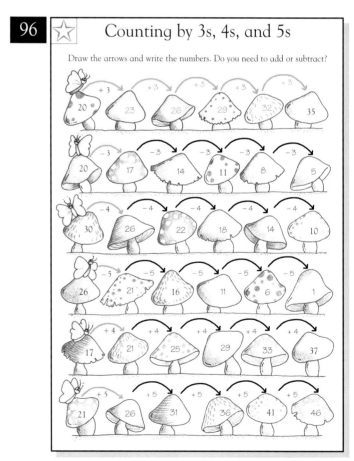

Draw the arrows and write the numbers. Do you need to add or subtract?

Some children may be able to add or subtract the appropriate number, but most will count by groups of 1s.

## 97

## Patterns of 2, 5, and 10

Count, color, and find a pattern.

Count by 2s and color them green.

| 1 | 2 | 3 | 4 | 5 | 6 | 7 | 8 | 9 | 10 |
|---|---|---|---|---|---|---|---|---|----|
| 11 | 12 | 13 | 14 | 15 | 16 | 17 | 18 | 19 | 20 |
| 21 | 22 | 23 | 24 | 25 | 26 | 27 | 28 | 29 | 30 |
| 31 | 32 | 33 | 34 | 35 | 36 | 37 | 38 | 39 | 40 |
| 41 | 42 | 43 | 44 | 45 | 46 | 47 | 48 | 49 | 50 |

Count by 5s and color them purple.

| 1 | 2 | 3 | 4 | 5 | 6 | 7 | 8 | 9 | 10 |
|---|---|---|---|---|---|---|---|---|----|
| 11 | 12 | 13 | 14 | 15 | 16 | 17 | 18 | 19 | 20 |
| 21 | 22 | 23 | 24 | 25 | 26 | 27 | 28 | 29 | 30 |
| 31 | 32 | 33 | 34 | 35 | 36 | 37 | 38 | 39 | 40 |
| 41 | 42 | 43 | 44 | 45 | 46 | 47 | 48 | 49 | 50 |

Count by 10s and color them yellow.

| 1 | 2 | 3 | 4 | 5 | 6 | 7 | 8 | 9 | 10 |
|---|---|---|---|---|---|---|---|---|----|
| 11 | 12 | 13 | 14 | 15 | 16 | 17 | 18 | 19 | 20 |
| 21 | 22 | 23 | 24 | 25 | 26 | 27 | 28 | 29 | 30 |
| 31 | 32 | 33 | 34 | 35 | 36 | 37 | 38 | 39 | 40 |
| 41 | 42 | 43 | 44 | 45 | 46 | 47 | 48 | 49 | 50 |

For the second section, make sure that children do not omit the multiples of 10, which are also part of the set of counting by 5s.

## 98

## Fractions of shapes

Color one third $\left(\frac{1}{3}\right)$.

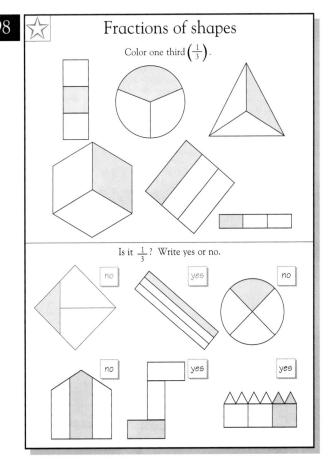

Is it $\frac{1}{3}$? Write yes or no.

no    yes    no

no    yes    yes

Explain why some of the pictures in the second section do not show one third, even though each shape is cut into three pieces. (The pieces are not all of equal size.)

## Ordering

Write the numbers in order.

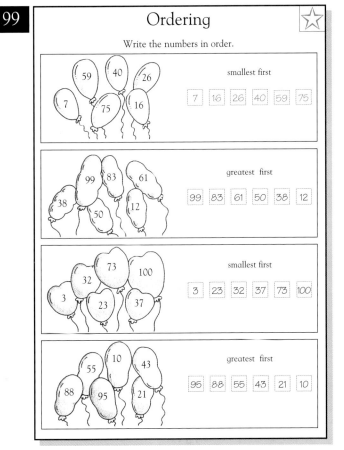

smallest first

| 7 | 16 | 26 | 40 | 59 | 75 |

greatest first

| 99 | 83 | 61 | 50 | 38 | 12 |

smallest first

| 3 | 23 | 32 | 37 | 73 | 100 |

greatest first

| 95 | 88 | 55 | 43 | 21 | 10 |

Watch for possible reversals such as reading 16 as 61. In the third section, 23, 32, 37, and 73 have been included to deal with such reversals. Ask children to identify the place values of the digits in 37 and 73.

## 100

## Doubles

Write the missing numbers.

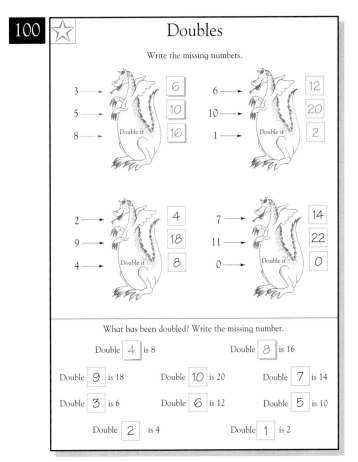

3 → 6
5 → 10
8 → Double it → 16

6 → 12
10 → 20
1 → Double it → 2

2 → 4
9 → 18
4 → Double it → 8

7 → 14
11 → 22
0 → Double it → 0

What has been doubled? Write the missing number.

Double 4 is 8          Double 8 is 16

Double 9 is 18     Double 10 is 20     Double 7 is 14

Double 3 is 6      Double 6 is 12      Double 5 is 10

Double 2 is 4          Double 1 is 2

Explain that doubling is the same as adding two sets of the same number. If children cannot yet double in their heads, use counters to make two sets of the number, and add them.

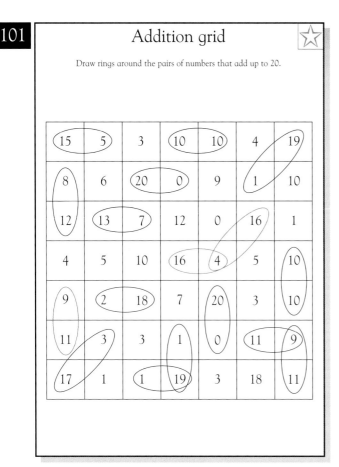

## 101 — Addition grid ☆

Draw rings around the pairs of numbers that add up to 20.

| | | | | | | |
|---|---|---|---|---|---|---|
| 15 | 5 | 3 | 10 | 10 | 4 | 19 |
| 8 | 6 | 20 | 0 | 9 | 1 | 10 |
| 12 | 13 | 7 | 12 | 0 | 16 | 1 |
| 4 | 5 | 10 | 16 | 4 | 5 | 10 |
| 9 | 2 | 18 | 7 | 20 | 3 | 10 |
| 11 | 3 | 3 | 1 | 0 | 11 | 9 |
| 17 | 1 | 1 | 19 | 3 | 18 | 11 |

If children find this page difficult, encourage them to find 20 objects, such as counters or pennies and find different ways of separating them into 2 groups, such as 2 and 18, 15 and 5. Children can then look for these pairs of numbers.

## 102 — ☆ Number wall

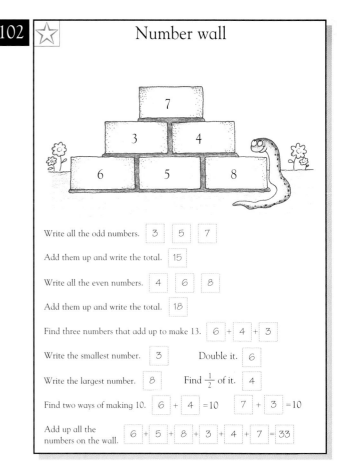

Write all the odd numbers. [3] [5] [7]

Add them up and write the total. [15]

Write all the even numbers. [4] [6] [8]

Add them up and write the total. [18]

Find three numbers that add up to make 13. [6] + [4] + [3]

Write the smallest number. [3]  Double it. [6]

Write the largest number. [8]  Find $\frac{1}{2}$ of it. [4]

Find two ways of making 10. [6] + [4] =10  [7] + [3] =10

Add up all the numbers on the wall. [6] + [5] + [8] + [3] + [4] + [7] = [33]

Help children look for "easy options" when adding, for example, adding 4 and 6 to make 10 to which 8 can be added. Ask them to find other such addition pairs.

## 103 — Matching fractions ☆

Color the matching squares.

Use yellow for halves.
Use orange for thirds.
Use green for fourths.

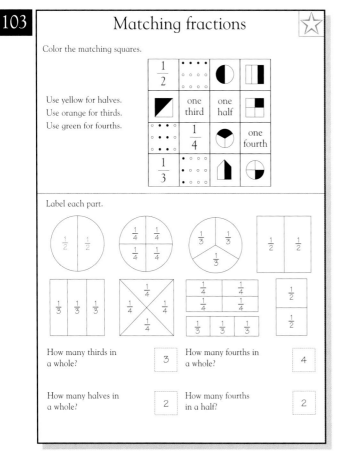

Label each part.

How many thirds in a whole? [3]  How many fourths in a whole? [4]

How many halves in a whole? [2]  How many fourths in a half? [2]

Children can look back at the drawings they labeled for help in answering the questions in the last section on the page.

## 104 — ☆ Counting

Count on forward or backward by 10s. Write the missing numbers.

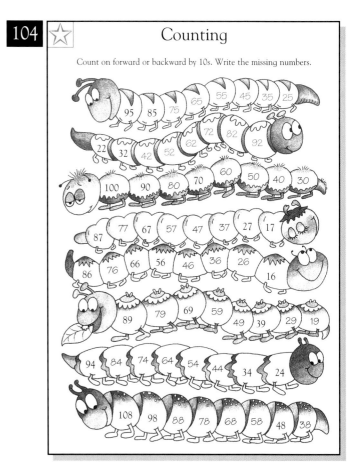

Children should determine whether the numbers are increasing or decreasing. They can then decide whether to count forward or to count back. Children should see that the ones digits remain unchanged; the tens digits increase or decrease.

## Venn diagrams ☆

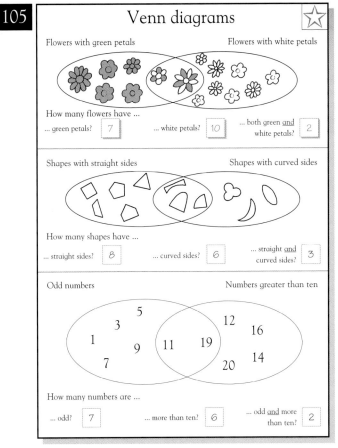

Flowers with green petals

Flowers with white petals

How many flowers have ...

... green petals? **7**   ... white petals? **10**   ... both green *and* white petals? **2**

Shapes with straight sides

Shapes with curved sides

How many shapes have ...

... straight sides? **8**   ... curved sides? **6**   ... straight *and* curved sides? **3**

Odd numbers

Numbers greater than ten

5
3
1   11   19   12   16
9
7   20   14

How many numbers are ...

... odd? **7**   ... more than ten? **6**   ... odd *and* more than ten? **2**

Make sure children understand that the items in the part of the diagram where the two ovals intersect are part of both sets of items. They must be included when counting either of the main sets.

## ☆ Comparing

Complete the boxes.

| 2 less | number | 2 more |
|---|---|---|
| 51 | 53 | 55 |

| number | between | number |
|---|---|---|
| 96 | 97   98 | 99 |

| number | between | number |
|---|---|---|
| 20 | 21  22  23 | 24 |

| 3 less | number | 3 more |
|---|---|---|
| 27 | 30 | 33 |

| 2 less | between | 2 more |
|---|---|---|
| 27 | 29 | 31 |

| number | between | number |
|---|---|---|
| 18 | 19  20  21 | 22 |

| number | between | number |
|---|---|---|
| 131 | 132  133 | 134 |

| 10 less | number | 10 more |
|---|---|---|
| 109 | 119 | 129 |

| 5 less | number | 5 more |
|---|---|---|
| 80 | 85 | 90 |

| number | between | number |
|---|---|---|
| 40 | 41  42  43  44 | 45 |

| number | between | number |
|---|---|---|
| 99 | 100  101 | 102 |

| 5 less | number | 5 more |
|---|---|---|
| 151 | 156 | 161 |

Make sure children understand the meanings of *more*, *less*, and *between*. Have them give examples such as 3 more or 3 less than 10. Children should see that they are filling in a number that makes a sequence with the numbers before and after.

## Odd or even?

Add or subtract to find the answers.
Choose two colors. Color the odd houses one color and the even houses another color.

32
+4
**36**
even

23
−4
**19**
odd

10
−5
**5**

11
+ 2
**13**

25
−6
**19**

20
+ 7
**27**

23
−7
**16**

35
−5
**30**

30
−6
**24**

16
+ 8
**24**

25
− 10
**15**

28
−8
**20**

17
+ 9
**26**

36
− 10
**26**

Children may notice that adding or subtracting an odd and an even number results in an odd number. Adding or subtracting two even numbers gives an even number, and adding or subtracting two odd numbers results in an even number.

## ☆ Clocks

Write the times under the clocks.

4 o'clock   half past 8   10 o'clock

half past 5   half past 1   6 o'clock

Draw the hands.

half past 7   half past 2   10 o'clock

half past 11   3 o'clock   9 o'clock

The lengths of the clock hands are important to make sure that times such as half past 12 and 6 o'clock are not confused. Remind children that the long hand is the minute hand and that the short hand is the hour hand.

# Fact families

Use the 3 numbers to write 4 different facts.

| | | | |
|---|---|---|---|
| 6 + 7 = 13 | 7 + 6 = 13 | 13 − 7 = 6 | 13 − 6 = 7 |
| 16 + 4 = 20 | 4 + 16 = 20 | 20 − 4 = 16 | 20 − 16 = 4 |
| 6 + 5 = 11 | 5 + 6 = 11 | 11 − 5 = 6 | 11 − 6 = 5 |
| 7 + 8 = 15 | 8 + 7 = 15 | 15 − 7 = 8 | 15 − 8 = 7 |
| 8 + 12 = 20 | 12 + 8 = 20 | 20 − 8 = 12 | 20 − 12 = 8 |
| 10 + 8 = 18 | 8 + 10 = 18 | 18 − 10 = 8 | 18 − 8 = 10 |
| 8 + 9 = 17 | 9 + 8 = 17 | 17 − 9 = 8 | 17 − 8 = 9 |
| 9 + 7 = 16 | 7 + 9 = 16 | 16 − 9 = 7 | 16 − 7 = 9 |
| 14 + 6 = 20 | 6 + 14 = 20 | 20 − 14 = 6 | 20 − 6 = 14 |
| 11 + 8 = 19 | 8 + 11 = 19 | 19 − 11 = 8 | 19 − 8 = 11 |

Lead children to understand that if they know one addition fact, they can form three other facts: one more addition fact and two subtraction facts. For example, 6 + 7 = 13 allows the formation of 7 + 6 = 13, 13 − 6 = 7, and 13 − 7 = 6.

# Identifying patterns

Continue each pattern.

| | | | | | |
|---|---|---|---|---|---|
| 0 | 6 | 12 | 18 | 24 | 30 |
| 0 | 7 | 14 | 21 | 28 | 35 |
| 60 | 52 | 44 | 36 | 28 | 20 |

Continue each pattern.

| | | | | | | | |
|---|---|---|---|---|---|---|---|
| 3 | 9 | 15 | 21 | 27 | 33 | 39 | 45 |
| 2 | 9 | 16 | 23 | 30 | 37 | 44 | 51 |
| 1 | 9 | 17 | 25 | 33 | 41 | 49 | 57 |
| 7 | 15 | 23 | 31 | 39 | 47 | 55 | 63 |
| 7 | 13 | 19 | 25 | 31 | 37 | 43 | 49 |
| 7 | 12 | 17 | 22 | 27 | 32 | 37 | 42 |

Continue each pattern.

| | | | | | | | |
|---|---|---|---|---|---|---|---|
| 71 | 65 | 59 | 53 | 47 | 41 | 35 | 29 |
| 90 | 82 | 74 | 66 | 58 | 50 | 42 | 34 |
| 56 | 49 | 42 | 35 | 28 | 21 | 14 | 7 |
| 72 | 66 | 60 | 54 | 48 | 42 | 36 | 30 |
| 96 | 88 | 80 | 72 | 64 | 56 | 48 | 40 |
| 48 | 42 | 36 | 30 | 24 | 18 | 12 | 6 |

Continue each pattern.

| | | | | | | | |
|---|---|---|---|---|---|---|---|
| 36 | 43 | 50 | 57 | 64 | 71 | 78 | 85 |
| 61 | 55 | 49 | 43 | 37 | 31 | 25 | 19 |
| 0 | 7 | 14 | 21 | 28 | 35 | 42 | 49 |
| 7 | 14 | 21 | 28 | 35 | 42 | 49 | 56 |
| 4 | 12 | 20 | 28 | 36 | 44 | 52 | 60 |

Point out that some of the patterns show an increase and some a decrease. Children should check that the operation that turns the first number into the second, also turns the second number into the third. They can then continue the pattern.

# Real-life problems

Look at the picture. Answer the questions.

What time is it ? 4:30

Today is Friday. What day was it yesterday? Thursday

How many cupcakes can each person have? 2

If half of the apples were eaten, how many would be left? 3

If each person had 2 drinks, how many drinks would there be altogether? 8

How many more sandwiches are there than apples? 4

If 13 candies were eaten, how many would be left? 7

Each package contains 2 presents. How many presents are there altogether? 6

What shape are the sandwiches? triangle

Is there an odd or an even number of chairs? even

Children have to decide what each question is asking for and then find a way of arriving at each answer. For example, they should recognize that the fifth question can be answered by counting by 2s.

# Addition fact families

Circle the number sentence that is in the same fact family.

| 12 − 5 = 7<br>5 + 7 = 12 | 12 − 4 = 8 | (7 + 5 = 12) | 12 + 12 = 24 |
|---|---|---|---|
| 10 − 8 = 2<br>8 + 2 = 10 | 8 − 6 = 2 | (2 + 8 = 10) | 8 − 2 = 6 |

Circle the number sentence that is in the same fact family.

| 7 − 8 = 15<br>8 + 7 = 15 | 7 + 5 = 12 | (15 − 8 = 7) | 8 − 7 = 1 |
|---|---|---|---|
| 17 − 6 = 11<br>11 + 6 = 17 | (17 − 11 = 6) | 17 + 6 = 12 | 5 + 6 = 11 |
| 14 − 5 = 9<br>14 − 9 = 5 | 9 − 3 = 6 | 14 + 9 = 23 | (5 + 9 = 14) |
| 9 + 7 = 16<br>7 + 9 = 16 | (16 − 9 = 7) | 16 + 7 = 23 | 9 − 7 = 2 |
| 19 − 9 = 10<br>19 − 10 = 9 | 9 + 3 = 12 | (9 + 10 = 19) | 18 − 8 = 10 |
| 4 + 7 = 11<br>11 − 4 = 7 | 11 + 4 = 15 | (7 + 4 = 11) | 7 + 7 = 14 |

Write the fact family for each group of numbers.

| 5, 6, 11 | 6, 10, 4 | 5, 13, 8 |
|---|---|---|
| 5 + 6 = 11 | 6 + 4 = 10 | 5 + 8 = 13 |
| 6 + 5 = 11 | 4 + 6 = 10 | 8 + 5 = 13 |
| 11 − 6 = 5 | 10 − 6 = 4 | 13 − 8 = 5 |
| 11 − 5 = 6 | 10 − 4 = 6 | 13 − 5 = 8 |

Children should understand that subtraction "undoes" addition. You may want to use counters to show the addition fact families.

## Real-life problems

Solve the problem and then write the answers.

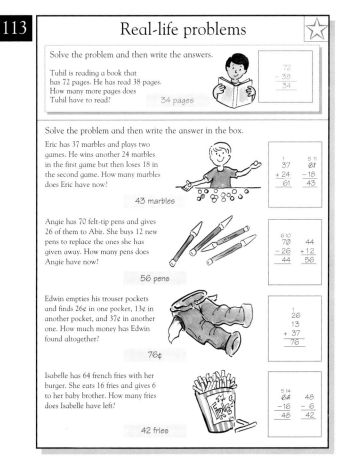

Tuhil is reading a book that has 72 pages. He has read 38 pages. How many more pages does Tuhil have to read?

**34 pages**

$$\begin{array}{r} 72 \\ -\ 38 \\ \hline 34 \end{array}$$

Solve the problem and then write the answer in the box.

Eric has 37 marbles and plays two games. He wins another 24 marbles in the first game but then loses 18 in the second game. How many marbles does Eric have now?

**43 marbles**

$$\begin{array}{r} \overset{1}{3}7 \\ +\ 24 \\ \hline 61 \end{array} \qquad \begin{array}{r} \overset{5\ 11}{6\cancel{1}} \\ -\ 18 \\ \hline 43 \end{array}$$

Angie has 70 felt-tip pens and gives 26 of them to Abir. She buys 12 new pens to replace the ones she has given away. How many pens does Angie have now?

**56 pens**

$$\begin{array}{r} \overset{6\ 10}{7\cancel{0}} \\ -\ 26 \\ \hline 44 \end{array} \qquad \begin{array}{r} 44 \\ +\ 12 \\ \hline 56 \end{array}$$

Edwin empties his trouser pockets and finds 26¢ in one pocket, 13¢ in another pocket, and 37¢ in another one. How much money has Edwin found altogether?

**76¢**

$$\begin{array}{r} \overset{1}{2}6 \\ 13 \\ +\ 37 \\ \hline 76 \end{array}$$

Isabelle has 64 french fries with her burger. She eats 16 fries and gives 6 to her baby brother. How many fries does Isabelle have left?

**42 fries**

$$\begin{array}{r} \overset{5\ 14}{6\cancel{4}} \\ -\ 16 \\ \hline 48 \end{array} \qquad \begin{array}{r} 48 \\ -\ 6 \\ \hline 42 \end{array}$$

These problems require children to perform multiple operations. If they have difficulty, discuss the problems and "walk" them through the steps needed.

---

## Adding

Write the answer between the lines.

$$\begin{array}{r} 34 \\ +\ 42 \\ \hline 76 \end{array} \qquad \begin{array}{r} 28 \\ +\ 11 \\ \hline 39 \end{array} \qquad \begin{array}{r} 75 \\ +\ 14 \\ \hline 89 \end{array}$$

Write the answer between the lines.

| | | | |
|---|---|---|---|
| $\begin{array}{r}24\\+\ 14\\\hline 38\end{array}$ | $\begin{array}{r}36\\+\ 23\\\hline 59\end{array}$ | $\begin{array}{r}45\\+\ 13\\\hline 58\end{array}$ | $\begin{array}{r}61\\+\ 17\\\hline 78\end{array}$ |
| $\begin{array}{r}63\\+\ 14\\\hline 77\end{array}$ | $\begin{array}{r}71\\+\ 16\\\hline 87\end{array}$ | $\begin{array}{r}48\\+\ 10\\\hline 58\end{array}$ | $\begin{array}{r}53\\+\ 16\\\hline 69\end{array}$ |
| $\begin{array}{r}60\\+\ 36\\\hline 96\end{array}$ | $\begin{array}{r}46\\+\ 21\\\hline 67\end{array}$ | $\begin{array}{r}54\\+\ 33\\\hline 87\end{array}$ | $\begin{array}{r}83\\+\ 6\\\hline 89\end{array}$ |
| $\begin{array}{r}28\\+\ 31\\\hline 59\end{array}$ | $\begin{array}{r}53\\+\ 36\\\hline 89\end{array}$ | $\begin{array}{r}74\\+\ 25\\\hline 99\end{array}$ | $\begin{array}{r}38\\+\ 21\\\hline 59\end{array}$ |
| $\begin{array}{r}57\\+\ 22\\\hline 79\end{array}$ | $\begin{array}{r}65\\+\ 14\\\hline 79\end{array}$ | $\begin{array}{r}79\\+\ 10\\\hline 89\end{array}$ | $\begin{array}{r}47\\+\ 12\\\hline 59\end{array}$ |
| $\begin{array}{r}35\\+\ 13\\\hline 48\end{array}$ | $\begin{array}{r}46\\+\ 22\\\hline 68\end{array}$ | $\begin{array}{r}57\\+\ 31\\\hline 88\end{array}$ | $\begin{array}{r}68\\+\ 40\\\hline 108\end{array}$ |
| $\begin{array}{r}44\\+\ 25\\\hline 69\end{array}$ | $\begin{array}{r}53\\+\ 34\\\hline 87\end{array}$ | $\begin{array}{r}26\\+\ 33\\\hline 59\end{array}$ | $\begin{array}{r}62\\+\ 17\\\hline 79\end{array}$ |
| $\begin{array}{r}50\\+\ 37\\\hline 87\end{array}$ | $\begin{array}{r}47\\+\ 11\\\hline 58\end{array}$ | $\begin{array}{r}66\\+\ 22\\\hline 88\end{array}$ | $\begin{array}{r}45\\+\ 32\\\hline 77\end{array}$ |

These are straightforward addition problems with no regrouping needed. This page prepares children for the next page, which involves regrouping.

---

## Adding

Write the answer between the lines.

$$\begin{array}{r} 15 \\ +\ 20 \\ \hline 35 \end{array} \qquad \begin{array}{r} 25 \\ +\ 40 \\ \hline 65 \end{array} \qquad \begin{array}{r} 55 \\ +\ 5 \\ \hline 60 \end{array}$$

Write the answer between the lines.

| | | | |
|---|---|---|---|
| $\begin{array}{r}50\\+\ 25\\\hline 75\end{array}$ | $\begin{array}{r}70\\+\ 15\\\hline 85\end{array}$ | $\begin{array}{r}90\\+\ 5\\\hline 95\end{array}$ | $\begin{array}{r}20\\+\ 45\\\hline 65\end{array}$ |
| $\begin{array}{r}65\\+\ 30\\\hline 95\end{array}$ | $\begin{array}{r}25\\+\ 40\\\hline 65\end{array}$ | $\begin{array}{r}35\\+\ 50\\\hline 85\end{array}$ | $\begin{array}{r}85\\+\ 10\\\hline 95\end{array}$ |
| $\begin{array}{r}30\\+\ 25\\\hline 55\end{array}$ | $\begin{array}{r}60\\+\ 35\\\hline 95\end{array}$ | $\begin{array}{r}55\\+\ 30\\\hline 85\end{array}$ | $\begin{array}{r}75\\+\ 20\\\hline 95\end{array}$ |
| $\begin{array}{r}25\\+\ 15\\\hline 40\end{array}$ | $\begin{array}{r}45\\+\ 5\\\hline 50\end{array}$ | $\begin{array}{r}65\\+\ 25\\\hline 90\end{array}$ | $\begin{array}{r}15\\+\ 15\\\hline 30\end{array}$ |
| $\begin{array}{r}75\\+\ 10\\\hline 85\end{array}$ | $\begin{array}{r}15\\+\ 25\\\hline 40\end{array}$ | $\begin{array}{r}35\\+\ 25\\\hline 60\end{array}$ | $\begin{array}{r}45\\+\ 15\\\hline 60\end{array}$ |
| $\begin{array}{r}65\\+\ 35\\\hline 100\end{array}$ | $\begin{array}{r}45\\+\ 25\\\hline 70\end{array}$ | $\begin{array}{r}5\\+\ 65\\\hline 70\end{array}$ | $\begin{array}{r}55\\+\ 35\\\hline 90\end{array}$ |
| $\begin{array}{r}35\\+\ 45\\\hline 80\end{array}$ | $\begin{array}{r}45\\+\ 35\\\hline 80\end{array}$ | $\begin{array}{r}15\\+\ 30\\\hline 45\end{array}$ | $\begin{array}{r}75\\+\ 5\\\hline 80\end{array}$ |
| $\begin{array}{r}5\\+\ 95\\\hline 100\end{array}$ | $\begin{array}{r}50\\+\ 35\\\hline 85\end{array}$ | $\begin{array}{r}45\\+\ 45\\\hline 90\end{array}$ | $\begin{array}{r}80\\+\ 15\\\hline 95\end{array}$ |

Children must remember that when they regroup they must add 1 to the tens column.

---

## Subtracting

Write the answer between the lines.

$$\begin{array}{r} 36 \\ -\ 14 \\ \hline 22 \end{array} \qquad \begin{array}{r} 25 \\ -\ 13 \\ \hline 12 \end{array} \qquad \begin{array}{r} 57 \\ -\ 26 \\ \hline 31 \end{array}$$

Write the answer between the lines.

| | | | |
|---|---|---|---|
| $\begin{array}{r}27\\-\ 14\\\hline 13\end{array}$ | $\begin{array}{r}35\\-\ 12\\\hline 23\end{array}$ | $\begin{array}{r}47\\-\ 32\\\hline 15\end{array}$ | $\begin{array}{r}63\\-\ 20\\\hline 43\end{array}$ |
| $\begin{array}{r}54\\-\ 23\\\hline 31\end{array}$ | $\begin{array}{r}38\\-\ 16\\\hline 22\end{array}$ | $\begin{array}{r}47\\-\ 12\\\hline 35\end{array}$ | $\begin{array}{r}56\\-\ 21\\\hline 35\end{array}$ |
| $\begin{array}{r}44\\-\ 32\\\hline 12\end{array}$ | $\begin{array}{r}57\\-\ 24\\\hline 33\end{array}$ | $\begin{array}{r}65\\-\ 32\\\hline 33\end{array}$ | $\begin{array}{r}78\\-\ 35\\\hline 43\end{array}$ |
| $\begin{array}{r}66\\-\ 26\\\hline 40\end{array}$ | $\begin{array}{r}75\\-\ 35\\\hline 40\end{array}$ | $\begin{array}{r}84\\-\ 64\\\hline 20\end{array}$ | $\begin{array}{r}93\\-\ 33\\\hline 60\end{array}$ |
| $\begin{array}{r}87\\-\ 34\\\hline 53\end{array}$ | $\begin{array}{r}76\\-\ 45\\\hline 31\end{array}$ | $\begin{array}{r}67\\-\ 33\\\hline 34\end{array}$ | $\begin{array}{r}49\\-\ 28\\\hline 21\end{array}$ |
| $\begin{array}{r}56\\-\ 35\\\hline 21\end{array}$ | $\begin{array}{r}73\\-\ 40\\\hline 33\end{array}$ | $\begin{array}{r}47\\-\ 25\\\hline 22\end{array}$ | $\begin{array}{r}54\\-\ 32\\\hline 22\end{array}$ |
| $\begin{array}{r}79\\-\ 38\\\hline 41\end{array}$ | $\begin{array}{r}45\\-\ 21\\\hline 24\end{array}$ | $\begin{array}{r}76\\-\ 43\\\hline 33\end{array}$ | $\begin{array}{r}75\\-\ 12\\\hline 63\end{array}$ |
| $\begin{array}{r}43\\-\ 30\\\hline 13\end{array}$ | $\begin{array}{r}55\\-\ 12\\\hline 43\end{array}$ | $\begin{array}{r}67\\-\ 33\\\hline 34\end{array}$ | $\begin{array}{r}53\\-\ 12\\\hline 41\end{array}$ |

Children will not need to regroup to subtract the numbers on this page. Discuss any mistakes with them to determine whether they are due to lapses of concentration or show a basic misunderstanding of subtraction.

## Subtracting

Write the answer between the lines.

$$\begin{array}{r} {}^{1}2{}^{1}3 \\ 23 \\ -\ 16 \\ \hline 7 \end{array} \qquad \begin{array}{r} {}^{2}3{}^{1}4 \\ 34 \\ -\ 17 \\ \hline 17 \end{array} \qquad \begin{array}{r} {}^{3}4{}^{1}3 \\ 43 \\ -\ 18 \\ \hline 25 \end{array}$$

Write the answer between the lines.

| | | | |
|---|---|---|---|
| 36 − 28 = 8 | 41 − 35 = 6 | 53 − 46 = 7 | 65 − 47 = 18 |
| 44 − 27 = 17 | 35 − 18 = 17 | 62 − 24 = 38 | 73 − 44 = 29 |
| 56 − 46 = 10 | 37 − 18 = 19 | 43 − 26 = 17 | 68 − 49 = 19 |
| 34 − 12 = 22 | 45 − 18 = 27 | 63 − 46 = 17 | 37 − 15 = 22 |
| 60 − 43 = 17 | 47 − 24 = 23 | 63 − 40 = 23 | 86 − 29 = 57 |
| 73 − 34 = 39 | 56 − 47 = 9 | 48 − 36 = 12 | 80 − 45 = 35 |
| 54 − 38 = 16 | 70 − 45 = 25 | 37 − 18 = 19 | 53 − 26 = 27 |
| 34 − 18 = 16 | 71 − 44 = 27 | 25 − 17 = 8 | 83 − 29 = 54 |

Most of the questions on this page require regrouping. Make sure that children do not neglect to do this where necessary.

---

## Choosing the operation

Write either + or − in the box to make each problem correct.

15 + 25 = 40     30 − 8 = 22     50 − 25 = 25

Write either + or − in the box to make each problem correct.

| | | |
|---|---|---|
| 45 − 12 = 33 | 48 − 14 = 34 | 31 + 15 = 46 |
| 17 + 13 = 30 | 60 − 35 = 25 | 70 − 35 = 35 |
| 27 − 15 = 12 | 26 + 18 = 44 | 50 + 12 = 62 |
| 65 − 25 = 40 | 80 − 35 = 45 | 63 − 23 = 40 |

Write either + or − in the box to make each problem correct.

| | |
|---|---|
| 12 yd + 5 yd = 27 yd | 34 ft − 18 ft = 16 ft |
| 29 cm − 17 cm = 12 cm | 42 in. + 20 in. = 62 in. |
| 28 in. + 28 in. = 56 in. | 60 cm − 15 cm = 45 cm |
| 40 ft − 8 ft = 32 ft | 90 cm − 35 cm = 55 cm |
| 28 cm + 15 cm = 43 cm | 70 yd − 29 yd = 41 yd |
| 90 in. − 12 in. = 78 in. | 28 m + 21 m = 49 m |

Write the answer in the box.

| | | | |
|---|---|---|---|
| I start with 12 apples and end up with 18 apples. How many have I added or subtracted? | added 6 | A number is added to 14 and the result is 20. What number has been added? | 6 |
| I start with 14 pens. I finish up with 9 pens. How many pens have I lost or gained? | lost 5 | I take a number away from 30 and have 12 left. What number did I take away? | 18 |

Children should realize that if the answer is larger than the first number then they must add, and if the answer is smaller than the first number then they must subtract. They should check some of their answers to make sure that they are correct.

---

## Tables and graphs

Look at this bar graph.  **Rashir's marbles**

How many green marbles does Rashir have?   10

Number of marbles

Look at this bar graph.

**Ines' marbles**

How many green marbles does Ines have?   5

Ines has 7 marbles of which color?   red

How many clear marbles does Ines have?   6

Of which color does Ines have the most marbles?   blue

How many marbles does Ines have altogether?   26

Number of marbles

Complete the table.

**Favorite pets**

| Pets | tally marks | total |
|---|---|---|
| hamsters | ⊦⊦⊦ \| \| | 7 |
| mice | \| \| \| \| | 4 |
| gerbils | \| \| \| | 3 |
| rats | ⊦⊦⊦ | 5 |

Number of children

How many more children have hamsters than have rats?   2

Which animal is owned by 4 children?   mice

The first section requires children to notice that the units on the scale are in twos rather than ones. To answer some of the questions about the bar graph, children will have to add and compare data.

---

## Identifying patterns

Complete each pattern.

| | | | | | | | |
|---|---|---|---|---|---|---|---|
| 48 | 42 | 36 | 30 | 24 | 18 | 12 | 6 |
| 44 | 41 | 38 | 35 | 32 | 29 | 26 | 23 |

Complete each pattern.

| | | | | | | | |
|---|---|---|---|---|---|---|---|
| 21 | 19 | 17 | 15 | 13 | 11 | 9 | 7 |
| 38 | 34 | 30 | 26 | 22 | 18 | 14 | 10 |
| 36 | 31 | 26 | 21 | 16 | 11 | 6 | 1 |
| 55 | 50 | 45 | 40 | 35 | 30 | 25 | 20 |
| 42 | 37 | 32 | 27 | 22 | 17 | 12 | 7 |
| 52 | 48 | 44 | 40 | 36 | 32 | 28 | 24 |
| 62 | 57 | 52 | 47 | 42 | 37 | 32 | 27 |
| 35 | 31 | 27 | 23 | 19 | 15 | 11 | 7 |
| 41 | 39 | 37 | 35 | 33 | 31 | 29 | 27 |
| 38 | 33 | 28 | 23 | 18 | 13 | 8 | 3 |
| 42 | 36 | 30 | 24 | 18 | 12 | 6 | 0 |
| 50 | 44 | 38 | 32 | 26 | 20 | 14 | 8 |
| 63 | 57 | 51 | 45 | 39 | 33 | 27 | 21 |
| 37 | 34 | 31 | 28 | 25 | 22 | 19 | 16 |
| 58 | 53 | 48 | 43 | 38 | 33 | 28 | 23 |
| 78 | 70 | 62 | 54 | 46 | 38 | 30 | 22 |
| 67 | 60 | 53 | 46 | 39 | 32 | 25 | 18 |

Point out that some of the patterns show an increase and some a decrease. Children should check that the operation that turns the first number into the second, also turns the second number into the third. They can then continue the pattern.

## Odds and evens

Write the answer in the box.

$3 + 3 =$ 6    $4 + 6 =$ 10    $7 + 3 =$ 10    $2 + 6 =$ 8

Add the even numbers to the even numbers.

$4 + 8 =$ 12    $12 + 6 =$ 18    $10 + 6 =$ 16    $8 + 14 =$ 22

$20 + 14 =$ 34    $14 + 12 =$ 26    $16 + 10 =$ 26    $30 + 20 =$ 50

$14 + 16 =$ 30    $18 + 6 =$ 24    $22 + 8 =$ 30    $20 + 40 =$ 60

What do you notice about each answer?   All the answers are even numbers.

Add the odd numbers to the odd numbers.

$7 + 9 =$ 16    $5 + 7 =$ 12    $11 + 5 =$ 16    $9 + 5 =$ 14

$7 + 7 =$ 14    $9 + 3 =$ 12    $15 + 5 =$ 20    $13 + 7 =$ 20

$11 + 3 =$ 14    $17 + 9 =$ 26    $15 + 9 =$ 24    $13 + 15 =$ 28

What do you notice about each answer?   All the answers are even numbers.

Add the odd numbers to the even numbers.

$3 + 8 =$ 11    $9 + 12 =$ 21    $5 + 18 =$ 23    $7 + 14 =$ 21

$11 + 4 =$ 15    $13 + 10 =$ 23    $15 + 6 =$ 21    $21 + 4 =$ 25

$7 + 20 =$ 27    $13 + 30 =$ 43    $9 + 12 =$ 21    $17 + 6 =$ 23

What do you notice about each answer?   All the answers are odd numbers.

Add the even numbers to the odd numbers.

$6 + 7 =$ 13    $8 + 5 =$ 13    $10 + 9 =$ 19    $2 + 17 =$ 19

$10 + 29 =$ 39    $14 + 3 =$ 17    $8 + 13 =$ 21    $12 + 5 =$ 17

$14 + 7 =$ 21    $8 + 51 =$ 59    $16 + 9 =$ 25    $30 + 17 =$ 47

What do you notice about each answer?   All the answers are odd numbers.

Children should notice that adding two even numbers results in an even number; adding two odd numbers results in an odd number, and adding an odd and an even number results in an odd number. The order in which they are added is not important.

---

## Real-life problems

Write the answer in the box.

Sarah has eight wrenches and is given six more. How many wrenches does she have now?

$8 + 6 = 14$

Write the answer in the box.

Karl has 20 marbles but loses 12 in a game of marbles. How many marbles does he have left?   $20 - 12 = 8$

After buying some candies for 30¢, Naomi still has 65¢ left. How much did she have to begin with?   $30¢ + 65¢ = 95¢$

Billy takes 20 balls out of a barrel and leaves 15 in the barrel. How many balls are there altogether?   $20 + 15 = 35$

June collected 150 stamps and her father gave her 60 more. How many stamps does June have now?   $150 + 60 = 210$

Angela puts 40 toys in a box that already has 35 toys in it. How many toys are in the box now?   $40 + 35 = 75$

Patrick leaves 45¢ at home and takes 50¢ with him. How much money does Patrick have altogether?   $45 + 50 = 95¢$

Don gives some of his allowance to his sister. He gives his sister 80¢ and has 60¢ left. How much allowance did Don have in the first place?   $80¢ + 60¢ = \$1.40$

Five letters of the alphabet are vowels. How many letters of the alphabet are not vowels?   $26 - 5 = 21$

These problems test whether children know when to add and when to subtract. Some words, such as *altogether*, may need to be explained.

---

## Symmetry

The dotted line is a mirror line. Complete each shape.

Complete each shape.

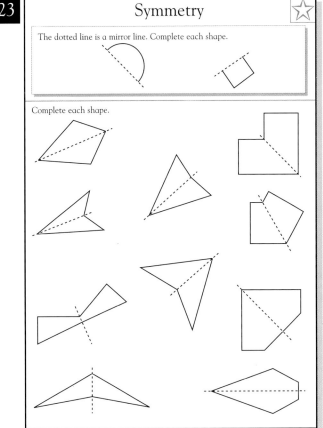

If children have difficulty with these shapes let them use a mirror. Even if they are confident, let them check the shapes with a mirror when they finish.

---

## Adding

Write the answer between the lines.

| 35 | 18 | 24 |
|----|----|----|
| 17 | 14 | 16 |
| + 16 | + 17 | + 19 |
| 68 | 49 | 59 |

Write the answer between the lines.

| 12 | 17 | 15 | 12 | 18 |
|----|----|----|----|----|
| 13 | 10 | 13 | 14 | 10 |
| + 13 | + 11 | + 11 | + 12 | + 11 |
| 38 | 38 | 39 | 38 | 39 |

| 17 | 19 | 16 | 12 | 19 |
|----|----|----|----|----|
| 26 | 13 | 21 | 25 | 32 |
| + 12 | + 14 | + 31 | + 33 | + 12 |
| 55 | 46 | 68 | 70 | 63 |

| 20 | 30 | 40 | 50 | 60 |
|----|----|----|----|----|
| 32 | 26 | 42 | 21 | 14 |
| + 16 | + 25 | + 25 | + 21 | + 8 |
| 68 | 81 | 107 | 92 | 82 |

| 25 | 35 | 45 | 55 | 65 |
|----|----|----|----|----|
| 15 | 25 | 15 | 35 | 15 |
| + 5 | + 5 | + 5 | + 5 | + 5 |
| 45 | 65 | 65 | 95 | 85 |

| 23 | 34 | 45 | 56 | 67 |
|----|----|----|----|----|
| 45 | 32 | 16 | 16 | 12 |
| + 32 | + 13 | + 9 | + 7 | + 8 |
| 100 | 79 | 70 | 79 | 87 |

Children should add the ones column first, making sure they regroup when necessary. In some of the questions, children must add 20 to the tens column, rather than 10.

## Subtracting

Write the answer between the lines.

| 57 | 42 | 36 |
|---|---|---|
| − 15 | − 16 | − 29 |
| 42 | 26 | 7 |

Write the answer between the lines.

| 40 | 60 | 70 | 50 | 90 |
|---|---|---|---|---|
| − 18 | − 23 | − 37 | − 18 | − 27 |
| 22 | 37 | 33 | 32 | 63 |

| 41 | 62 | 85 | 64 | 71 |
|---|---|---|---|---|
| − 14 | − 15 | − 37 | − 45 | − 36 |
| 27 | 47 | 48 | 19 | 35 |

| 45 | 65 | 75 | 95 | 85 |
|---|---|---|---|---|
| − 18 | − 34 | − 69 | − 49 | − 38 |
| 27 | 31 | 6 | 46 | 47 |

| 73 | 82 | 74 | 81 | 64 |
|---|---|---|---|---|
| − 27 | − 38 | − 47 | − 39 | − 47 |
| 46 | 44 | 27 | 42 | 17 |

| 61 | 52 | 61 | 53 | 73 |
|---|---|---|---|---|
| − 14 | − 17 | − 19 | − 23 | − 44 |
| 47 | 35 | 42 | 30 | 29 |

| 70 | 63 | 83 | 53 | 47 |
|---|---|---|---|---|
| − 26 | − 7 | − 56 | − 36 | − 43 |
| 44 | 56 | 27 | 17 | 4 |

Most of the subtraction problems on this page require regrouping.

---

## 2 times table

Count in 2s, color, and find a pattern.

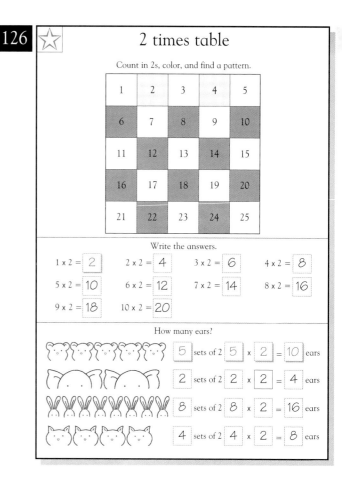

Write the answers.

1 x 2 = 2  2 x 2 = 4  3 x 2 = 6  4 x 2 = 8

5 x 2 = 10  6 x 2 = 12  7 x 2 = 14  8 x 2 = 16

9 x 2 = 18  10 x 2 = 20

How many ears?

5 sets of 2  5 x 2 = 10 ears

2 sets of 2  2 x 2 = 4 ears

8 sets of 2  8 x 2 = 16 ears

4 sets of 2  4 x 2 = 8 ears

---

## Multiplying by 2

Write the problems.

How many pairs of feet?
2 sets of 2 = 4
2 x 2 = 4

How many pairs of feet?
4 sets of 2 = 8
4 x 2 = 8

How many pairs of feet?
7 sets of 2 = 14
7 x 2 = 14

How many pairs of feet?
6 sets of 2 = 12
6 x 2 = 12

How many pairs of feet?
5 sets of 2 = 10
5 x 2 = 10

How many pairs of feet?
1 set of 2 = 2
1 x 2 = 2

Draw different pictures to go with these problems.

| Child's drawing | Child's drawing |
|---|---|
| 8 x 2 = 16 | 10 x 2 = 20 |

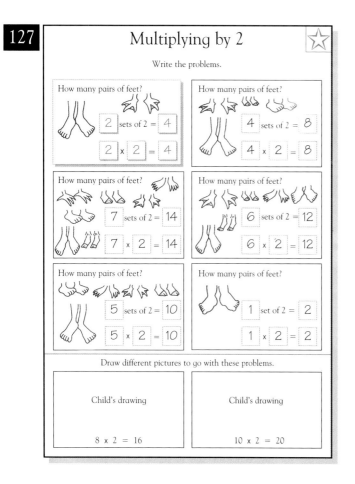

---

## Dividing by 2

Share the eggs equally between the nests.

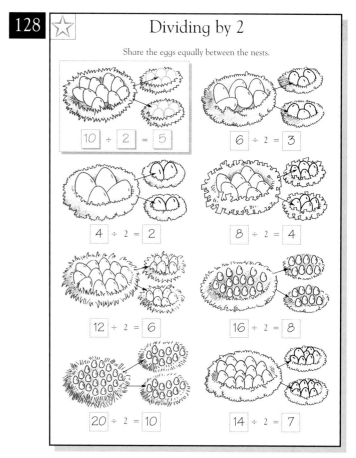

10 ÷ 2 = 5    6 ÷ 2 = 3

4 ÷ 2 = 2    8 ÷ 2 = 4

12 ÷ 2 = 6    16 ÷ 2 = 8

20 ÷ 2 = 10    14 ÷ 2 = 7

## Using the 2 times table

Write the problems to match the stamps.

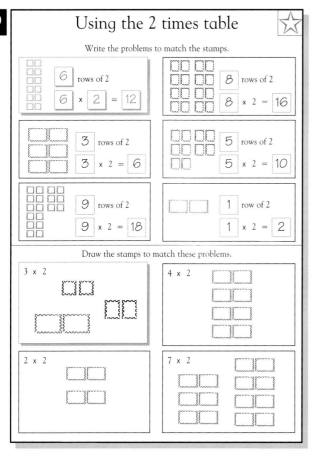

| | |
|---|---|
| 6 rows of 2 | 8 rows of 2 |
| 6 x 2 = 12 | 8 x 2 = 16 |
| 3 rows of 2 | 5 rows of 2 |
| 3 x 2 = 6 | 5 x 2 = 10 |
| 9 rows of 2 | 1 row of 2 |
| 9 x 2 = 18 | 1 x 2 = 2 |

Draw the stamps to match these problems.

3 x 2

4 x 2

2 x 2

7 x 2

## Using the 2 times table

Each face stands for 2. Join each set of faces to the correct number.

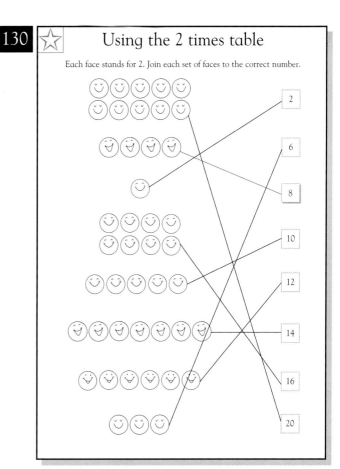

2

6

8

10

12

14

16

20

## Using the 2 times table

How many eyes?

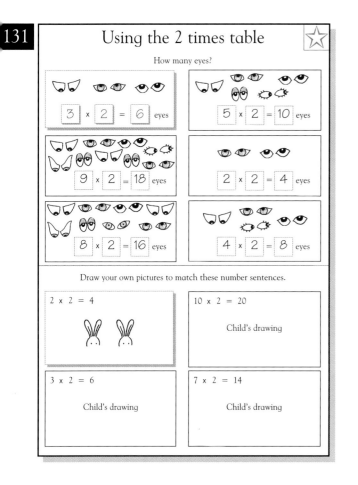

3 x 2 = 6 eyes

5 x 2 = 10 eyes

9 x 2 = 18 eyes

2 x 2 = 4 eyes

8 x 2 = 16 eyes

4 x 2 = 8 eyes

Draw your own pictures to match these number sentences.

2 x 2 = 4

10 x 2 = 20

Child's drawing

3 x 2 = 6

Child's drawing

7 x 2 = 14

Child's drawing

## 5 times table

Count in 5s, color, and find a pattern.

| 1 | 2 | 3 | 4 | 5 | 6 | 7 | 8 | 9 | 10 |
|---|---|---|---|---|---|---|---|---|---|
| 11 | 12 | 13 | 14 | 15 | 16 | 17 | 18 | 19 | 20 |
| 21 | 22 | 23 | 24 | 25 | 26 | 27 | 28 | 29 | 30 |
| 31 | 32 | 33 | 34 | 35 | 36 | 37 | 38 | 39 | 40 |
| 41 | 42 | 43 | 44 | 45 | 46 | 47 | 48 | 49 | 50 |
| 51 | 52 | 53 | 54 | 55 | 56 | 57 | 58 | 59 | 60 |
| 61 | 62 | 63 | 64 | 65 | 66 | 67 | 68 | 69 | 70 |
| 71 | 72 | 73 | 74 | 75 | 76 | 77 | 78 | 79 | 80 |
| 81 | 82 | 83 | 84 | 85 | 86 | 87 | 88 | 89 | 90 |
| 91 | 92 | 93 | 94 | 95 | 96 | 97 | 98 | 99 | 100 |

Write the answers.

1 x 5 = 5    2 x 5 = 10    3 x 5 = 15    4 x 5 = 20

5 x 5 = 25    6 x 5 = 30    7 x 5 = 35    8 x 5 = 40

9 x 5 = 45    10 x 5 = 50

How many candies?

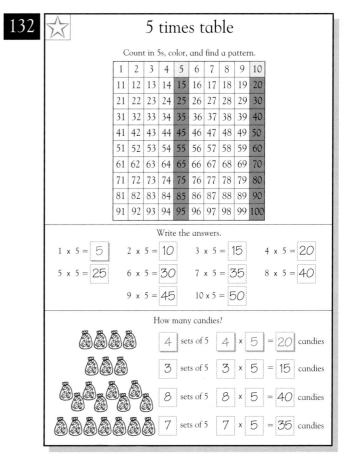

4 sets of 5   4 x 5 = 20 candies

3 sets of 5   3 x 5 = 15 candies

8 sets of 5   8 x 5 = 40 candies

7 sets of 5   7 x 5 = 35 candies

# Multiplying by 5

Draw a ring around rows of 5. Complete the problem.

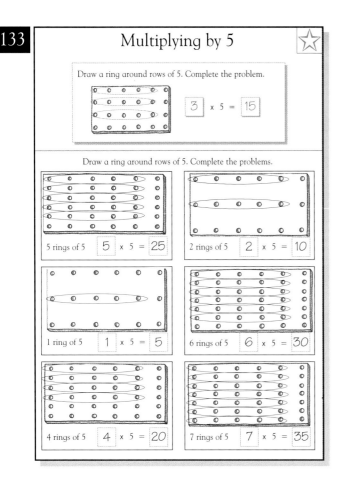

$3$ x 5 = $15$

Draw a ring around rows of 5. Complete the problems.

5 rings of 5   $5$ x 5 = $25$

2 rings of 5   $2$ x 5 = $10$

1 ring of 5   $1$ x 5 = $5$

6 rings of 5   $6$ x 5 = $30$

4 rings of 5   $4$ x 5 = $20$

7 rings of 5   $7$ x 5 = $35$

# Dividing by 5

Write a number sentence to show how many cubes are in each stack.

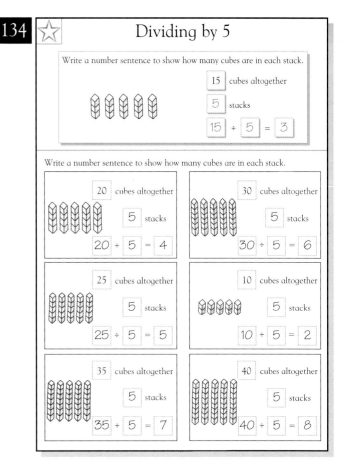

$15$ cubes altogether

$5$ stacks

$15$ ÷ $5$ = $3$

Write a number sentence to show how many cubes are in each stack.

$20$ cubes altogether   $5$ stacks
$20$ ÷ $5$ = $4$

$30$ cubes altogether   $5$ stacks
$30$ ÷ $5$ = $6$

$25$ cubes altogether   $5$ stacks
$25$ ÷ $5$ = $5$

$10$ cubes altogether   $5$ stacks
$10$ ÷ $5$ = $2$

$35$ cubes altogether   $5$ stacks
$35$ ÷ $5$ = $7$

$40$ cubes altogether   $5$ stacks
$40$ ÷ $5$ = $8$

# Using the 5 times table

Write the number that is hiding under the star.

$4$ x 5 = 20

Write the number that is hiding under the star.

$2$ x 5 = 10    3 x 5 = $15$

$5$ x 5 = 25    1 x 5 = $5$

$10$ x 5 = 50    8 x 5 = $40$

$9$ x 5 = 45    0 x 5 = $0$

$7$ x 5 = 35    6 x 5 = $30$

# Using the 5 times table

Each frog stands for 5. Join each set of frogs to the correct number.

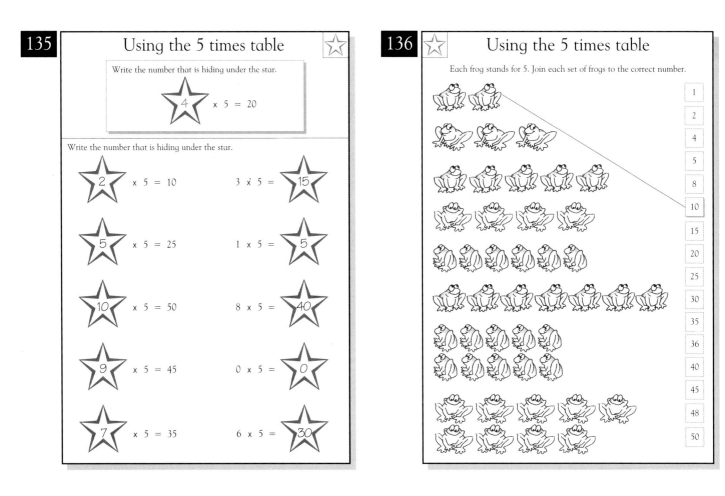

1
2
4
5
8
10
15
20
25
30
35
36
40
45
48
50

## Using the 5 times table

How many altogether?

Georgia had 7 cats. Each cat had 5 kittens. How many kittens were there altogether? $7 \times 5 = 35$ kittens

How many altogether?

Charlie had 6 boxes. He had 5 trains in each box. How many trains did he have altogether? $6 \times 5 = 30$ trains

Zoe had 3 jackets. Each jacket had 5 buttons. How many buttons were there altogether? $3 \times 5 = 15$ buttons

Yan had 8 fish tanks. Each tank had 5 fish in it. How many fish were there altogether? $8 \times 5 = 40$ fish

How many in each?

Joe had 45 pencils and 5 pencil cases. How many pencils were in each case? $45 \div 5 = 9$ pencils

How many in each?

Heather had 10 mice and 5 cages. How many mice were in each cage? $10 \div 5 = 2$ mice

Shannon had 35 candies in 5 bags. How many candies were in each bag? $35 \div 5 = 7$ candies

Mark put 25 seeds into 5 pots. How many seeds were in each pot? $25 \div 5 = 5$ seeds

## 10 times table

Count in 10s, color, and find a pattern.

| 1 | 2 | 3 | 4 | 5 | 6 | 7 | 8 | 9 | 10 |
|---|---|---|---|---|---|---|---|---|----|
| 11 | 12 | 13 | 14 | 15 | 16 | 17 | 18 | 19 | 20 |
| 21 | 22 | 23 | 24 | 25 | 26 | 27 | 28 | 29 | 30 |
| 31 | 32 | 33 | 34 | 35 | 36 | 37 | 38 | 39 | 40 |
| 41 | 42 | 43 | 44 | 45 | 46 | 47 | 48 | 49 | 50 |
| 51 | 52 | 53 | 54 | 55 | 56 | 57 | 58 | 59 | 60 |
| 61 | 62 | 63 | 64 | 65 | 66 | 67 | 68 | 69 | 70 |
| 71 | 72 | 73 | 74 | 75 | 76 | 77 | 78 | 79 | 80 |
| 81 | 82 | 83 | 84 | 85 | 86 | 87 | 88 | 89 | 90 |
| 91 | 92 | 93 | 94 | 95 | 96 | 97 | 98 | 99 | 100 |

Write the answers.

$1 \times 10 = 10$　$2 \times 10 = 20$　$3 \times 10 = 30$　$4 \times 10 = 40$

$5 \times 10 = 50$　$6 \times 10 = 60$　$7 \times 10 = 70$　$8 \times 10 = 80$

$10 \times 10 = 100$　$9 \times 10 = 90$

Each box contains 10 crayons. How many crayons are there altogether?

2 sets of 10　$2 \times 10 = 20$ crayons

4 sets of 10　$4 \times 10 = 40$ crayons

6 sets of 10　$6 \times 10 = 60$ crayons

9 sets of 10　$9 \times 10 = 90$ crayons

## Multiplying and dividing

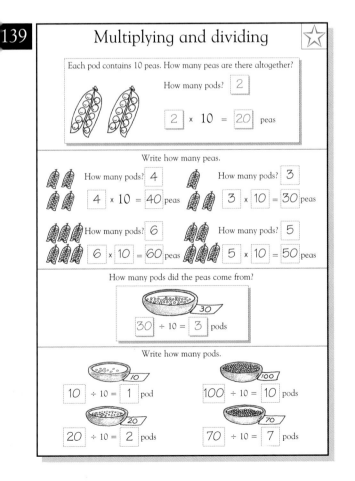

Each pod contains 10 peas. How many peas are there altogether?

How many pods? 2

$2 \times 10 = 20$ peas

Write how many peas.

How many pods? 4　　$4 \times 10 = 40$ peas

How many pods? 3　　$3 \times 10 = 30$ peas

How many pods? 6　　$6 \times 10 = 60$ peas

How many pods? 5　　$5 \times 10 = 50$ peas

How many pods did the peas come from?

30

$30 \div 10 = 3$ pods

Write how many pods.

$10 \div 10 = 1$ pod　　$100 \div 10 = 10$ pods

$20 \div 10 = 2$ pods　　$70 \div 10 = 7$ pods

## Dividing by 10

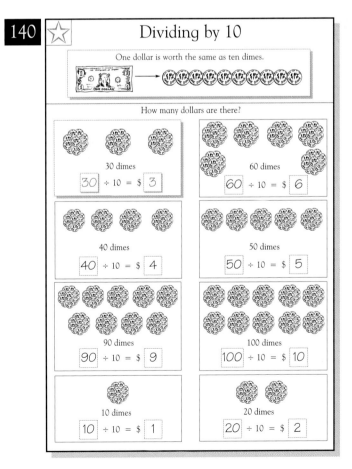

One dollar is worth the same as ten dimes.

How many dollars are there?

30 dimes
$30 \div 10 = \$ 3$

60 dimes
$60 \div 10 = \$ 6$

40 dimes
$40 \div 10 = \$ 4$

50 dimes
$50 \div 10 = \$ 5$

90 dimes
$90 \div 10 = \$ 9$

100 dimes
$100 \div 10 = \$ 10$

10 dimes
$10 \div 10 = \$ 1$

20 dimes
$20 \div 10 = \$ 2$

## 141 — Using the 10 times table

### How many altogether?
The squirrels had 4 food dens. Each den had 10 acorns. How many acorns were there altogether?

$4 \times 10 = 40$ acorns

### How many altogether?
The monkeys had 6 trees. There were 10 bananas in each tree. How many bananas did they have altogether?

$6 \times 10 = 60$ bananas

The frogs had 2 ponds. Each pond had 10 lily pads. How many lily pads were there altogether?

$2 \times 10 = 20$ lily pads

The snakes had 5 nests. Each nest had 10 eggs in it. How many eggs were there altogether?

$5 \times 10 = 50$ eggs

The lions had 7 cubs. Each cub already had 10 teeth. How many teeth did the cubs have altogether?

$7 \times 10 = 70$ teeth

### How many in each?
The crows had 40 eggs and 10 nests. How many eggs were in each nest?

$40 \div 10 = 4$ eggs

### How many in each?
There were 90 mice living in 10 nests. How many mice were in each nest?

$90 \div 10 = 9$ mice

There were 60 foxes hiding in 10 dens. How many foxes were in each den?

$60 \div 10 = 6$ foxes

## 142 — Using the 10 times table

Match each dog to the right bone.

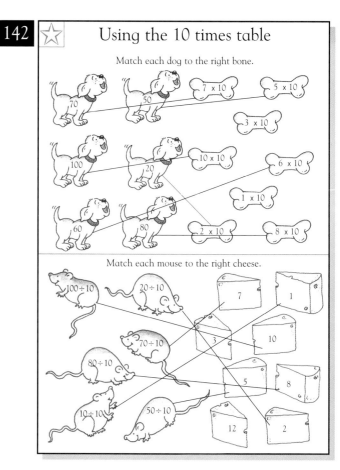

Match each mouse to the right cheese.

## 143 — Using the 10 times table

Write in the missing numbers.

| | | |
|---|---|---|
| $3 \times 10 = 30$ | | |
| $10 \times 3 = 30$ | | |
| $30 \div 3 = 10$ | | |
| $30 \div 10 = 3$ | | |

| | | |
|---|---|---|
| $5 \times 10 = 50$ | | |
| $10 \times 5 = 50$ | | |
| $50 \div 10 = 5$ | | |
| $50 \div 5 = 10$ | | |

| | | |
|---|---|---|
| $7 \times 10 = 70$ | | |
| $10 \times 7 = 70$ | | |
| $70 \div 10 = 7$ | | |
| $70 \div 7 = 10$ | | |

| | | |
|---|---|---|
| $9 \times 10 = 90$ | | |
| $10 \times 9 = 90$ | | |
| $90 \div 10 = 9$ | | |
| $90 \div 9 = 10$ | | |

| | | |
|---|---|---|
| $2 \times 10 = 20$ | | |
| $10 \times 2 = 20$ | | |
| $20 \div 10 = 2$ | | |
| $20 \div 2 = 10$ | | |

| | | |
|---|---|---|
| $4 \times 10 = 40$ | | |
| $10 \times 4 = 40$ | | |
| $40 \div 10 = 4$ | | |
| $40 \div 4 = 10$ | | |

| | | |
|---|---|---|
| $8 \times 10 = 80$ | | |
| $10 \times 8 = 80$ | | |
| $80 \div 10 = 8$ | | |
| $80 \div 8 = 10$ | | |

| | | |
|---|---|---|
| $6 \times 10 = 60$ | | |
| $10 \times 6 = 60$ | | |
| $60 \div 10 = 6$ | | |
| $60 \div 6 = 10$ | | |

## 144 — 3 times table

Count in 3s, color, and find a pattern.

| 1 | 2 | 3 | 4 | 5 |
|---|---|---|---|---|
| 6 | 7 | 8 | 9 | 10 |
| 11 | 12 | 13 | 14 | 15 |
| 16 | 17 | 18 | 19 | 20 |
| 21 | 22 | 23 | 24 | 25 |

Write the answers.

$1 \times 3 = 3$    $2 \times 3 = 6$    $3 \times 3 = 9$    $4 \times 3 = 12$    $5 \times 3 = 15$

How many flowers?

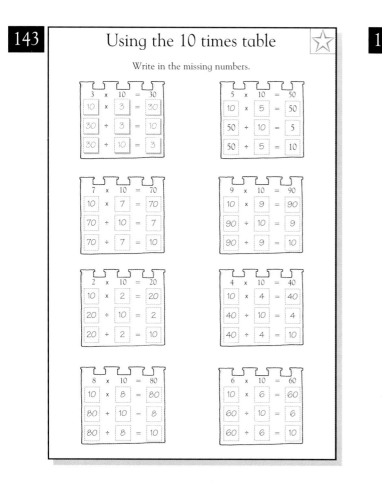

2 sets of 3    $2 \times 3 = 6$

3 sets of 3    $3 \times 3 = 9$

4 sets of 3    $4 \times 3 = 12$

5 sets of 3    $5 \times 3 = 15$

# Multiplying by 3

Write the number sentences to match the pictures.

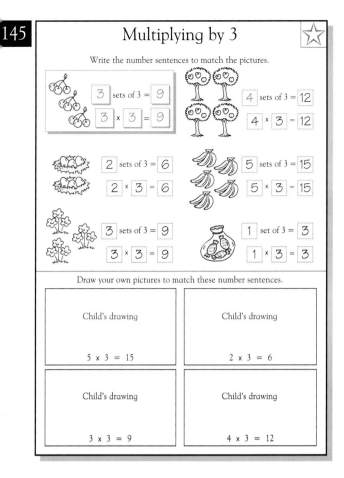

3 sets of 3 = 9
3 x 3 = 9

4 sets of 3 = 12
4 x 3 = 12

2 sets of 3 = 6
2 x 3 = 6

5 sets of 3 = 15
5 x 3 = 15

3 sets of 3 = 9
3 x 3 = 9

1 set of 3 = 3
1 x 3 = 3

Draw your own pictures to match these number sentences.

| Child's drawing | Child's drawing |
|---|---|
| 5 x 3 = 15 | 2 x 3 = 6 |
| Child's drawing | Child's drawing |
| 3 x 3 = 9 | 4 x 3 = 12 |

# Dividing by 3

Divide the money equally among the purses.
Write a problem to show what you have done.
You might find it easier to change all the money into 1¢ coins.

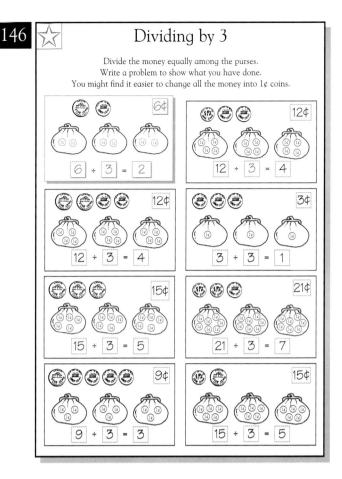

6¢
6 ÷ 3 = 2

12¢
12 ÷ 3 = 4

12¢
12 ÷ 3 = 4

3¢
3 ÷ 3 = 1

15¢
15 ÷ 3 = 5

21¢
21 ÷ 3 = 7

9¢
9 ÷ 3 = 3

15¢
15 ÷ 3 = 5

# 4 times table

Count in 4s, color, and find a pattern.

| 1 | 2 | 3 | 4 | 5 |
|---|---|---|---|---|
| 6 | 7 | 8 | 9 | 10 |
| 11 | 12 | 13 | 14 | 15 |
| 16 | 17 | 18 | 19 | 20 |
| 21 | 22 | 23 | 24 | 25 |

Write the answers.

1 x 4 = 4    2 x 4 = 8    3 x 4 = 12    4 x 4 = 16    5 x 4 = 20

How many flowers?

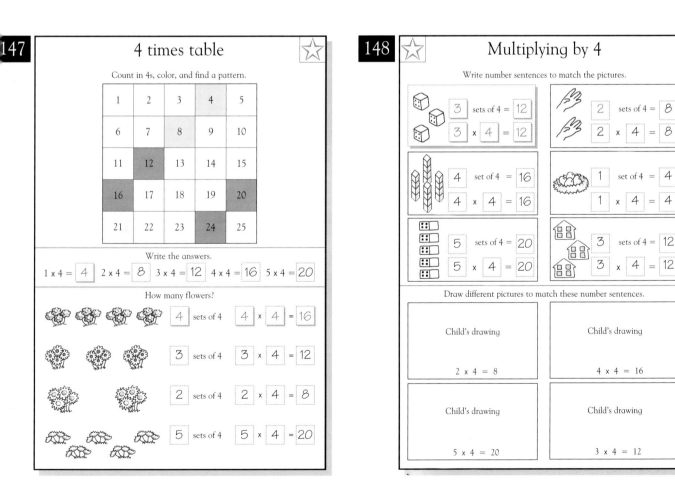

4 sets of 4    4 x 4 = 16

3 sets of 4    3 x 4 = 12

2 sets of 4    2 x 4 = 8

5 sets of 4    5 x 4 = 20

# Multiplying by 4

Write number sentences to match the pictures.

3 sets of 4 = 12
3 x 4 = 12

2 sets of 4 = 8
2 x 4 = 8

4 set of 4 = 16
4 x 4 = 16

1 set of 4 = 4
1 x 4 = 4

5 sets of 4 = 20
5 x 4 = 20

3 sets of 4 = 12
3 x 4 = 12

Draw different pictures to match these number sentences.

| Child's drawing | Child's drawing |
|---|---|
| 2 x 4 = 8 | 4 x 4 = 16 |
| Child's drawing | Child's drawing |
| 5 x 4 = 20 | 3 x 4 = 12 |

## Dividing by 4

How many on each plate?

There are 4 children. How many things will each child have?
Draw the objects in the circles.

**8 sandwiches**

$8 \div 4 = 2$ each

**12 cookies**

$12 \div 4 = 3$ each

**4 drinks**

$4 \div 4 = 1$ each

**20 cherries**

$20 \div 4 = 5$ each

**16 cupcakes**

$16 \div 4 = 4$ each

**8 cheese triangles**

$8 \div 4 = 2$ each

---

## Mixed tables

How many pegs are there in each pegboard?

$3$ rows of $4$

$3 \times 4 = 12$

How many pegs are there in each pegboard?

$4$ rows of $5$

$4 \times 5 = 20$

$2$ rows of $6$

$2 \times 6 = 12$

$6$ rows of $3$

$6 \times 3 = 18$

$5$ rows of $5$

$5 \times 5 = 25$

$6$ rows of $2$

$6 \times 2 = 12$

$1$ row of $5$

$1 \times 5 = 5$

$4$ rows of $3$

$4 \times 3 = 12$

$3$ rows of $4$

$3 \times 4 = 12$

---

## Mixed tables

Divide the 12 pennies equally. Draw the coins
and write the problem to show how many each person gets.

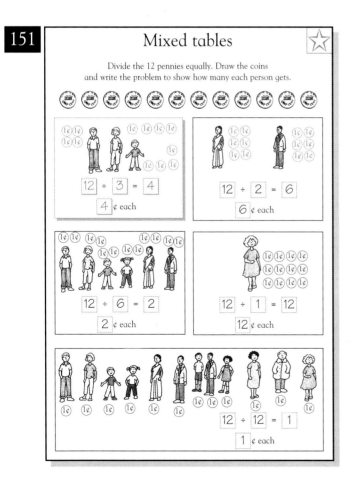

$12 \div 3 = 4$

$4$ ¢ each

$12 \div 2 = 6$

$6$ ¢ each

$12 \div 6 = 2$

$2$ ¢ each

$12 \div 1 = 12$

$12$ ¢ each

$12 \div 12 = 1$

$1$ ¢ each

---

## Mixed tables

How much will they get paid?

| Price List for Jobs | |
|---|---|
| Dust bedroom | 3¢ |
| Feed rabbit | 2¢ |
| Put toys away | 6¢ |
| Fetch newspaper | 5¢ |
| Walk dog | 10¢ |

Write a problem to show how much money
Joe and Jasmine will get for these jobs.

Feed 4 rabbits $\quad 4 \times 2¢ = 8¢$

Dust 2 bedrooms $\quad 2 \times 3¢ = 6¢$

Walk the dog 4 times $\quad 4 \times 10¢ = 40¢$

Put the toys away 3 times $\quad 3 \times 6¢ = 18¢$

Fetch the newspaper 5 times $\quad 5 \times 5¢ = 25¢$

How much will they get for these jobs?
Use the space to work out the problems.

Dust 3 bedrooms and walk
the dog twice

$3 \times 3 = 9$
$2 \times 10 = 20$

$9¢ + 20¢ = 29¢$

Feed the rabbit 10 times and
put the toys away twice

$10 \times 2 = 20$
$2 \times 6 = 12$

$20¢ + 12¢ = 32¢$

## 153 Mixed tables

Write the numbers that the raindrops are hiding.

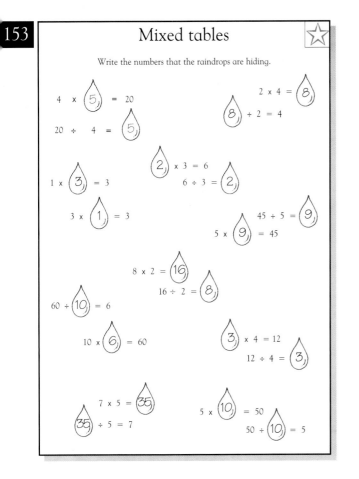

$4 \times \boxed{5} = 20$

$20 \div 4 = \boxed{5}$

$2 \times 4 = \boxed{8}$

$\boxed{8} \div 2 = 4$

$1 \times \boxed{3} = 3$

$\boxed{2} \times 3 = 6$

$6 \div 3 = \boxed{2}$

$3 \times \boxed{1} = 3$

$45 \div 5 = \boxed{9}$

$5 \times \boxed{9} = 45$

$8 \times 2 = \boxed{16}$

$16 \div 2 = \boxed{8}$

$60 \div \boxed{10} = 6$

$10 \times \boxed{6} = 60$

$\boxed{3} \times 4 = 12$

$12 \div 4 = \boxed{3}$

$7 \times 5 = \boxed{35}$

$\boxed{35} \div 5 = 7$

$5 \times \boxed{10} = 50$

$50 \div \boxed{10} = 5$

## 154 Mixed tables

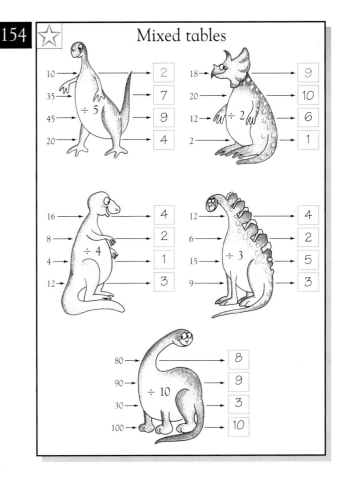

$\div 5$

$10 \rightarrow \boxed{2}$
$35 \rightarrow \boxed{7}$
$45 \rightarrow \boxed{9}$
$20 \rightarrow \boxed{4}$

$\div 2$

$18 \rightarrow \boxed{9}$
$20 \rightarrow \boxed{10}$
$12 \rightarrow \boxed{6}$
$2 \rightarrow \boxed{1}$

$\div 4$

$16 \rightarrow \boxed{4}$
$8 \rightarrow \boxed{2}$
$4 \rightarrow \boxed{1}$
$12 \rightarrow \boxed{3}$

$\div 3$

$12 \rightarrow \boxed{4}$
$6 \rightarrow \boxed{2}$
$15 \rightarrow \boxed{5}$
$9 \rightarrow \boxed{3}$

$\div 10$

$80 \rightarrow \boxed{8}$
$90 \rightarrow \boxed{9}$
$30 \rightarrow \boxed{3}$
$100 \rightarrow \boxed{10}$

## 155 Mixed tables

$\times 2$

$7 \rightarrow \boxed{14}$
$8 \rightarrow \boxed{16}$
$10 \rightarrow \boxed{20}$
$3 \rightarrow \boxed{6}$
$5 \rightarrow \boxed{10}$

$\times 3$

$2 \rightarrow \boxed{6}$
$5 \rightarrow \boxed{15}$
$1 \rightarrow \boxed{3}$
$4 \rightarrow \boxed{12}$
$3 \rightarrow \boxed{9}$

$\times 4$

$5 \rightarrow \boxed{20}$
$3 \rightarrow \boxed{12}$
$4 \rightarrow \boxed{16}$
$2 \rightarrow \boxed{8}$
$1 \rightarrow \boxed{4}$

$\times 5$

$9 \rightarrow \boxed{45}$
$0 \rightarrow \boxed{0}$
$6 \rightarrow \boxed{30}$
$8 \rightarrow \boxed{40}$
$10 \rightarrow \boxed{50}$

$\times 10$

$8 \rightarrow \boxed{80}$
$6 \rightarrow \boxed{60}$
$10 \rightarrow \boxed{100}$
$2 \rightarrow \boxed{20}$
$5 \rightarrow \boxed{50}$

## 156 Mixed tables

Work out how many.

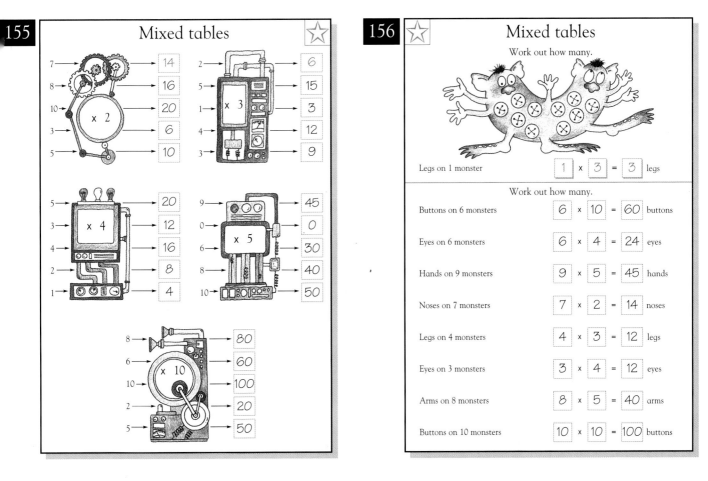

Legs on 1 monster $\quad \boxed{1} \times \boxed{3} = \boxed{3}$ legs

Work out how many.

Buttons on 6 monsters $\quad \boxed{6} \times \boxed{10} = \boxed{60}$ buttons

Eyes on 6 monsters $\quad \boxed{6} \times \boxed{4} = \boxed{24}$ eyes

Hands on 9 monsters $\quad \boxed{9} \times \boxed{5} = \boxed{45}$ hands

Noses on 7 monsters $\quad \boxed{7} \times \boxed{2} = \boxed{14}$ noses

Legs on 4 monsters $\quad \boxed{4} \times \boxed{3} = \boxed{12}$ legs

Eyes on 3 monsters $\quad \boxed{3} \times \boxed{4} = \boxed{12}$ eyes

Arms on 8 monsters $\quad \boxed{8} \times \boxed{5} = \boxed{40}$ arms

Buttons on 10 monsters $\quad \boxed{10} \times \boxed{10} = \boxed{100}$ buttons